Breaking the Silence of the Lambs

A Clinician's Memoir and Private Letters from the Predator who Inspired "The Silence..."

Jack A. Apsche, Ed.D., ABPP
and
Jerry L. Jennings, Ph.D.

Published by ePrintedBooks.com
2014

Cover art by Melissa Apsche

Dedication

This book is dedicated to Jack Apsche, who passed away shortly after its publication. Jack was an extraordinary person and brilliant clinician. As his friend and co-author, I was enriched by Jack's big heart, deep soul, free spirit, and laughter – and by his courage and integrity in sharing his personal struggles in a way that can hopefully enrich others.

Copyright © Statement

No part of this book may be reproduced or transmitted in any form or by any means, electronic or mechanical, including recording, photocopying, or by any information storage and retrieval system, without the Publisher's written permission.

Non-fiction Statement

This book was the non-fiction winner of the 2012 Public Safety Writer's Association writing competition under the title, "Greetings From the Crypt: A Dark Journey Through the Letters of Gary M. Heidnik."

Author contact information:

jxj100@gmail.com

Contents

Summary 4

I. THE CASE 5
The Untold Story of Gary M. Heidnik 5
Meet the Devil 10
Was Heidnik Truly Crazy? 17
Was I Crazy? A Review of My Case 32

II. THE CORRESPONDENCE 45
"I'm Not Available" 45
"Who's Exploiting Me?" 48
"The Special Olympics of Churches" 54
"It Piques Me Extremely" 64
"This Vacuum of Belonging" 70
"As Interesting as a Dried Prune" 85
"My Injustices of 78" 94
"Is That Love or What??" 113
"Now I'm Going to Play a Game With You" 133
"Here Lies Gary M. Heidnik" 143
"A Distant Chord But No Music" 146
"Prunes Could Turn Into Plums" 155
"Persecution Is My Middle Name" 159
"I Promised You a Juicy Story" 186
"Put Yourself in the Criminal's Mind" 201
"Let Her Know I Am Remorseful" 208
"Greetings From the Crypt" 215

III. THE SCHISM 220
"The Local Drug Lord" 220
"Don't Open That Can of Worms" 228
"Your Hostile Perspective" 240
"Expose Him From the Grave" 245
"YOU That's Right You!" 247
"A Failure to Communicate" 253
"The Quintessential Cruel Ghoul" 258
"My Last Letter to You" 263
"I've Got a Lot of Nerve, Don't I?" 269
Postscript 276

Summary Guide to Gary Heidnik's Letters 278
Other Books by the Authors 280

Summary

"Breaking the Silence of the Lambs" is a unique and fascinating story within a story. It is, first, a dark journey into the secret world of the infamous *"Silence of the Lambs"* serial killer, Gary M. Heidnik. It presents 26 secret letters from Death Row that reveal the truth of how Heidnik made a fortune in the stock market and conducted church services in his living room, while a harem of starving sexual slaves were chained in the cellar beneath their feet. It is also the story of Jack Apsche, Gary Heidnik's psychologist and the recipient of these personal letters, who is prepared to "break the silence of the lambs" by revealing Heidnik's secret letters and his own simultaneous struggle with the dark side.

When the case begins, Jack is still deeply haunted by the horrors of Vietnam, mired in a self-destructive life of drug abuse, criminal violence and sex orgies. Letter by letter, the book takes the reader through the inside experience of being Heidnik's psychologist and the emotional toll of dealing with the infamous killer's cunning and the uncensored revelations of his perverse crimes. At the same time, in a personal narrative that is harrowing in its honesty, Jack reveals the truth of his simultaneous struggle with his own dark side, of death and killing in Vietnam, depression and self-destruction, reckless gangsterism, and cocaine-charged orgies.

During the course of his unblinking investigation of Heidnik's ultimate human evil, Jack becomes transformed by the emerging power of love – for his daughter, his new wife and stepfamily, and finally, himself – and it yields the path to healing and hope. By the end of the story, Jack has used his insights from the Heidnik case to create an innovative new treatment for helping violent and disturbed adolescents and has redeemed himself as a husband, father and citizen.

I. THE CASE

Chapter 1
The Untold Story of Gary M. Heidnik

In March 1987, the national media exploded with the story of a horrific sexual murder in Philadelphia. In seventeen weeks of terror, Gary M. Heidnik kidnapped, imprisoned, raped, and tortured six women in his basement, killing two and dismembering one. Like most people, I read the newspaper accounts with curiosity and revulsion, but I never imagined that I would come to play a key role in the case that inspired *The Silence of the Lambs*.

Over 25 years later, Gary Heidnik remains one of the most notorious sex criminals in history. His crimes continue to fascinate and haunt. Hundreds of books, articles, TV shows and internet sites have documented the bizarre and shocking exploits of this man who kidnapped and tortured a harem of sexual slaves, while making a fortune in financial investments and started his own church. Yet, for all the attention that this infamous case has received, there is another Heidnik story that has never been told.

What no one knows is that Heidnik wrote a series of 26 intimate letters from Death Row. In over 150 hand-written pages, Heidnik revealed his life, his personality, and the motivations and thinking that drove his violent sexual atrocities. Those personal letters were written to me, Jack Apsche, the psychologist on his defense team.

This book will reveal the extraordinary story of how and why I became the confidant to Heidnik's secrets. It will present these private letters in their entirety for the first time, analyze their meaning, and chronicle the roller-coaster relationship between this crazy serial killer and me, a half-crazy Vietnam veteran. In fact, the letters are comprehensive enough to serve as Heidnik's autobiography, the genuine "inside story," told in his own words. As such, it is a grim portrayal of loneliness, pain, and destruction. But it is also <u>my</u> story, which is a story of redemption.

When the Heidnik case first began, my life was in ruins – a mess of post-traumatic nightmares, drug abuse, sexual addiction, explosive violence, divorce, and self-contempt. The freak chance to become part of Heidnik's defense team in September 1987 became a chance to revitalize and redeem myself. In the three years that covered Heidnik's trial and this correspondence, I was challenged both personally and professionally. When this strange odyssey began, I shared too many qualities with Heidnik. We were the same age and the same height and build. We were both failed husbands. We had both killed and we had both engaged in obsessive sexual behavior. We both hated our current situations and had no promise for our futures. And we were both, arguably, crazy.

By the end of the Heidnik period, I could be proud of myself as a good father, husband, and citizen, and an accomplished psychologist. I would never credit Heidnik with my transformation but, for better or worse, Heidnik was my dark companion on the journey to health. The story in these pages reveals the darkest depths of human ugliness and despair – for both Heidnik and me. But also, I hope, it conveys the promise and triumph of human goodness and love.

It was very difficult to write this book. It was hard enough to write my first book about the Heidnik case, which was published in 1993 under the title, *Probing the Mind of a Serial Killer*. That book used excerpts from a few of the letters presented here and was intended as a serious psychological analysis of Heidnik and serial killers. To be honest, the book was flawed and incomplete, partly due to my exhaustion from dealing with Heidnik himself. I was depleted by the project and the quality of the book likely suffered.

Since that time, however, my career has remained inextricably linked to Heidnik. I continue to receive as many requests for interviews as I did when the case was fresh. For that reason, I have always wanted to revisit the case and write a better book that would explain the deeper psychopathology of Gary Heidnik. To reach that depth, I felt that I needed to be brutally honest about myself during that same time period. But did I dare to confess the reprehensible and humiliating details of my own past in order to explain the mystery of Heidnik? Such candor would be risking my personal and professional reputation. I needed help and encouragement.

Enter my good friend and colleague, Jerry Jennings, another clinical psychologist. I told Jerry about my experiences with Heidnik and that I had a trove of his personal letters packed somewhere in my attic. Jerry urged me to find them. After reading through Heidnik's many letters, he had a great idea. We would use the letters in their exact words and chronology to give a live voice to Gary Heidnik. The series of letters would be like private clinical sessions between Heidnik and me. We would analyze each letter as forensic psychologists, but I would also reveal what it was like, as a person, to deal with such a complex, manipulative, and repulsive criminal. Through most of this book, I discuss Heidnik as a professional. But many times I take my tie off and speak personally, revealing the gut level reality of how I felt and what it was like to struggle with the depravity of Heidnik.

With the infusion of Jerry's energy and talent, we have created a uniquely personal and professional forensic investigation of an infamous serial killer that is the first of its kind. Other investigators have used letters or transcripts of interviews to analyze their subjects. But we don't believe that any published criminal forensic study has ever had an original correspondence of such volume to literally fill a book that could sustain readers' interest.

In February 1989, Heidnik began his fifteenth letter with the words, "Greetings from the Crypt." Written shortly after his umpteenth suicide attempt, the words convey the narcissistic bravado and idiosyncratic flair for words that characterize Heidnik's correspondence with me. Each Heidnik letter is a chapter in this book. Each chapter is titled using a distinctive phrase from that given letter. The letters vary in length from one to 28 pages and vary in attitude as well. At times, Heidnik's transparent efforts to justify and minimize his crimes are tedious and irksome. This is Heidnik the criminal – arrogant, crass, and manipulative. Yet, many times he is surprisingly candid and reveals the deep insecurities that drove his abominations. This is Heidnik the person, a vulnerable mental patient. Through Heidnik's letters, we can observe the continually shifting balance between bravado and inadequacy, between deception and honesty, between controlling manipulation and child-like helplessness.

Our intention is for the reader to experience the emotions, mystery, and discomfort of these letters as if they are private sessions in a therapy room. As much as possible, we allow Heidnik to "speak" at length before interrupting his letter narratives to analyze his meaning or to point out the workings of his disordered and criminal mind. But we also attempt to show my personal experience of the relationship. What was it like for me to interact with Heidnik and be immersed in the dark ink of his psyche? How did the ugliness of revisiting his atrocities and the egotism of his self-serving explanations drain me emotionally? How did my own personal ugliness and on-going struggle with sex, drugs, and depression play into our dynamic? You might mistake my attitude and frank disclosures as arrogance or even egotism, but it is honest and direct. I share my worst side because I think this story demands the truth, not because I am proud of it.

Hopefully, Jerry and I have succeeded in creating something unique, interesting, and worthwhile. In describing what this book is intended to be, we also should be clear on what this book is not. It is not sensationalist pulp for those seeking titillating stories of the macabre. It is not a citation-heavy academic monograph meant for clinical forensic professionals. It is not a treatise about the legal issues of the insanity defense as applied to Heidnik. In my first book, I drew evidence from a few of these private letters to buttress my argument that Heidnik was insane. In this book, we present the full collection of Heidnik's letters in their original chronology, <u>not</u> to add more convincing evidence to a forensic proof, but to reveal the actual thinking of this cunning, but mentally disordered criminal.

And now, in the words of Gary Heidnik from letter #9, "You are about to take a ride on a literary roller coaster. At all times I endeavor to be entertaining… BUT I'm warning you ahead of time, you have to be wary of me…" Wary, indeed.

AUTHORS' NOTE: WITH THE EXCEPTION OF THE INDIVIDUALS AND VICTIMS WHOSE NAMES ARE PART OF THE PUBLIC AND COURT RECORDS OF THE HEIDNIK CASE, THE IDENTITIES OF OTHER PEOPLE, SUCH AS <u>HEIDNIK'S CHILDREN</u>, HAVE BEEN REPLACED WITH GENERIC FALSE NAMES LIKE <u>DOE</u>, <u>SMITH</u>, AND <u>NORTON</u>.

Chapter 2
Meet the Devil

When the Heidnik case began in September 1987, I was a psychologist, but I was not a trained specialist in the field of forensic psychology. I just happened to have a lawyer friend, who was the cousin of Gary Heidnik's defense attorney, the sharp and charismatic A. Charles Peruto. My friend introduced me to Peruto, who hired me as a fact witness researcher for the case. To be honest, I lacked the forensic qualifications and probably should have declined his offer, but I recognized that this was the chance of a lifetime. I would be probing the deepest, darkest secrets of a <u>notorious serial killer in a nationally televised court case.</u> Peruto made no promises of any pay for my services, but said he would do his best. I didn't care. I was thrilled to take the opportunity.

My unexpected new job began with two big boxes stuffed with a jumble of arrest records, psychiatric reports, and information related to Heidnik. I had to somehow organize this chaos into a cogent and comprehensive understanding of Heidnik's extensive psychiatric and criminal history and then connect it to his mental condition at the time of the killings. The boxes were an apt metaphor. I was trying to sort out Heidnik's life from two big messy boxes at the same time that I was trying to sort out my own messed up life. My problem was that I didn't have any boxes to organize my life and I didn't know where to begin to organize his.

I was forty years old and had just earned my doctorate in psychology, but the newly crowned "Doctor" Apsche had no clue. I was living in a cloud of cocaine and alcohol and frequent flashbacks of combat in Vietnam. I had recently lost my closest friend and caretaker, my older brother Bill, to cancer. My marriage of 13 years was ending in a bitter and excruciating divorce and her lawyer was out for my blood. He insultingly demanded to know how many children I had killed in Vietnam. I suggested that if he wanted to find out if I was baby killer, he could read my fucking military record or enlist himself. He declined to confirm that I had a shitload of medals or anything else that would redeem my honorable service for Uncle Sam. I'm sure that my hostility made him doubt that I had ever been capable of enough "good conduct" to actually earn a Good Conduct Medal. Yes, the poison was flying and I was paying the price. The worst blow was losing custody of my only child, Melissa, who was then about eight years old.

I loved my daughter more than life. I always was a person who loved children and would often babysit when I was growing up. One of my recurring nightmares from Vietnam was of trying to save the life of a 3 year old baby who was hit by an A-Cav armored vehicle in a convoy somewhere around Sui Cat. I saw the accident and ran from my own A-Cav to rescue the child. He was crushed and covered in blood, but I immediately began mouth to mouth resuscitation until the medics could arrive. We were able to medi-vac him to base-camp, but he was just too badly injured to survive. I asked to be part of the detail to return the baby's body to his family. I tried to console his parents through an interpreter, but they cursed us all. I felt horribly guilty and their curse penetrated to my deepest soul. I became completely dead of feelings. I would never forget being covered in the blood of that little crushed baby. The memory would return in a thousand nightmares.

Flashbacks. Night terrors. Numbness. Sudden violent outbursts. In September 1987, Vietnam still dominated my life. I had been counseling Vietnam veterans for five years under a federal grant program that had just expired. I was an actively post-traumatic combat veteran trying to help other actively post-traumatic veterans. Other mental health professionals would consider this to be a classic case of "the wounded healer." But I didn't give a shit. I had a duty to bring my brothers home, because our country never did, nor did the politicians, protesters or hawks. Once you are wounded, either physically or mentally, you are damaged goods and you get tossed on the heap of weak and vulnerable. I had to help my peers even though it took a heavy toll on me emotionally to revisit Vietnam on a daily basis. Hearing the stories of my fellow vets meant that I was still slugging through the hot jungle and riding shotgun in a chopper over the A Shau Valley – Monday through Saturday. I was still being visited nightly by the dead and dying faces of my past, especially one old farmer in a straw hat, a man whom I unfortunately killed and that changed me forever. I felt like I owed that old man my life and my soul, yet there was no way to repay him in this lifetime.

So this was my condition in September 1987. I was trying to overcome Vietnam, drug and sex addictions, and the pain of losing my wife, brother, and daughter – and I was doing it by starting a brand new career in forensic psychology. For too many reasons, the Heidnik case was a lifeline for yours truly – or a noose.

I had no idea what I was getting into or how far it would take me. Professionally, I was a novice and in way over my head. But, as they say, failure was not an option. To make up for my lack of experience, I determined that I would become the consummate expert on Gary M. Heidnik and serial murderers. I dedicated myself to researching and knowing more about the subject than anyone else in the world. I searched and studied anything and everything that I could find on the topic. I scoured through every page of those two 40-pound file boxes. From the chaos, I organized a detailed understanding of the case. (I also had huge help from my girlfriend and future wife, Joanne, who had everything tabbed and highlighted). In this way, I had every fact and date down cold – Heidnik's diagnoses, hospitalizations, suicide attempts, crimes, every bizarre and abusive act – and it gave me confidence when it came time to testify in court.

After three months of intensive study, I knew every

detail of Heidnik's life, but I had not yet met him. I first interviewed him at the old Holmesburg Prison in Philadelphia in January 1988. The prison guards escorted him to a small, bare room in the mental health unit where I was waiting. He was wearing his orange prison jump suit. I was struck by our similarity in age, 40, height, over six feet, and build. As far as I could tell, Heidnik wasn't struck by me at all. He was a career mental patient who was streetwise to psychologists and psychiatrists. By my count, he had been hospitalized 22 times and saw over 150 psychiatrists and psychologists during a 26 year period. He knew the game and was averse to yet another mental status exam and clinical interview. He was polite and respectful, but his eyes were suspicious and his responses were guarded and short. He spoke softly, but made it clear from the start that, in his own words, "I may be crazy, Doc, but I'm not stupid."

Admittedly, I'm not known for my patience. After ten minutes of his evasions, I got pissed off and decided to call him out. "Listen," I said, "when I was in Vietnam, I killed more people than the Manson family, so let's cut the shit." This unorthodox move intrigued Heidnik and he looked at me differently. He quickly became more engaged in the interview. He was impressed, even flattered, by how much I already knew about his life from my detailed record reviews. He spoke openly after that. This meeting would be the first of five or six interviews with Heidnik at the jail, each lasting about two hours. It marked the beginning of a unique trust that eventually led to the extraordinary personal correspondence between Heidnik and me that is featured in this book.

The Heidnik trial began on Monday, June 20, 1988. My job as the psychologist for the defense was to help prove that Heidnik was legally insane in that he did not understand the nature or quality of the crimes he committed at the time of his offenses. I was called to testify as a fact witness on Thursday and Friday. The day started badly. I was caught in traffic and arrived late and frazzled. When Peruto saw me, he followed me to the bathroom where we could confer privately. While I was standing at the urinal, he said, "You better be good, Jack, because MacKenzie just fucked up." Dr. Clancy McKenzie was the psychiatrist serving as Peruto's expert witness for the defense. This only added to my anxiety when I was called to the witness stand in front of a courtroom that was packed with reporters and people attracted by this sensational national news story.

I testified for eight hours in a brutally hot courtroom. It was a typical Philadelphia summer week, high 90s and high humidity. I took my jacket off and still felt like I was in a sauna. The judge, Lynne M. Abraham, was kind and joked with me. Three years later she would be elected as Philadelphia's first female district attorney and she held the position for four terms, longer than anyone in the city's history. I remember that she liked to nibble on candy during the trial (juju beads, I think) and at one point she gave me a few and said, "You're doing a good job." For a rookie like me, it was reassuring.

When the court adjourned that day, I had only one thought in mind: grab my girlfriend Joanne from the courtroom gallery and run to the nearest air conditioned bar for some ice cold beer. But I was immediately swarmed by newspaper and TV reporters, who hounded me as we fled City Hall. Since I was under a gag order, I could not answer any questions. All I could do was smile in front of the TV cameras.

The next morning I arrived for another day of testimony. The courtroom was sweltering hot again and Judge Abraham pulled me aside. "I saw you on TV last night," she remarked. "You were smiling. Let's see if you keep your smile today." I was on the stand for another hour and a half and felt that it went well. When I was dismissed, Heidnik stood up and surprised me and the rest of the court with a military salute. He refused to sit down until, embarrassed, I felt obliged to return his salute. Charles Peruto then asked me to join him and Heidnik at the defense table. Heidnik was wearing the same ridiculous Hawaiian shirt that he wore every day of the five-day trial. He leaned over and whispered that the prosecutor, Charles Gallagher, was wearing mismatched brown shoes with his blue suit.

Ultimately, on June 30, after two and half days of deliberation, the jury found Heidnik guilty of murder in the first degree and he was sentenced to death by electrocution. The gracious and dignified prosecution expert, Dr. Robert Sadoff, had handed us a "guilty but mentally ill" plea on a silver platter. But Charles Peruto and Heidnik were determined to get a verdict of "<u>not</u> guilty for reasons of mental defects." I sincerely believed, and still do, that Heidnik was legally insane and really did not understand the nature or quality of the crimes he committed <u>at</u> <u>the</u> <u>time</u> of the acts.

I was devastated by the outcome. I felt like a failure. My one great chance for professional and personal redemption had been crushed. I was exhausted from dragging around my own 40-pound box of emotional defects. I felt that I couldn't go back to being a therapist and my estranged wife had hired an expensive lawyer to find the hidden treasures of my lost Dutchman's mines. It was understood that I was not going to be paid for my trial work and I was broke. All I could do was go have a drink (or ten) to ease the sting of failure. As always, getting drunk didn't work and I felt more depressed and down on myself.

My girlfriend Joanne helped by inviting me to move in with her that summer. We were in love, but our new life was far from easy. Joanne was raising her daughter and son and neither one liked me. I could understand. I was an intruder who was sleeping with their mom. But on a deeper level, I didn't like myself much either.

Then I had a brainstorm. I'll write a Heidnik book! Though we had failed at the trial, Heidnik was very happy with my efforts on his behalf. Wouldn't he be happy to cooperate? Plus I could set the record straight and prove that we were right about Heidnik's insanity. I might even change how the world looks at serial killers and return my bank account to a positive balance. I could be a crusader for justice and write a best seller at the same time, right!?

Wrong. In August 1988, I wrote to Heidnik about my idea for a book. He refused. By this time, Heidnik was incarcerated on Death Row at the State Correctional Institution at Pittsburgh. Unlike the polite Gary Heidnik during the trial, I would soon learn that post-trial Heidnik was an annoying, manipulative pain-in-the-ass. He had nothing but time on Death Row and liked to play games. My style is to be direct. I like to speak my mind and have others do the same. But now I had to play Heidnik's game by <u>his</u> rules. Our match was about to begin: Crazy, manipulative Heidnik in one corner and half-crazy, impatient Jack in the other.

Chapter 3
Was Heidnik Truly Crazy?
A Review of the Case

Before turning to my "unholy" alliance with Heidnik, it is important to summarize the case. The Heidnik letters contain a lifetime of names and events and it will be difficult to keep track of who's who without some kind of summary of the people, places, and events.

The Power of Deviant Sexual Fantasies

The vast majority of serial killers who have pled not guilty by reason of insanity have, like Heidnik, lost in court. The rituals and compulsions of the sexual predator/serial killer often appear to indicate careful planning and logical thinking. Individuals like Heidnik appear so skilled and diabolical in their detailed planning and deception, that ordinary people cannot believe the killer is not sane and clearly in control of his actions.

The answer to this paradox is that the planning and premeditation are expressions of the powerful compulsions that drive the sexual predator/serial killer. Their obsessive sexual domination fantasies are often highly scripted, rehearsed to perfection, and repeatedly reinforced with masturbation and orgasm. Beginning in youth, fantasy life is an area where a social outcast can enjoy power, control, and pleasure. Fantasy, especially sexual fantasy, is a self-stimulating, self-reinforcing behavior that feeds itself and is strengthened in frequency and potency by the powerful reinforcement of orgasm.

There is no counter-balance to the narcissistic fantasy life of the isolated loner because he lacks support from family and friends and the pleasures and diversity of normal social activities, such as scouts, sports, music, and school groups. The sexual fantasies provide some semblance of self-pride and competence for someone who otherwise feels small, worthless, incompetent, and deformed. In his fantasy life, the sexual predator/serial killer imagines himself as all powerful, having control over people who fear and admire him. This reversal from self-disgust to self-grandiosity, even if momentary, combined with sexual pleasure, is an extremely powerful reinforcement of his deviant sexual fantasy life.

At the same time, the pursuit of power and control becomes a substitute for the natural human instinct for intimacy and bonding. When a child like Heidnik grows up with frequent or severe physical abuse, emotional humiliation, and parental rejection, he is deprived of experiences of closeness, safety, and bonding. His capacity to form relationships becomes impaired. Wary of rejection, shame, and punishment, such a child becomes increasingly anxious, withdrawn, avoidant, and guarded.

Gary Heidnik's childhood is a classic example of this developmental pattern. His mother was a severe alcoholic and depressive, who was married five times and eventually committed suicide when he was 27. Heidnik's father divorced his mother when he was two years old because of her volatile behavior. But Gary Heidnik and his little brother Terry remained in her custody for the next four years. Undoubtedly, her unpredictable emotional swings made a poor environment for a child to learn intimacy or how to reliably read and respond to social cues.

Subsequently, at the age of 6, Heidnik's father and new stepmother took over responsibility for raising the brothers. Gary described his father as a "strict disciplinarian," but denied any physical abuse. In particular, he denied his brother's claim that their father "hit Gary on the head with a board and hung him out of his third floor bedroom window by his feet." Gary was a lifelong bed-wetter and his father would display his son's bed-sheets to shame him into learning bladder control. He struggled in school, failed second grade, and was about to fail for a second time when his father intervened. Gary credits his father with rigorous tutoring that forced him to learn. Though he continued to struggle in school, he learned to compensate by studying many extra hours. He developed a genuine liking for reading and it filled the void of his isolation and loneliness. According to Terry Heidnik, the other kids made fun of Gary's odd-shaped skull and called him "football head." Gary felt alien and disconnected from people and peers, baffled by ordinary social interactions, and increasingly avoided relationships. His hours of solitude contributed to the development of an intense fantasy life. He quit school in 9th grade, but his father persuaded him to enroll in Staunton Military Academy. For two years, the extreme structure of the military school may have helped to disguise Gary's lack of interpersonal skills, but he quit after two years. He remained a loner without the normal peer outlets of sports, clubs, play or friendships. He returned to public high school once again, but soon dropped out and joined the army at age 17.

This brief history illustrates the psychological ingredients that characterize the development of serial killers. Even though a child like Heidnik is deprived of opportunities to learn or experience human intimacy, he continues to crave it. He will try to manage his fears, loneliness, and insecurity through control, which gives the illusion of security through empowerment. Acts of violence and dominance over others becomes a substitute for intimacy with others. Thus, the quality of his relationships is dictated by his ability or inability to be in control. A child like Heidnik cannot control his painful world, he cannot control his insecurity and fear, he cannot control whether he gets love from his relationships – but he can control everything when it comes to his fantasy life and later, as an adult, his ability to terrorize others into subservience. For the sexual predator/serial killer who never experienced normal bonding or intimacy, control and power over victims is substituted for intimacy. For Heidnik, the craving for intimacy is eventually released in the form of total control through kidnapping, imprisonment, rape, and torture of his victims.

But the emergence of an obsessive sexual fantasy is just the beginning. Repetition of the same sexual fantasy becomes boring. Its capacity to generate arousal and orgasm decreases. Like the heroin addict who needs more heroin to attain the same high, the fantasy must be elaborated or heightened. The sexual predator/serial killer is compelled to do more to gain the desired sexual satisfaction. The fantasies escalate to entail more power over the victims, more violence, more sadism, and more deviance to achieve the desired payoff. Ultimately, the sexual predator/serial killer feels compelled to act out his internal fantasy on real victims and, once this occurs, the deviant urges can become reinforced by the more intensive thrill of terrorizing and brutalizing real victims, even killing them.

This dynamic of escalating sexually violent fantasies can be even more powerful for a person like Heidnik with a major psychotic disorder, such as schizophrenia, schizoaffective disorder, or bipolar disorder. Insatiable obsessions and sexual mania can be exacerbated by paranoia, delusional thoughts, and hallucinations. The psychotic serial killer may imagine voices, even commands from God, telling him to rape and kill to destroy his imagined enemies or restore a righteous world.

Gary Heidnik was a paranoid schizophrenic with delusional thinking, command hallucinations, and escalating obsessive deviant sexual fantasies. While in Fairview State Hospital for the Criminally Insane, Heidnik remained mute for three years (1,005 days from 1978 until 1981) because "the devil put a cookie in my throat." In a series of Parole Board hearings, which took place over several months, he communicated exclusively by passing notes. He also brought a Bible to one meeting in which he had highlighted passages about Satan removing voices and biblical characters who became mute. At the end of the meeting, Heidnik signed his name as "G. M. Kill" instead of G. M. Heidnik. His muteness continued until the day he entered a church and his voice magically returned during the service – restored, in his mind, by God.

There are many examples of psychotic delusional thinking in Heidnik's psychiatric history, including religious obsessions. He said that he frequently conversed with God and that Jesus appeared to him in bright lights and made him feel warm and tingly. He received a Divine message commanding him to start a church. Heidnik's psychotic religious delusions and sexually deviant obsessions proved to be a deadly egotistical mix.

Heidnik's History

The first diagnosis of Heidnik's mental illness appears in August 1962 at the age of 18. After one year of service in the Army, Heidnik sought medical help for symptoms that included severe headaches, vertigo, blurred vision, and nausea. Although diagnosed with stomach flu, the hospital neurologist also detected symptoms of mental illness, including seizure-like behaviors that were thought to be hallucinatory and delusional. He was prescribed Stelazine, an anti-psychotic medication typically used for schizophrenia. Two months later, Heidnik was transferred from Germany to a military hospital in Philadelphia, where he was diagnosed with "schizoid personality disorder" and honorably discharged from military service with a medical disability. Clearly, his symptoms were serious because Heidnik was soon committed to a civilian psychiatric hospital for three months of intensive evaluation and treatment.

Based on his brief training as a medic in the Army, Heidnik pursued a career in nursing. In 1964, he completed one year of training as a licensed practical nurse and did an internship at the now-defunct Philadelphia General Hospital. He took classes at the University of Pennsylvania to become an RN and got a job at the university's hospital. But he soon dropped out of classes and was fired for poor performance. He next tried working as a psychiatric nurse at a Veterans hospital in Coatesville, where he was terminated for poor attendance and, notably, inappropriate and rude behavior with the patients.

Nevertheless, Heidnik continued in nursing, likely attracted by the authority of the position. He obtained a job at the Elwyn Institute, which primarily served individuals with intellectual disabilities. In 1967, Heidnik bought a 3-story house in the same west Philadelphia neighborhood at 4706 Cedar Avenue. He lived in one apartment and rented the other two. His job at Elwyn proved to be a turning point because Heidnik discovered the victim category that he would prey upon in the years to come: women with intellectual disabilities. Heidnik exploited his position of authority over his intellectually challenged clients. One of his duties was to escort them during outings in the neighborhood. He realized that he could finish these excursions by taking the women to his home for sex. Using his charm and authority, he took full advantage of the women's limited intelligence and inability to consent to sexual intercourse. He found a social group, both at work and outside of work, that he could dominate and over whom he could feel supremely powerful. His friends were mentally challenged men, his sex partners were mentally challenged women, and nearly all were African American. His longest relationship lasted ten years from 1968 to 1978, when he cohabitated with Dorothy Knox, who suffered from chronic mental illness and a severe intellectual disability. Previously, from 1967 to 1968, Heidnik dated and fathered a child by Lynn Wilson, another African-American woman with an intellectual disability. Notably, he gave first expression to his deviant fantasies of multiple partners by seducing her adult daughter as well.

Heidnik was a king over his intellectually weak subjects. He could act out his narcissistic fantasies of supremacy and sexual dominance. But it was not enough to sate his hunger for power. Deviant sexual fantasies lose their arousing appeal for the serial abuser, who is driven to more extreme fantasies and behavior to gain arousal. In 1971, Heidnik had a severe episode of florid psychosis. One morning, he got into his 1964 Plymouth to get coffee and donuts. But he just kept driving and driving as if possessed. Heidnik drove westward until he could drive no further, stopping at the ocean in Malibu, California, where he had command hallucinations from God to return home and start a church. In October 1971, he recruited five people with intellectual disabilities to create his new United Church of the Ministers of God – with himself as Bishop, supreme leader. By adding the authority of God's word to his dominance, Heidnik's flock would admire and worship him and be even more submissive to his will.

Heidnik's obsessive sexual fantasies became more and more extreme. He became more aroused by sadism and bondage pornography, and he even dug a three foot pit in the basement – the prototype for the sexual torture chamber he will later build to hold multiple victims at the same time.

Inevitably, even establishing himself as a pseudo-god was not enough to quench his insatiable obsession with power. Wealth would further enhance his dominance. In 1976, Heidnik invested $15,000 in the stock market and had extraordinary success in amassing a fortune of between $350,000 and $600,000 (an amount worth $1.2 to $2.1 million in today's dollars), which he partly attributed to "stock tips from god." He used the tax-exempt status of his so-called church to avoid taxes. He started living the high life, purchasing a fleet of luxury cars, including a Rolls Royce, Cadillac, and Lincoln Continental, and even had a van customized to his tastes. He sold his first house and bought a new one. The trappings of wealth gave him more power than ever. He flashed his money around and used his expensive cars to impress and attract new victims. But he also lost control one day with one of his tenants, who was refusing to pay rent. He fired a gun at his head, nicking the victim in the cheek. (In Letter #12, Heidnik describes this episode as nothing but a bluff to scare the man). Heidnik was charged with aggravated assault and unlawful possession of a firearm.

In June 1977, Heidnik befriended another vulnerable African-American woman, who had been discharged, penniless and homeless, from a facility for persons with intellectual disabilities. Heidnik quickly made Anjeanette Norton into his girlfriend and brought her into his home with his ten-year common law wife, Dorothy. This was significant as Heidnik's first experiment with maintaining multiple wives and sex partners. Anjeanette soon became pregnant. In March 1978, she gave birth to a child who was promptly taken away by authorities and placed in foster care. Heidnik liked the feeling of power he gained from becoming a father and his fragile self-esteem was crushed when the child was taken by authorities. Soon after, in May 1978, he devised a plan that escalated his fantasies to the next level. He drove with Anjeanette to the state institution for intellectual disabilities at Selinsgrove, where they signed out her sister, Alberta Norton, for a supposed home visit. Heidnik expected that no one would notice that she did not return. They drove back to Philadelphia where he imprisoned, raped, and sodomized Alberta for ten days in his basement. He had delusional ideas of fathering another child who the authorities could not take away from him. Heidnik was arrested and charged with kidnapping, unlawful restraint, false imprisonment, rape, involuntary deviant sexual intercourse, and interfering with the custody of a committed person.

Heidnik's crime had every key feature of the serial kidnapping, rape, and imprisonment that he committed nine years later. If the crime had not been discovered early, he may well have escalated his fantasies of sexual domination by adding other sexual slaves to his basement prison. He was prevented by over four years of incarceration.

In November 1978, Heidnik was sentenced to seven years in prison. He served almost four and half years, three years of which were spent in secure mental health units rather than the general prison. He was paroled in April 1983, but with clear concerns. When interviewed by a psychiatrist in 1984, Heidnik was found to have persecutory delusions, grandiose thinking, and severely impaired judgment, and the clinician predicted that Heidnik would commit heinous crimes or hurt himself.

Nevertheless, Heidnik was released from prison. Though he retained a sizeable fortune, he lived in his van for a few months before purchasing his final house in the fall of 1984. The property at 3250 N. Marshall Street was located in a run down neighborhood in North Philadelphia, but had a garage to protect his luxury cars. He returned to his former way of life. He advertised his "church" to area residents and befriended an intellectually disabled black man named Cyrus "Tony" Green as his part-time handy man. Tony Green became Heidnik's professed best friend. During this period, Heidnik enjoyed "around the clock companionship" with Tony, Tony's girlfriend Sandra Lindsay (later to become his second victim), and others who roomed in his home. Notably, Heidnik described this as the "favorite time" of his life (Letter #5). Heidnik's primary regret, however, was that, in his own words, "Still there was a vacuum in my life. I needed bonding and closeness of a wife and children" (also Letter #5).

It did not take long for the sexual fantasies and obsession with power to rise again. Instead of another victim with intellectual disabilities, Heidnik used his money to devise a new scheme to get a mail-order bride. After two years of letters, Heidnik lured Betty Pappas, a 22-year old Filipino woman, to come to the United States to marry him on October

3, 1985. "Falsely thinking that oriental women would be the greatest wives ever in existence," (letter #5) he expected Betty to be stereotypically subservient and knew she would be helpless as a foreigner in a new country without friends, family, or means. Almost immediately, Heidnik unleashed his deviant sexual obsessions on his new wife. He began to rape and beat her and tried to force her to have group sex with three other women. In less than three months, Betty fled the abuse and the marriage dissolved. Heidnik was arrested and charged with assault, rape, and involuntary deviant sexual intercourse. The charges were dropped, but he fell apart emotionally. In February 1986, a month after separating, Heidnik nearly committed suicide by car exhaust. He was committed to a locked psychiatric ward in the Veteran's Hospital in Coatesville from March to August.

Three months later, on Thanksgiving Day of 1986, Heidnik launched his plan to create a "harem" of ten sex slaves who would bear his many children "Indian style," that is, naturally. He escalated from the kidnapping, rape, and torture of a single victim to the kidnapping and abuse of an entire group of victims. Heidnik started by picking up a 25-year old, part-time prostitute named Josephina Rivera and lured her to his house, where he choked her until she was unconscious and carried her to the prison pit he had dug in his basement. The fact that his victim was not intellectually disabled would prove his undoing. Josephina used her intelligence to outwit him and escape, but not before he had committed one of the most unspeakable series of atrocities in modern criminal history.

Seventeen Weeks of Terror

After kidnapping Josephina Rivera on Thanksgiving Day, Heidnik kept her imprisoned and half-naked in his cold basement and raped her repeatedly each day. He attached metal clamps to her ankles, which were chained to a pipe in the ceiling. She watched as he used a shovel and pick to expand and deepen the pit to hold more victims. For food, he gave her nothing but bread and water. When she tried to escape and scream for help, he beat her with a board and covered the hole with a piece of plywood. Josephina endured the cramped space, hearing only the heavy metal music that Heidnik blasted from the radio to muffle any cries for help.

Just one week later, on December 3, 1986, Heidnik kidnapped his second victim, 24-year old Sandra Lindsay. This victim was probably the easiest to capture because she was intellectually disabled and already known to him as the girlfriend of his best friend, Tony Green. Heidnik chained Sandra to a beam alongside his first victim. She, too, was subjected to repeated rape and beatings. When visitors came to the house, including Sandra's relatives, he gagged both women and threatened them to be silent. If either victim disobeyed, he would punish her by hanging her from a pipe by one handcuffed wrist for hours at a time.

Three weeks later, on December 23, Heidnik went cruising for prostitutes to obtain his third sex slave. He pulled up to 19 year old Lisa Thomas, who angrily told him that she was not a prostitute. Heidnik apologized, started a conversation and offered her a ride. Impressed by his silver and white Cadillac Coupe De Ville and fooled by his charm, Lisa got in. He took her to a restaurant for dinner and lured her back to his house with promises of wine, new clothes, and luxuries. After she passed out from the wine that he had drugged, Heidnik dragged Lisa to the basement pit with Josephina and Sandra.

Just ten days later, on January 2, 1987, Heidnik abducted his fourth victim, Deborah Dudley, age 23, from the streets of north Philadelphia. From the start, Deborah was a fighter, who resisted Heidnik's rules of imprisonment and thwarted his wishes. For each rebellion, Heidnik beat her severely, but he never succeeded in gaining her submission in the eleven nightmarish weeks to come.

During this period, Heidnik's obsession with sexual power and dominance became more demanding and perverse. In addition to routine oral and genital rape, he now forced the women to engage in group sex. He also found pleasure in the illusion of having the women compete for his favor. He accomplished this by pitting the women against each other. The victims would be required to "rat" on each other or they would be punished. He continued to feed them little more than starvation rations of bread and water, but would add the occasional "treat" of spoiled leftovers and canned dog food.

Meanwhile, after so many weeks in captivity, Josephina had found ways to ingratiate herself with her captor in order to escape the worst of his abuses. She became Heidnik's special favorite and, as a survival strategy, she increasingly played the role of his assistant. Emboldened by this false loyalty and his continuing success in keeping four victims under control, Heidnik went cruising in north Philadelphia for a fifth victim. On January 18, 1987, Heidnik picked up an 18-year old prostitute named Jacqueline Askins and lured her to his house where he overpowered and chained her with the other prisoners.

It is notable that the kidnappings now stopped for more than two months. It would appear that Heidnik was struggling to manage five sexual slaves, including the active resistance and defiance of one of them, Deborah Dudley. But the biggest factor may have been the horror that occurred three weeks later. On February 5, 1987, after ten long weeks of imprisonment, Sandra Lindsay attempted to escape and was discovered by Heidnik. As punishment, she was hung by one handcuffed wrist from an overhead beam for two days. When he finally released her, she was barely conscious and obviously sick. But Heidnik attributed her vomiting and fever to her refusal to eat and forced food in her mouth because he believed she was pregnant with his child (she was not). When she collapsed in deliria, he regarded it as faking, and threw her back into the pit. When he returned later, Sandra had died.

Heidnik enlisted the help of his favorite slave, Josephina Rivera, and they carried the body to a bathroom upstairs where Heidnik used a power saw to dismember the corpse. According to Lisa Thomas, Heidnik eventually fed her and other victims parts of the body of Sandra Lindsay. The flesh was ground up, cooked, and mixed with dog food and rice. The remaining body parts were stored in the freezer. At this time, Heidnik narrowly escaped capture when a rookie police officer came to the house because neighbors had complained of the stench. Heidnik convinced the officer that he had merely burned a meal.

This near discovery by the police led Heidnik to another atrocity. To prevent his prisoners from hearing when he was in or out of the house, he bound the victims and systematically punctured their ear drums with a screwdriver. All were brutally deafened except for Josephina, his favorite, who Heidnik now considered more as a partner than a prisoner.

Yet another six weeks of unspeakable misery passed after the killing. Heidnik continued his daily abuse and rape, monitoring the women for signs of desired impregnation. He also escalated the level of his perverse power by adding a new method of torture: electric shocks. He would touch the open wires of an electric cord to the metal chains and handcuffs of the women. Here too, Josefina Rivera was exempted from the torture. By this time, she had succeeded in winning his trust, which meant that he would take her from the basement for sex and to watch TV together. He even took her out to eat a few times. Josefina lived in better conditions, but she still lived in dread terror of Heidnik and did not yet dare to attempt an escape.

Given his insatiable demand for total domination, Heidnik devised a more horrible punishment to control his sex slaves. On March 18, he ordered Josephina to fill the pit with water. As the terrified women stood in the shallow pool, Heidnik applied the electric wire. The women screamed hysterically, but Deborah Dudley received a lethal blast when the wire directly touched her shackles. She convulsed and collapsed dead. Showing no emotion over the death, Heidnik calmly went upstairs to get dog food for his victims and a pen and paper. He forced Josephina to write a confession of her participation in the killing and forced the two shaken survivors to add their names to the document. Leaving the corpse with Lisa and Jacquelyn for the night, he took Josephina upstairs to his bedroom. The next morning, he wrapped Deborah's corpse in plastic and stuffed it into the freezer.

Incredibly, on the very next day, March 19, Heidnik resumed his obsession to capture and impregnate a harem of ten women. With Josefina Rivera riding beside him, he cruised the streets of north Philadelphia, looking for his next victim. They encountered Agnes Adams, a 24-year old prostitute who happened to know Josefina from a local club where they had once worked as strippers. Josephina introduced Heidnik as her boyfriend and they readily convinced Agnes to come with them. Within hours, she too would be chained half-naked in Heidnik's basement pit.

Three days later, Heidnik and Josefina loaded Deborah Dudley's frozen corpse into his van and drove to a remote forested area of southern New Jersey known as the Pine Barrens. As Heidnik buried the body, Josephina Rivera waited in the van. She knew there was no longer any limit to Heidnik's violence. Still terrified of him, she knew she had to do something soon to escape. She convinced Heidnik that she needed to visit her family to show that she was safe and promised to come back with another woman to add to his harem. He agreed to drive her to her family's house and wait nearby until she returned with the next slave. Instead Josephina went to the police. It was March 24, 1987, almost four months to the day after she became the first of Heidnik's prisoners. The ordeal was over.

Steps in Heidnik's Pattern of Escalating Deviant Behavior

1962-1964: Emergence of mental illness and development of deviant sexual fantasies of dominance and power.

1964-1966: Chooses career in nursing because it gives him power and authority.

1967-1969: Internal deviant sexual fantasies acted out externally on real victims: sexual exploitation of vulnerable people with intellectual disabilities.

1968: Expresses sexual fantasy of multiple sex partners by seducing adult daughter of his girlfriend.

1971-1975: Sexual power fantasies/behavior are expanded to greater domination of victims by starting a "church" with himself as Bishop and leader.

1975 Deviance escalates to bondage pornography and digging first prison pit in basement.

1976: Wealth fuels the pursuit of still greater power – new house, luxury cars, living the high life.

1977: Adds a second "wife" to his household for multiple sex partners.

1978: Deviant sexual fantasies/behavior escalate to the next level: kidnapping, rape, abuse and imprisonment of an actual victim.

1984: After prison, he returns to his primary victim pool and re-starts his church.

1985: Deviance escalates to the next level when Heidnik tries to exploit a new type of vulnerable victim: he "buys" a Filipino mail-order bride. Deviant fantasies escalate as he tries to force his wife into group sex with himself as master.

1986: Deviance escalates to highest level: kidnapping, rape and torture of an entire group of victims.

CHAPTER 4
Was I Crazy? A Review of My Case

So we've seen just how crazy Gary Heidnik was. The question now is how crazy was I when I entered the picture in 1987? The answer, for me, is Vietnam and why I volunteered to fight there twenty years before. The story starts with the death of my father. He died unexpectedly in a filling station bathroom in 1952 when I was almost 5 years old. I remember a lot about him, like how he held me on his lap while I watched cartoons. I knew that he was gone forever. It was devastating. I can remember the adults treating me oddly and talking in whispers and hushed tones. They shipped me off to my aunt's farm while the adults took care of the funeral. My mother's sister said to me, "Well, we won't have to clean out his ash trays anymore." A four year old may not know how to say "fuck you," but I never spoke to my aunt again unless commanded by my mother.

My father had built a successful business, but after his death, my mother was bamboozled by two slick lawyers into signing it over to them. Suddenly my childhood went from a large house with maids to a tiny one with my mother and two older brothers. We moved repeatedly and ended up in a cramped basement apartment. My mother had to work hard to make ends meet. The only way to get any money was to earn it myself.

Living with my mother was difficult. She had an emotionally deprived childhood and it often manifested itself in her deficient child-rearing and lack of warmth. Some of my earliest memories are of my mother telling me, and anyone who would listen, that she didn't want me. According to the family folklore, she demanded that the doctor take me back because she wanted a girl. In fact, she <u>did</u> send me back with a nurse on several occasions as she often claimed till she was 85. Naturally, if my own mother didn't want me, then who would? I felt unlovable. And my dad was dead. So I shut down my hurt feelings and acted like it didn't matter. I decided I would take care of myself.

My two older brothers reinforced this independence. There was no room for self-pity or tears. If I suffered a fall or beating, they taught me to stand up, dust myself off, and move forward. I remember episodes of extreme anxiety and depression, even as a pre-teen and teenager, but I always concealed my emotions. I often felt sick with worry and I threw up in every school that I ever attended, but no one suspected that it was anxiety. My brothers made doubly sure that I could never show any fear. I was simply not allowed to lose a fight. One time I was beaten by a neighbor boy, who was bigger and two years older. My brothers cleared the living room furniture to create a gladiator pit for a win-or-die fight. It was savage and ended with me nearly choking him to death. I might have killed him if my brothers did not tear me away. I am not proud of this, but no one dared to mess with me after that because I would become a raging animal.

I was angry at my Dad dying, at my self-centered mother, at my brothers for using me as punching bag, and at myself for being unlovable. My response was to shut down any feelings. The other kids feared me as a tough guy, but I didn't feel like one. I never knew where I fit into the various clubs and cliques. I was not impressed by the smart kids, or the cool kids, or the fake tough kids. But I had a strong sense of social justice and whenever I saw a weak kid who was getting picked on, I would take care of the bully. I had some good friends, including one who I love to this day. He and his Italian family were like my second family and it felt good to share in their open and easy expressions of love and emotion.

I think that losing my father at such a young age was part of my life-long problem with authority figures. I excelled in baseball and sports, and I might have been some kind of star athlete, but I clashed with coaches. I felt like I had to prove myself by being tough and fearless. I often did things that were dangerous and foolhardy. In particular, I grew up with the idea that I had to live up to the family legacy of my Uncle Harry, the war hero. He was in the 2nd Rangers in World War II and scaled the cliffs at Pointe du Hoc during the Normandy invasion to knock out the German artillery guns. He was a certified bad ass, who saw a lot of combat in Europe. He was later captured and spent the last 10 months of the war as a POW. Eventually Uncle Harry came home, suffering from severe headaches. He went to the VA for medication and evidently took the entire bottle of pills to ease the pain. He was coming home on a streetcar and dropped dead.

I took the family legacy to heart and felt it was my personal duty to represent Uncle Harry. My oldest stepbrother had failed in that task. He faked stuttering to avoid serving in the Korean War. He was a big guy who could really fight, which made him a coward in my eyes. So, when Vietnam came along, I volunteered, entering Officer Candidate School at age 18. I don't consider myself to be brave or a hero or anything like that, neither then or now. I was just trying to do something to uphold Uncle Harry's hero legacy. Given my issues with authority, I had no tolerance for the bullshit I saw in OCS. I soon quit and they sent me to Vietnam with 13 days leave. I was glad to go – at the time.

In the Nam, I did a lot of recon and was frequently out on ambush patrol. We operated with the 11th Armored Cavalry Regiment in war zones II and IV. One time, in January 1968, our platoon had to attack a village. We torched the huts to burn it to the ground, but one of the villagers, an old man in a straw hat, tried to put out the fire. One trooper felled him with the butt end of his rifle. The old man lurched toward something that looked like a weapon and I instinctively fired. I shot him three times in the head. It turned out that he was reaching for a pitch fork. It is horrible to admit, but I didn't care about killing him at that moment. But I did later, and I do now, and with more regret and self-hatred than you can imagine. For the rest of my life, I have seen that old man in my dreams. Maybe I always will – and should.

That was the day I decided that I had had enough of the ground war. I requested a transfer to the air and became a helicopter door gunner with the First Cav, 227th and 228th. Being a door gunner was no less dangerous, probably a lot worse, but at least I could get my ass out of the steaming jungle. My skin was ravaged with some kind of jungle rot and my crotch was always itching and burning. I also had an infection from ripping a leach off my skin. My infections finally began to heal as I could get some regular showers. We choppered into every hot LZ in our zone and lost a lot of men. Sometimes we flew medi-vacs and I sadly remember loading dead and wounded marines during the battle of Hue City in February 1968.

In the fall of 1968, I received a 30 day leave to go back home. After we landed in Seattle, we were told that we could get a hot shower, clean uniforms, and a steak dinner. The shower and clean uniform were the most inviting to me. Later I caught a ride to the airport. I remember the amazing sight of mini-skirts, long straight hair, and "hippies." It was the first time I had seen beautiful, round-eyed women in a long time and they were unbelievably hot. As luck would have it, a pretty hippie girl said hello and flopped on my lap. At first, I thought she was just messing with a Nam vet. But then she kissed me and rubbed my crotch. I immediately decided to stay for an unforgettable night of sex, weed, and wine. For that one night, I was able to totally forget the horrors of the Nam. What a welcome home. Nothing like my homies. Many Vietnam vets talk of coming home to be spit on and called "baby killers." I always felt bad for them and guilty over my night of mercy sex. Thank you, Lisa, wherever you are.

I made it back home with the expectation of returning to Vietnam for another year. But then my mother was rushed to the hospital for a gall bladder attack, followed by a heart attack. I was sitting in the ICU when my buddy Frank called from Portland. He was also on 30-day leave and asked for some money so that he could fly to Philly to see me. I said it was too hectic and I would see him back in Phu Bai.

As it turned out, I never returned. Given my mother's condition, I was afraid that the stress of returning to Vietnam would kill her, so I asked to be reassigned stateside. I survived the Nam by not going back, but Frank was killed in the A Shau Valley. My friend had saved my life and was ready to cross the country just to hang with me for a few days. But I said no. It's another one of those bad decisions that stays with me forever.

Ultimately, I was stationed at Fort Dix in New Jersey to finish my time. One day, in May or June 1969, I learned that my high school friend Gary had been wounded on Hamburger Hill and was hospitalized on base. I was horrified to see him maimed and stooped in the hallway with bandages across his chest and a catheter bag that was overflowing. He was too good of a kid to suffer like this. Blind with tears and rage, I grabbed his nurse and dragged her over to his urine-drenched bed. I was rubbing her face in the wet sheets when I was restrained and cuffed by the MPs.

I guess they empathized with my outburst because they let me go without charges. Soon after, I had a severe migraine, one of many that plagued me over the years. I went to the clinic and they gave me a bottle of Darvon with morphine. I don't remember taking them all, nor do I remember driving my car to Bristol, PA where my mother lived. I woke up the next morning with my face in a pool of vomit and didn't know where or who I was. A kindly state trooper let me go home. Unlike my Uncle Harry, I had escaped a similar death by overdose. In my bleary mind, however, I thought that I had failed again – by not living up to his legacy. Despite my shitload of war medals, I felt like an imposter. I wasn't a war hero like him and now I couldn't even die like him.

As I look at the high rates of suicide of combat veterans, I think I have some insight into the death of my Uncle Harry and my own self-destructive behavior. After experiencing so much killing and horror in war, you become hollow and numb except for a nagging feeling of pain. In my case, I also had an unrelenting buzzing white noise in my head. I think combat veterans take pills, drugs, and alcohol to stop the constant pain, even for a moment. It is an intentional overdose that can easily slip into intentional or accidental suicide. When I ingested those thirty morphine balls and passed out, the pain was finally gone – at least until I woke up again. For some vets, it seems that the only way to end their pain is to overdose and possibly die.

    The idea of not living up to my bad-assed uncle played a large role in my life as I continued to put myself in high risk situations. I would do stupid dangerous things without caring about the law or my own life. One time my friend "Saint Nick" asked me to help him with his business. He was a combat veteran, who made his living as a money lender and illegal pharmaceutical salesman. He needed to collect a large sum of money from a rival crew's territory, in fact, from the bar that was their headquarters. He tried to get others to go with him for the collection, but they all refused because it was too dangerous. I pulled on my black leather coat and leather gloves, stuffed four guns in my pockets, and we drove to the bar in a black Eldorado. We marched in like we owned the place. Nick ordered a shot of Seagram's at the bar, while I locked the front door and faced the crew with two drawn pistols. I had a Colt 45 automatic in one hand and a 9mm Smith and Wesson model 669 with a 20 round clip in the other. Nick made his demands for the money owed. No one moved a muscle. Nick finished his whiskey, picked up the money, and sauntered out. I followed, back-stepping out of the bar, and jammed the door latch with a screwdriver that I brought along for that purpose. We drove over to an after-hours club called the Sherwood and celebrated by doing lines of coke.

    Let me tell you why I called him "Saint Nick." It started on Christmas Eve in 1985 or 1986. A friend owned an apartment complex in northeast Philly and wanted us to evict some sleazy meth dealer and a woman who was five months behind on her rent. I was really pumped up and exploded through the door with my 45 and my 9 with Nick right behind me. I flattened the drug dealer and held him down while Nick confiscated his shotgun, 357, drug money, and inventory. After a brief counseling session, we evicted the dealer with the proviso that his return would be his end. We proceeded to visit the deadbeat renter next door. She turned out to be an old lady and the drug dealer had been extorting money from her, which is why she couldn't pay her rent, and she was too scared to call the cops. Nick and I assured her that she was safe and would not be evicted. In fact, we gave her the dealer's money to pay her back rent as well as six more months of rent as a Christmas present. She hugged us and we both felt like we were Santa Claus. And since Nick is on the fat side, I named him, "Saint Nick."

There are more stories I could tell, but you get the picture of what I mean by stupid dangerous behavior. It is important to recognize, however, that I did not just jump into my life as a gangster. It was a slow transition, not an implosion. I was a trained professional counselor, but after five years of dealing constantly and intensely with other Vietnam veterans (along with my own war trauma), my sense of reality was so blurred that I felt like I was back in the shit in Nam. You might think this is a bullshit excuse for bad behavior, but I can honestly say that such distortion and confusion was real. Yes, I am fully responsible for my gangster life, and do not blame it on PTSD, but I think these facts serve as a mitigation for some of my excesses.

There would be a dozen years of recklessness ahead of me – along with the migraines and nightmares, drug and alcohol abuse, and wild sexcapades – before I would encounter the three people that would enable me to turn my life around: first my daughter, then my second wife Joanne and, ironically, Gary M. Heidnik. Don't get me wrong. The intervening years weren't all horrible. I did manage to get married, graduate college, and start a profession. I met Carol, my first wife, while home on leave from Vietnam. She was 16 when we met and I was 19. I was struck by her brains and wit. After the war, in 1969, I enrolled at the University of Pittsburgh because Carol had a full scholarship there. We married in our junior year and shared a good life for several years. But it wasn't meant to last. I was young, wild, and fucked up by Vietnam. All the sex, drugs, and rock n' roll took its toll and we grew apart.

There was one purely good thing in the growing chaos and conflict in my marriage: my daughter Melissa, born in 1975. I can honestly say that, even in my worst moments, I got that part right. I was always an involved loving father. My daughter made me feel like I had done something right in my life. But I didn't stop partying. One day, after snorting a quarter ounce of blow on another three day run, I had a moment of clarity. I literally looked in the bathroom mirror and was disgusted with myself. I had wrecked my life, my marriage, and my future and, if I didn't change, my daughter would have to visit me in a penitentiary or a graveyard. For her sake, I determined to change myself that day. I began to seriously try (emphasis on try) to become a responsible adult. It took time. Years.

Meanwhile, in 1977, I completed my Masters degree in psychology at Temple University. I worked in mental health and enrolled in the doctoral program in 1982. From 1983 to 1987, I primarily did therapy with post-traumatic Vietnam vets on a five year outreach grant from the Veterans Administration. Eventually I earned my doctorate from Temple in May 1986. One month later, I separated from my wife. Shortly after that, I had my first date with my future wife, Joanne.

I had first met Joanne many months before at a doctor's office where I was doing some consulting on behaviorally disordered youth and she was working as a nurse. For some reason, this bright, beautiful woman liked me and we flirted. I waited until after my separation before I asked her on a date. It was summer 1986 and I drove up in my lipstick red Trans Am, wearing a white suit and light blue shirt. I took her to an outdoor restaurant with a wooden bridge crossing over a natural waterfall. It was a fabulous night and I was totally smitten, but I knew it was best to not get involved. I was a gangster living a dangerous, secret life of crazy stripper sex and parties fueled by cocaine and speed. I liked and respected Joanne too much to hurt her with that. We had a great rapport and I kept going back to see her, but I kept my distance for nearly a year – for her sake.

The turning point was in May 1987. I suggested a romantic weekend at the beach in Delaware. I took the top off of my Trans Am and off we went. The ride down was really fun as we talked about everything, kids, life, justice, injustice, and music, my favorite topic to this day. I loaded up on cassettes of Bob Marley, Def Leppard, Psychedelic Furs, Clash, Zeppelin, Pat Metheny, Miles Davis, and Coltrane. We got a lovely beachfront room – but it was right next to a construction site! The pounding was like 155mm howitzers as we began to unpack. I had brought enough clothes for a year along with my Mossberg semi automatic, 200 rounds of buckshot, tracers, incendiary rounds, 9mm pistol, and 300 rounds of hollow points. It looked like I was going on a combat mission in the A Shau Valley, not a trip to the beach. Joanne asked if I was expecting an invasion.

We put on our shorts and took a long walk along the shore. One of the things that I had talked to Joanne about was quitting drugs, all drugs, no exceptions. She never said "you better," or "you should," or made any sort of ultimatum. Instead, she just listened and made it safe for me to reveal my inner world of numbness, pain, and hopelessness. As we strolled the beach, I felt utterly exhausted and weak, as if I was "running on empty," to quote Jackson Browne. Joanne suggested that we go back to the room. The jack hammers were gone and we could hear the waves. After a shower, I fell asleep. I didn't awaken for another 24 hours. When I did, I expected Joanne to be angry. Instead she was kind and took me to breakfast, simple toast and coffee. We took another walk and then just sat and talked on a bench overlooking the ocean, my favorite place in the world.

That was our romantic weekend, sleeping, talking, a little food, and more sleeping. I don't think we even had sex because everything else was so wonderful, especially relating to a woman in a totally honest and equal way. Joanne remembers going out to dinner and I put a piece of broccoli in my ear to make her laugh. Her laugh was intoxicating and touched my heart. It was fun to let that side of me out, as I had been a soldier, a gangster, a father, a tough guy, a sex maniac, but never my child self. I had been acting grown up since my father died. For the first time, I was just being my pure self and it felt great to be accepted. I went off all drugs that weekend and knew that I had found my soul mate for life. I had also begun to find myself.

Of course, quitting drugs is just the starting point. Now I had to learn to live without them – just as I was embarking on my dark journey with Gary M. Heidnik. And that brings us back to September 1987, when Charles Peruto hired me for the Heidnik defense team. A month later, catastrophe struck. On Halloween night, Joanne and I went to surprise my brother Bill. Joanne was dressed as a gangster in a suit and fedora with a semi-automatic Mossberg pump shotgun, stockings, and garter. I was totally naked in a pervert's trench coat. I flashed my brother and he laughed so hard that he went into a coughing fit and couldn't catch his breath. He was thin and gaunt and I realized something was seriously wrong. It was lung cancer and his time was very short. On the night before Thanksgiving, I was hanging with Bill and feeling depressed about losing custody of my daughter in court the day before. He was the closest thing to a real father for me because he raised me and gave me love throughout my life. Bill told me to "never give up, never quit, no one can beat you." Those words have remained my mantra at the various times in my life when I've lost hope. The very next day I got a call that Bill was dying. I raced to the hospital at 120 mph. I ran up to find the distorted crying faces of his family outside the room and rushed in to see him. I told Bill that I loved him and watched a tear run down his face. After a long day, he died holding my hand. It was something I'd done too many times before in Vietnam, watching the life drain out of young men whose only sin in life was being from families without means. We were the product of the select draft, for the poor and the expendable.

My brother's death hit me really hard. He represented all that was good and right in the world. He was a dedicated English teacher, loyal husband, and father loved by all of his children. He was my anchor to the world, the key to maintaining some faith in righteousness, justice, and hope. I looked at myself as the opposite, the embodiment of all that was selfish, damaged, and wrong. I wanted to trade places with Bill so that he could live. It was wrong that Bill, the good one, should die and that I should live.

I was overwhelmed by the pain of losing him. He was my brother, father, friend, and hope. I was desperate to stop the agony of my grief and escape into sleep. So I started taking valium and benzos, two and three at a time, until they were all gone. Joanne came in and discovered me barely breathing. I was drifting in and out of consciousness and she wanted to take me to a hospital, but I refused. Now, understand when I say refuse, I mean fucking REFUSE, as in a stubborn bad-ass soldier who is raging and ready to fight the world. It was a long night, but she got me into the shower, walked me around, and saved my life. I wasn't trying to kill myself. I just wanted to stop the pain of losing my brother, along with a line of brothers in bloodied and mangled jungle fatigues. I still miss and love my brother as much today and can still feel his hand let go of mine when he let go of this world.

Now, as 1987 came to close, I had an agonizing case of grief to add to my other problems. I was in the thick of my nasty divorce, still fighting for custody of my daughter, and clinging to my new-found sobriety. I was also unemployed, penniless, and working for free on Heidnik's defense team. But, as my brother Bill told me on our last night together, "Never quit fighting," and I never have.

KEY TO PHOTOS ON THE OPPOSITE PAGE:

Top left: Jack, age 16, at the beach in Wildwood NJ, 1964.

Top middle: Door Gunner Jack cleaning his M-60 machine gun at Phu Bai, Vietnam, 1968.

Top right: Mr. Tamborine Man, at Phu Bai, June 1968.

Middle left: Jack giving peace sign at firebase near Cambodia, early 1967.

Middle right: Mom welcomes Jack back from the Nam, fall 1968.

Bottom right: Jack with daughter Melissa, age 8, 1986.

Bottom left: Jack's "Miami Vice" gangster look, 1986.

II. THE CORRESPONDENCE

LETTER #1
"I'm Not Available"

August 12, 1988

Three months after the Heidnik trial ended in failure, I was unemployed, fighting for custody of my daughter, and living with Joanne and her two kids. Then I came up with my seemingly brilliant plan to write a best seller that would tell Heidnik's story and explain why he should have been found not guilty by reason of insanity. I wrote to him in early August and waited excitedly for his response.

His letter arrived in a tan Department of Corrections envelope and took the form that all of his letters would. He always wrote in black pen in hand-printed letters and never in cursive. He nearly always wrote on 14 inch yellow lined legal paper and typically used every line on the page. He also made a ton of spelling and grammatical errors. These errors are marked with an asterisk throughout this book because they sometimes provide insights into his thinking and level of education and sophistication, or lack thereof.

I was not expecting the response I received.

NOTE: INSTANCES OF SIGNIFICANT MISSPELLING BY HEIDNIK ARE MARKED WITH AN ASTERISK * IN HIS LETTERS THROUGHOUT THIS BOOK.

August 12, 1988
Your letter arrived today and I was glad to hear from you.

There seemed to be a touch of urgency in your communication. Also it seemed to be a little cryptic. You said you'd like to "tell my story." Does this mean you're also writing another book? No offense, but you'll find a lot of competition. It seems a lot of people are doing that same thing. I am ashamed and disgusted with what happened, and have no intentions of writing a book, making any speeches, news casts etc. All this sensational publicity has caused me to be beaten up three times, and landed me on Death Row. Nobody believes those two deaths were not murders but accidents. They think I deliberately* committed murder with a pair of handcuffs. If I had really wanted to kill, I'd have used a gun or knife or something, but because of all the adverse publicity, such logic is beyond people.

Sorry, but I'm not available* for a book, but thank you very much for your extensive help at my trial.
Respectfully
Gary M. Heidnik

I was stunned and disappointed that Heidnik wasn't interested in my book. I was irritated by his boast that "you'll find a lot of competition." How was I going to get this crazy SOB to cooperate? In my former cocaine-filled head, I had deceived myself into believing that I was the only person he would trust to get inside his secret thinking.

I pondered his letter. In the aftermath of his trial and conviction, I first thought that Heidnik's complaint of being "ashamed and disgusted" might suggest genuine remorse over torturing and killing his victims. But a closer look shows nothing of the sort. He is ashamed and disgusted with "what happened," not with what he has done. Rather than remorse, Heidnik blames "sensational publicity" as the cause of his conviction. In his mind, he would be a free man if the story had simply not been blown out of proportion. Otherwise people would easily see that he could not have deliberately killed his victims by using handcuffs. The miscarriage of justice caused by the media is what disgusts Heidnik, not his crimes.

He also boasts that several entities are "competing" to write books about him, and fantasies himself giving speeches on the evening news. He recognizes, however, that such publicity will also result in more violent beatings from his African American prison mates, who are avenging the fact that nearly all of his victims were African-American women. So Heidnik's real concern for rejecting my book proposal was to escape any more attention that will bring violent retribution from the other inmates. He is torn between his narcissistic desire for attention and the practical necessity of avoiding attention for self-preservation. That is the reason he declined my offer. But Heidnik's egotism will eventually prevail – as revealed in his second letter to me.

LETTER #2
"Who's Exploiting Me?"

October 14, 1988

Given Heidnik's surprising refusal and my empty bank account, I now pondered a different approach and how, if necessary, I could write my best seller without his participation. I decided to research everything I could find on sexual homicide and serial killers. This was good for me because it strengthened my mastery of the topic and provided a healthy intellectual challenge that could distract me from the continuing temptations of my former cocaine and sex addiction.

At this time, I had the important idea of applying my own experience to better understand how Heidnik, or any human being, could be driven to commit such horrendous acts. My years in Vietnam had shown me how otherwise normal young men can be trained to kill and then driven by insane circumstances (and a regimen of mind-altering substances) to cross the boundaries of human restraint to do things that would be unthinkable in civilian life. I also knew, first hand, that one can cross boundaries when high on cocaine and speed that one would never cross when sober, or even when drunk on alcohol. Although Heidnik did not do drugs, I wondered if his mental illness manifested itself in a similar obsessive sex drive and loss of inhibitions. I theorized that Heidnik's psychosis was causing him to behave as if he was on a permanent obsessive speed trip. Perhaps his brain was hard-wired to generate deviant sexual urges and desires that he could not resist in the same way that cocaine and speed had removed the normal inhibitions that restrained my own sexual urges and desires.

In considering my theory, I looked frankly at my own coke-fueled sex-capades, which might rival Caligula, if not

Charlie Sheen. In the year before Heidnik, I would drink and hang out at a strip joint owned by my friend. I made friends with several of the dancers and two, in particular, were grateful to me for forcibly extracting the abusive boyfriends from their lives. After the club closed for the night, we would go back to one of their apartments to continue drinking, smoke weed, and do cocaine or speed. It was just me and two sexy, consenting women. We'd gradually ramp up from kissing and fooling around to more XXX-rated action. Sometimes we'd have porn movies rolling and try to keep up, or even try to do better and make our own. One of the effects of the drugs was to prevent orgasm, so I was able to perform for hours on end. I had insatiable sexual desire for these women and we would go all night long.

Like any good addict or alcoholic, I would often be disgusted with myself on the morning after. But then the urges and opportunity would return and it would start again. The marathon sex sessions morphed into larger parties, multiple partners, and Spider Man sex positions, and the attitude was anything goes. Many sober years later, it is both embarrassing and a marvel to me that I could have been so utterly amoral. But at the time, it was like a double addiction – sex <u>and</u> drugs – with double the strength. The combination made it almost unbearable to live without either. In the summer and fall of 1988, I was still struggling hard to resist these sexual and drug urges and stay clean, but my desires remained extremely powerful.

By looking at myself, I could see that, even though my sexploits were volitional, the obsessive drive is incredibly powerful and, under the influence of disinhibiting drugs, almost irresistible. In the case of Heidnik or another sexual killer, I theorized that the obsessive urge and fantasy must become similarly irresistible. Fortunately for me, Joanne gave me the extra motivation to resist the obsessive sexual and drug cravings. We had married in August and I committed myself to becoming a good husband and stepdad – and I was renewed in my determination to regain custody of my own daughter. Her faith in me revived my belief in myself. I decided to try again and wrote a second request to Heidnik in October.

Friday, Oct 14, 88

Dear Dr. Apsche,
 Your letter arrived today and it raised some questions I'd appreciate your answers to.
 1. About the book Serial Killers. *Is that the one I'm in?*
 2. If so could you send me a copy; I'll pay for it.
 3. I know you wrote that other book, you gave Peruto a copy but not me. Could you send me a copy of your book also? I'm willing to pay for it also.
 4. I'd like to see your writing* style.
 5. I'd like to see your article on McNaughton which you mentioned.
 6. Who's exploiting me?
 7. Mr. Peruto told me he paid you something like 5 or 10 thousand. You say you were unpaid. Is that true?
 8. I never trusted Dr. Bora. What makes you say that I did? And it was 82 not 78.
 9. Are there any other books about me, and if so what are their names.
 Gary M. Heidnik

I took it as a good sign that Heidnik wrote back as soon as he received my second letter. He is clearly excited by the idea of having a book written about himself. In Letter #1, he boasted of having competition to write his book. Here he wants to purchase a copy of the book, *Serial Killers*, which he presumes is written about him. In fact, the book predated

Heidnik's notoriety by a year and does not mention him. He further asks if there are more books about himself. He clearly imagines himself worthy of books. The advantage of using me, however, is that he can control the content of "his" book. He knows that I need his cooperation and he can use it as leverage. He writes, "I'd like to see your writing style," as if I'm going to audition to be his biographer.

I sure as hell did not want to be his biographer. But I was, for the moment, at his mercy and he knew it. The problem for Heidnik is his own paranoia. Can he trust me to do his bidding? This distrust underlies his list of nine numbered questions, which are tests of how well I can be trusted (and how easily I can be controlled).

In question #3, Heidnik asks about my "other book" and why I "gave a copy to Peruto, but not me." Four months after the trial, Heidnik is still insulted that I did not give him a copy of my book because he regards himself as an equal with attorney Charles Peruto and me. The book was *The Effects of Punishment on Human Behavior*, 1983, by Saul Axelrod and myself, and had nothing to do with serial killers. By reminding me of this event, he is both declaring his status and seeking a sample of my "writing style" to see if I am worthy of the honor of being his biographer.

For the same reason, Heidnik requests a copy of my McNaughton article in question #4. The so-called "McNaughton rule" (sometimes spelled M'Naghten) is a legal test of whether a mentally ill defendant understands the nature and quality of his crime at the time of commission and whether he knows the difference between right and wrong with regard to that crime. Historically, the rule derived from a famous case in English law in 1843 in which a Scotsman was acquitted of an assassination attempt because of mental illness. Although 170 years old, modern American law essentially continues to apply the same standard for the determination of sanity or insanity in criminal cases. My position, vis a vis the McNaughton rule, was that Heidnik suffered from psychotic delusions that were so severe that he both (1) did not understand the nature or quality of his acts at the time of the crime and (2) he did not see anything wrong with his crimes at the time of the crimes. I believe that Heidnik did, however, come to understand the difference between right and wrong <u>after</u> his terrible crimes. Defense attorneys often do not address this difference between insanity at the time of the crime and sanity after the act.

Heidnik's fundamental distrust and paranoia is revealed in the other questions. In question #6, the king of exploitation asks, "Who's exploiting me?" In question #8, he abruptly declares: "I never trusted Dr. Bora. What makes you say that I did? And it was 82 not 78." Dr. Bora was his psychiatrist at Graterford Prison, where he was incarcerated after kidnapping, raping, and imprisoning Alberta Norton in 1978. Heidnik first scolds me for the mistake of claiming that he trusted Dr. Bora and then gives me another little jab by correcting the dates. In essence, he is saying, "How can you ever write my book if you can't even get the facts right?" More importantly, in declaring that he didn't trust Dr. Bora, Heidnik is also revealing that, "I don't trust Dr. Apsche either."

The most remarkable part of Heidnik's second letter, for me, is item #6: "Mr. Peruto told me he paid you something like 5 or 10 thousand. You say you were unpaid. Is that true?" This comment is transparently manipulative. He suspects that Peruto and I may be in cahoots and wants to play us against each other by suggesting that Peruto is lying behind my back and cheating me. He thinks his ploy is subtle, suggesting that "You can't trust Peruto, but you can trust me." [Note: Both question #7 (Peruto's payment) and #8 (Dr. Bora) will reemerge in nearly the same exact words in Letter #16.]

The most important point of this letter is that Heidnik still does <u>not</u> agree to participate in my proposed book. But he clearly leaves the door open as a stalling technique to see what my next counter-offer will be.

Knowing how much he loved to read, I decided to try to win Heidnik over by sending him the requested book and article, as well as some extra gifts of newspapers and magazines. At the same time, I was fully prepared for his refusal. I figured I would try to interview other people who knew him personally, so I asked how I might find some of the members of his former "church." For the heck of it, I also asked his opinion of Harrison Marty Graham, another infamous serial killer, who had been arrested within months of Heidnik for very similar sexual crimes. I was curious about how Heidnik felt about his rival for the title of Philadelphia's greatest monster.

LETTER #3
"The Special Olympics of Churches"

November 5, 1988

Heidnik loved my gift box of books and articles. Although he still does not explicitly agree to the book idea, he positively dives into the project with this letter. He is so eager that he begins writing to me within minutes of receiving my letter. The game is on. With this letter, there is a definite turning point in our correspondence and Heidnik's true writing "style" emerges. Unlike his previous single-page letters, his third is four pages long. From this point forward, Heidnik's letters will be quite extensive, rambling, and informal, rarely less than three pages in length, frequently more than six, and often more than fifteen.

Saturday, Nov 5, 88

Dear Dr. Apsche,
Today, only about 15 minutes ago, the guards forwarded your material to me. To wit, the book, letters, newspaper clippings, etc. Apparently the information arrived a week or two ago, but they delayed giving it to me until it was reviewed and approved by the guard officer.
I've only made a cursory review so far, but will perform a more profound* study later. First, this letter and a few comments.
In your article, "Gary Heidnik, Serial Killers, etc-" you left out page 8. I haven't read it yet, but in organizing it, I noticed this oversight. Could you send me another page 8? The book "Effects of Punishment..." isn't apparently going to reveal to me what I was seeking, to know of your* literary style. I've gleaned from it so far that you've only edited it, and did none of the actual writing. Also you committed another oversight in this book you forgot to

autograph it. Shame on you ☺.
Seriously, have you written any other books or authored some pamphlets* or some other publications that would show me your literary capacity?

Heidnik's first and foremost concern is whether I have the "literary style" worthy of portraying him. He complains that my book is only co-edited by me and therefore lacks examples of my own writing. He further complains that my McNaughton article is too scholarly for what he imagines will be a popular best seller. He wants a more accessible style and is bothered that he cannot fully control how it will be written. Unlike his previous letter, however, Heidnik shows some subtlety in expressing this frustration. He attempts flattery by chastising me for failing to autograph my book and adds a smiley face to show that his "shame on you" remark is intended as humorous teasing. But Heidnik immediately reiterates his "serious" request for a writing sample that truly shows my "literary capacity."

Heidnik also wants to establish that he stands as an equal partner in writing this book, or better yet, the controlling partner. Though he cannot yet judge my writing style, he intends to show me that he is an able writer in his own "write." He inundates me with a dozen sophisticated vocabulary words in the next paragraph, such as gregarious, loquacious, appalling, and solicitous. He is obviously unfamiliar with these "$25 words." He misspells "unrepentant," "expatiated," and "prevailing." He misuses "regaled" and "intercession" and makes awkward use of "immured" and "spurious." His grandiose display of vocabulary is all for show. Once he thinks he has impressed me with his brilliant command of language, he promptly abandons his bunk-side thesaurus and does not use another grandiose word for the remainder of the letter.

The subject of his "loquacious" paragraph is Harrison "Marty" Graham. It is a quirk of history that two serial sex killers were arrested in the same section of the same city within months of each other for very similar crimes; that both suffered from chronic mental illness; that both pled insanity – unsuccessfully; and that they came to befriend each other in the same jail.

As for Marty Graham, I've had some personal experiences with him and thus feel compelled in making some comments. True, he is here, immured with me in the same prison*, but I've only seen him once, and all we did was say hello. I think he's somewhat depressed here, and is unpopular with the other inmates. They have him in administrative custody* for his own protection. I first met Marty several times in the holding cells of the Phila. City Hall courtroom. He was very gregarious and loquacious, and quite obviously very unrepentative*. He was not only willing to talk about his deeds, but he actually seemed to enjoy discussing them but expatiated* at some length, even to the point of making humorous remarks. He was also about the only black inmate who didn't show any hostility towards me, but even extended me the hand of friendship. He even refused some of the bitterness towards me and kept the other black inmates from assaulting me. To him, for this, I'm grateful. As you may already be aware of, I'm not very popular with the other inmates and many are seeking retribution towards me. One inmate even related the information to me that a certain black religious organization (Nation of Islam) has a $5,000 contract on me. This could be a spurious offer, related to me only for the purposes of further terrorizing*, but it does show the prevailing* attitudes. For certain, the inmates who assault me or even kill me are to be regaled as conquering heroes within the black community. As you may be aware of, I've been physically assaulted three times already since my arrest. The last time was on the bus from Graterford to S.C.I.P. I was beaten by 15 inmates and what makes this incident so appalling is they were actually encouraged by the *guards. I was taken to the hospital where I received 5 sutures in my face, assorted bruises and cuts and x-rayed for concussion and broken facial bones. Only God's intercession kept it from turning into a real massacre. Also, fortunately*, the guards here at S.C.I.P. have been very solicitous of my safety and I've haven't* been further assaulted, although I have been frequently taunted and harassed*. The guards can't protect me totally and it is probably only a matter of time till then...*

Professionally, I had just served as an expert advisor to Joel S. Moldovsky, the defense attorney for Marty Graham, so I was familiar with the case. Briefly, Graham was a 29 year old African American drug addict with mild retardation who would lure women to his apartment with the promise of drugs. After getting his victims high with drugs and alcohol, he would strangle them while having sex. His killing spree began with the sexual murder of his former girlfriend and another victim he had lived with. Like Heidnik, six of his seven victims were African American. As sexual predators, both men were obsessed with possessing and controlling women. Heidnik held them prisoner for months. Graham retained their corpses for months, sometimes wrapping them in sheets like mummies, dismembering some, and drawing macabre pictures of naked women and disconnected body parts. Unable to relinquish control, Graham clung to his victims' bodies until the corpses became putrid and the stench led his eventual discovery and arrest. As Graham said, "They were mine and weren't going nowhere."

Two psychiatrists evaluated Graham's competency to stand trial and had differing conclusions. One determined that he was incompetent because he had mental retardation (IQ of 63) and suffered from drug and alcohol abuse and psychotic illness with auditory hallucinations, blackouts, and paranoia. The other psychiatrist acknowledged that Graham was limited in capacity, but held that he was sufficiently coherent to respond logically to questions and could cooperate in his own defense. The court agreed with the latter. In May 1988, Marty Graham was found guilty of seven counts of murder and abuse of a corpse and sentenced to life in prison. Six years later, his case was reviewed by the Pennsylvania Supreme Court who unanimously determined that his original sentence was improper and he should be executed. Graham's execution was delayed for years, however, until the U.S. Supreme Court banned the execution of people with mental retardation in 2002. Ultimately, seventeen years after his trial, Marty Graham was deemed incompetent to be executed. He had "won" the insanity defense after all. Heidnik was executed in 1999. As final note, both Graham and Heidnik shared an intense religiosity. Whereas Heidnik became a self-proclaimed minister, Graham studied religion behind bars and became an ordained minister.

Given my familiarity with both Heidnik and Graham, I was curious whether they had encountered each other at the SCIP prison at Pittsburgh. Although they had only met there once in passing, he knew Graham quite well from previous encounters. He reveals strong mixed feelings about Graham. His predominant attitude is disdain. Graham is in competition for the limelight. Heidnik does not like the obvious similarities between them and wants to emphasize their differences. As someone who has ruled like a king over a world of intellectually disabled citizens, Heidnik presumes a fundamental superiority over Gardner, who is also intellectually disabled. He disapproves of Graham's cheerful willingness to tell the gory details of his exploits and make jokes about it. Heidnik declares that Graham is "quite obviously very unrepentative." It is something else that they have in common, but Heidnik, unlike Graham, knows better than to openly admit his crimes. To paraphrase Heidnik from letters #5 and #6, "I may be crazy, but I'm not stupid" – not like <u>that</u> guy.

Still, as much as Heidnik spurns his peer, he genuinely

likes Graham because he "kept the other black inmates from assaulting me" and "even extended me the hand of friendship." This is no small favor. Heidnik has endured three violent assaults from other inmates and has been threatened with death. (In fact, as described in letter #24, Heidnik remained grateful to Marty for single-handedly protecting him against the five assailants in the "Bullpen." Whether there really was a $5,000 contract on his head or not, Heidnik is clearly despised by the black inmates for his crimes against African American women. To emphasize the danger, Heidnik relates the terrifying experience of being greatly outnumbered and physically beaten by 15 black inmates on the prison bus. It is easy to see why, just three months before, Heidnik totally rejected the idea of doing a book about himself. He had just escaped death at the hands of a lynch mob and wanted to shrink from sight. But now that Heidnik is in a new prison where the guards are "very solicitous of my safety," he feels safe enough to pursue the book. He doesn't feel completely safe, however. He laments that "the guards can't protect me totally and it is probably only a matter of time till then…" The sentence is left hanging – as if he cannot bear to say that he will be killed.

It is notable that Heidnik's asserts that "only God's intercession" saved him from lynching. Clearly, his phrasing is not a simple figure of speech like, "thank God I survived." Rather he believes that God personally intervened to save his life. His ordeal could just as well be seen as a punishment from God for his sins, not deliverance. Similarly Heidnik describes the gang assault as a "massacre," which, by definition, involves multiple victims of attack, not just one. It seems to reflect his expansive sense of himself, like he is a Julius Caesar who could only be killed by a throng of lesser men.

Similar grandiosity is revealed in the second half of this letter as Heidnik proudly describes his "Special Olympics of Churches."

As to the whereabouts of Tony Green, I don't know where he is at present, but I can give some help in locating him. He often hangs out at the McDonalds at 40th & Walnut or the Roy Rogers at either 39th & Chestnut or 39th & Walnut. He'll probably be there with Gail, who follows him everywhere. At 40th & Samson is a sheltered workshop called Elwyn. They let out at 4 o'clock and some come into the McDonalds there for a while. Two of these people, Lonnie and Barbara, will know where Tony is living. Lonnie is about 5'2" and weighs 220 lbs. He's easily recognized. Barbara is short too and has a large streak of gray hair in the middle of her head. Lonnie and Barbara were both members of my church. Lonnie, like Tony, was a deacon, and had a 100% attendance record. He never missed one of my services.

As you may know my church was almost exclusively comprised of the handicapped. It was never intended to be a church for the handicapped, it just happened that way. The handicapped are more comfortable socially with other handicapped and preferred* a church where they could attend without fear of ridicule. This is a vacuum in your Main Line Churches, and I inadvertently filled it. It was a lot like the special Olympics of Churches. You don't expect to see anyone run a 4 minute mile, one only expects to see people do their best. Likewise my church. You didn't expect a perfect sermon from Rev. Evans, but he always tried his best. I did little actual preaching at these services, and let the others do the ministering. I simply acted like a guide and tried to gently keep things on track. One sermon, Rev. Evans preached so hard, he actually lost his voice. How's that for efforts? Also, as per the Churches Constitution there were no dues or collection plate. When I'd take members after services to restaurants, bowling, Great Adventure, etc. I paid those expenses out of my own pocket. As a church we had a good fellowship and plenty of activities. We'd usually meet at Rev. Evans' House or at my house. Believe it or not we once held services in my van. How's that for dedication.

Another church member whom I've known for about 20 years is Janice Morris. We were very close and I even made her an

honorary Reverend. The title was strictly honorary for she never held services or preached herself. She is a decent woman, kind at heart and bears no malice towards anyone... If you want to contact her she lives at xxx Street. She and Lonnie and Barbara may talk about the church. Tony although capable of reading and writing* and driving a car, has trouble getting his facts straight. He's absolutely terrified of policemen, and as such, told the cops any thing he thought they wanted to hear. That's how he got arrested. Well that's enough for this letter. I hope it's been helpful*.
Gary

    Heidnik is more than ready to help me find his former church flock. He gives detailed descriptions of five different congregants and where they can be found. He is utterly confident that they will have nothing but good things to say about him. Heidnik presents himself as a benevolent guardian of the handicapped, providing a sacred place where people with intellectual disabilities can worship "without fear of ridicule" or membership fees. He asserts that "the handicapped are more comfortable socially with other handicapped" and boasts of filling an important need in the Main Line spiritual community by providing an exclusive church for them. He takes great pride in his progressive social invention, comparing his church to the Special Olympics where people with intellectual disabilities are only expected to do the best they can. Instead of awarding medals, Heidnik bestows titles like "Reverend," "Honorary Reverend," and "Deacon," and gives people with intellectual disabilities the privilege of preaching from the pulpit. He views himself as magnanimous for standing back and "letting the others do the ministering." He boasts of "100% attendance" by his faithful congregation and describes how a disabled man preaches with such vehemence that he looses his voice in mid-sermon. Heidnik brags about their "good fellowship and plenty of activities" and takes credit for paying every expense as he treated his flock to restaurants, bowling, and amusement parks.

Heidnik is almost convincing in his idyllic portrayal of his church and it probably was true that his loyal and naive flock did enjoy many positive experiences together. But Heidnik's heavenly depiction evaporates as soon as we remember that "Bishop Gary" was not an ordained minister of any recognized denomination. This was no benevolent social services program for people with disabilities. This was Heidnik's power trip and pure exploitation. The purpose of his church was to fill his egotistical lust for power and to bask in the illusion of being loved and honored. The Church was a method to recruit unsuspecting victims for sex. It was even a clever scheme to avoid taxes. But it was no church.

Indeed, everything appears idyllic in Heidnik's story except for one thing. He warns me that Tony Green "has trouble getting his facts straight" and is prone to telling the cops whatever they want to hear. There is an interesting motive for this comment. When Heidnik was first arrested, he professed no knowledge of the women in his basement and instead encouraged the authorities to suspect Tony, who had also lived in his house. Conveniently enough for Heidnik, Tony made a false confession to the murders of both Sandra Lindsay and Deborah Dudley. Tony was the closest to being Heidnik's best friend, and even saved his life once (as we will see in letter #5), but Heidnik was ready to pin the killings on a scared, innocent man with intellectual disabilities. Fortunately, for Tony, he was released after the survivors' testimony confirmed that he had no part in the crimes.

Heidnik never seems to understand that I am trying to figure out the truth of why he enjoyed torturing defenseless women in his basement. Instead of an honest revelation about how he exploited vulnerable people, Heidnik presents himself as a saintly savoir of the weak and poor. He wants to warm our hearts with pictures of his happy parishioners singing hymns and enjoying communion in his living room – while starving women were hanging naked in chains beneath their feet in his basement. Even today, I am struck by this dichotomy between the good Bishop Gary holding church services upstairs, while his victims were being raped, starved and tortured below them. Heidnik's church was not just another manifestation of his obsession with control; it was a way to convince himself that he was a good person rather than a horrible fiend.

LETTER #4
"It Piques Me Extremely"

November 13, 1988

By his fourth letter, Heidnik is royally pissed at me and threatening to write his own book. The reason is that I had labeled him a serial killer and dared to ask about how he caused the death of Sandra Lindsey (and her unborn baby, which he discovered when he dismembered her corpse). He is outraged by my assertion and is determined to prove that Sandra's death was just a small glitch in his family planning. He can't imagine how she died. After all, she was only starving and hanging by a makeshift muffler clamp that he had rigged so that she needed to stand on her tiptoes for hours.

This next letter provides a revealing look inside his Jekyll and Hyde personality. Heidnik begins the letter as a friendly, charming Dr. Jekyll. He addresses me as "Jack" for the first time, compliments me as a war veteran, and playfully teases me about receiving a second mailing of materials on Veteran's Day. But just one page later, he is raging at me like Mr. Hyde and demanding a total retraction. The speed and virulence of his transformation is fascinating and revealing of his deep pathology.

Sunday, Nov. 13, 1988

Dear Jack,
    Imagine my surprise yesterday when the guard brought me a whole panoply of books, letters, college dissertations. I was particularly impressed when I noticed your letter was written Nov. 11, which of course is Veterans Day. What made it particularly impressive was it was in a large brown envelope that was mailed on

Nov 10. That's really amazing Jack. How did you do that? Get the post office to halt delivery so you could retroactively insert it? Shame* on you Jack for trying to impress me that way. How about being a little more candid with me in the future? O.K.?

I want to thank you for the books and articles etc. By the way here's a little trivia for you. In all those photographs of me in the newspapers, they always show me carrying that large brown envelope. Know what's in it? It holds a small version of the New Testament. I always carried it inside the envelope so no one could accuse me of being a hypocrite. It gave me much comfort having it too. The guards never allow us any books or magazines in court, but they made an exception with that small Bible.

I've perused your McNaughton article and the others, and it piques me extremely to be referred to by the epithet of "Serial Killer." I am by no means a serial killer. Those two deaths were purely accidental. There was no willful intent or premeditation on my part to kill anyone. As a matter of fact, the actual cause of their* death was ambiguous, in regards of what the coroner* said. He claimed it was murder since the body was mutilated. Bull S---!! Nobody knows how Sandy died. She may have strangled on a piece of food or had a heart attack or maybe a stroke. Nobody knows, but it WAS NOT MURDER!! The witnesses even testified I wasn't in the same room even at the actual time of death. They also testified that I didn't strangle, stab, shoot, or anything else. Declaring a pair of handcuffs as the murder weapon is preposterous. Nobody deliberately* kills someone with a pair of handcuffs. If you want to DELIBERATELY* kill someone you use a gun or a knife or something. And my purposes were to create life, with lots of babies, not to take lives. Also there is no pleasure or aura in me over those deaths. I do not get any joy or some kind of perverted sexual release out of other people's death or suffering. If I did I'd have stayed and watched them die, but in reality I wasn't even in the same room when they died. If I enjoyed seeing death, wouldn't I have stayed and watched? So please stop referring* to me as a serial killer. I'M NOT.

I have more to say on the subject of those two deaths and will send you a separate letter on the subject as soon as it's completed. Thus with this knowledge that I am <u>not</u> a ritualistic* serial killer, *your whole paper needs to be reworked. By the way, where did you get the information that my father hung me out the window by my feet? That never happened. My father was a strict disciplinarian, but he was never cruel. Also the part about I signed my name G. M. Kill. I don't remember that either and I'm skeptical. Could you send me a Xerox copy of that signature. That would show me something in my personality I'm not aware of myself.*

Having read the McNaughton article that he received from the week before, Heidnik is furious that I labeled him a ritualistic serial killer. In a strategy common to criminals, he decries this injustice by arguing strict legal definitions and technical distinctions – while blurring and ignoring the essential tragedy of the lives tortured and lost. He vociferously refutes the label of serial killer because he did not directly kill anyone. He admits that they died, of course, but not because he intentionally murdered them. He holds to the technical issue that no one, not even the coroner, knows the precise medical cause of Sandra's death, but ignores his responsibility for torturing her beyond human endurance and leaving her to die. Nor does he mention filling his prison pit with water and applying a lethal blast of electricity to Deborah Dudley. In both cases, Heidnik focuses on the legal criterion of intention. He repeatedly emphasizes his lack of intention to "DELIBERATELY" kill anyone and points to the logical absurdity of using handcuffs as a murder weapon. Indeed, in what may be his ultimate expression of gall, he declares the opposite intention: "my purposes were to create life, with lots of babies."

Heidnik applies the same semantics to refute the ritualistic sexual sadism that would define him as a serial killer. Since he "honestly" does not derive any perverse sexual pleasure from seeing the death of his victims, Heidnik asserts that he cannot, by definition, be labeled a serial killer.

Technically speaking (if he was willing to admit it), his deviant sexual pleasure was limited to domination and degradation of his victims, not murdering them. Therefore he urges me to "please stop referring to me as a serial killer. I'M NOT."

Heidnik forgets that the charade is over. He knows, I know, everyone knows what he did. Intentions aside, he is a sexually violent predator who took delight in brutalities against women that can and did cause death. He fixates on the injustice of being labeled incorrectly and ignores the pain and death he perpetrated.

Ironically, advances in the fields of forensic psychology and sex offender-specific treatment give some credence to Heidnik's complaint about his label. Today, Heidnik would be classified as a "sexually violent predator," which is a clinical category that was not fully formulated in the late 1980s. Most, but not all serial killers derive some sexual pleasure from killing their victims. But most sexual predators do not kill their victims. The key element that characterizes both categories is the obsessive sexual fantasies and compulsive ritualistic behavior.

In nearly every instance of serial killing, there is a component of sexual motivation, but it does not always entail sexual acts or take the form of orgasmic pleasure at the sight of the victim's death. For example, there have been serial killers of homosexual men, who did not sexually assault their victims. Their motivation was a deep-set self-loathing of their own forbidden homosexual desires. A few serial killers also have no apparent sexual motivation, such as the so-called Beltway Snipers, John Muhammad and Lee Malvo, who shot and killed 11 innocent people in 2002.

Conversely, only a very few sexually violent predators kill their victims for sexual pleasure. Many will rape multiple victims in a serial fashion, but killing for pleasure during the sexual act is relatively rare. It is more common for sexual predators to murder their victims to eliminate witnesses to their crimes. Both Harrison Marty Graham and Gary M. Heidnik were true sexual predators who were obsessed with deviant sexual fantasies. They both pursued victim after victim for primary sexual satisfaction. Whereas Graham gained orgasmic pleasure from strangling his partners during sex, Heidnik did not seek or derive climax through the act of killing during sex.

The upshot of Heidnik's fourth letter is his irritation at not being able to fully control "his" book. He cannot bear the idea that he might be depicted as a serial killer and lumped into a class of degenerates that would include someone as pathetic and mentally deficient as Harrison Marty Graham. This would be the ultimate insult to Heidnik, who was accustomed to being superior over his intellectually disabled flock.

Heidnik goes on to attack my mistaken claims that his father hung him out of the window by his feet and that he signed his name as "G.M. Kill." Heidnik is certain of my first error, declaring that his father was a strict disciplinarian, but "never cruel." Interestingly, however, he allows for the slim possibility of the second assertion. But he is "skeptical" and wants proof. With this small concession, Heidnik concludes his heated letter with a challenge: If I can prove that he really did write G. M. Kill, it "would show me something in my personality I'm not aware of myself."

His last words are intriguing. He believes that he is cognizant of every action he makes, that no deep hidden secrets or unconscious dynamics can possibly influence his behavior. Heidnik must control everything Heidnik. He cannot tolerate the idea that he might be driven by insecurities or perversions or childhood traumas (his denial of being abused not withstanding) or any weakness that is not in his complete conscious control.

In fact, I sent copies of several forms to Heidnik to prove that he had, indeed, signed his name as "G.M. Kill." I do not suggest anything unconscious here, I think he might have just wanted to get over and mess with the authorities. But, as with much of the information involved in this case, or many similar cases, we can only guess.

In any case, despite Heidnik's wall of denial, I was determined to press on. It seemed like the only option at the time. I was flat broke and needed money. I was being harassed by my wife's divorce lawyer. And, in between my cravings for drugs, I was trying to stay clean and faithful to my new wife and endeavoring to "win the hearts and minds" of her two young villagers, one who was starting to like me, and one had me confused with Heidnik.

LETTER #5
"This Vacuum of Belonging"

November 19, 1988

Despite his angry tirade in the previous letter, Heidnik continued playing our game. In this next letter, Heidnik really tries to make himself the victim. In many ways he was a victim, though not to the exclusion of hurting others. Is it possible that he truly believes the distortions that he describes here? For example, he is convinced that I arranged for my letter to be delivered on Veterans Day. Unless you are a paranoid schizophrenic like Heidnik, you would know that I'm way too loopy to pull that off. My point is that Heidnik perceived reality in a fundamentally different way. He was hospitalized 22 times and had double digit suicide attempts. He ate a light bulb and survived. He absolutely wanted to kill himself to end his torments of self-hatred and forbidden sexual urges. He tried his best to succeed. I'm not some gullible academic who is ready to buy a load of Heidnik's bullshit. But it changes everything to allow the idea that Heidnik is honestly describing his reality. At the time of these letters, and even now, I'm not sure of the answer.

One thing is certain. The sheer length of this 11 page letter shows that Heidnik is completely hooked on the book project. He is willing to answer my questions with lengthy and detailed expositions. Yet he is still out to impress me. He wants to be seen as equal, if not superior, in intelligence and authority. He flaunts his thesaurus vocabulary to sound intellectual and philosophical, even poetic ("two ships cast a drift"). His opening paragraphs are bloated with $25 words like homogenous, dutifully, exiled, ostracized, homily, virtually, ingratiating, gratification, fringes, vacuum and, of course, intellectual. In this letter, in particular, Heidnik's pretense may be more exaggerated and calculated than any of his other letters. Over time, he will dispense with the big vocabulary and philosophical tone and just let his thoughts flow onto the paper with little censure or foresight.

Nov. 19, 1988

As everybody knows, as much as America would like to think of itself as a homogeneous society it is not. America used to call itself the melting pot but no more. America is a complex social group consisting of many other social groups. The most dominant social group is the infamous WASPS of which by birth I am dutifully a member but of which we both know I am in reality an outcast of. Having being exiled and ostracized by my own social group was I condemned to live a life in limbo a virtual hermit or would I...? Would I what?

As we both know I am plagued with mental problems but I am not incompetent. This is a condition that can be summarized in the little homily "he's crazy but not stupid." So to satisfy this need for belonging (as you phrased it of bonding) I began to cast about looking for another social group to join. Since it was virtually impossible to join another group as a respected equal, the only way I could join was by ingratiating myself to them. The word ingratiating is properly used here since there could never be true acceptance. After many trials and disappointments I achieved moderate* success with some of the other fringes of black society. As I say though it wasn't true acceptance, and to belong I continually had to pay my dues. I did however achieve a measure of bonding with the companionship with an old mentally ill black woman. This junction however produced a bonding at only an emotional level, there was virtually no intellectual communication and perhaps to society's* gratification it produced no offspring. So we weren't interfered with and the union was preserved for about 10 years. I had of course desired children desperately and since I couldn't have any with Dorothy I began looking elsewhere. That was when I chanced upon lower society's* fellow rejects, Anjeanette Norton. She had been rejected and unloved by her own social group as well as her family, as I had been. We both experienced this ostracism, this vacuum of belonging. Two ships cast a drift in the night, searching and by luck we found each other. Perhaps because our needs were so great, it is that our love was so strong. We also shared a common desire to have children. Unfortunately for us though we were of different races she black and me white.

Whereas Dorothy and I couldn't have any children the bigots begrudgingly left us alone. But now with Anjeanette children were not only possible but one had arrived and more were in the offering. This was a situation racists couldn't permit to endure. So they undertook to separate Anjeanette and myself. Because of my mental illness and Anjeanette's functional retardation they resorted to the fact that I was crazy and took* advantage of the helpless. They succeeded in framing me for a crime that never occurred and putting me in jail for 5 years. Upon being released I sought to rejoin that social group which had given me the greatest measure of acceptance... the mentally handicapped. The mentally handicapped* do indeed form their own social group and it isn't influenced by things like race. Most handicapped are rejected by so called normal society and seek comfort and belonging with each other. Indeed this social group's pride even built my church. It was a territory no Main Line church was interested in since it was both poor and took a great measure of patience and time. Understanding if you will. By the handicapped I was readily accepted. I was compatible in two ways. Since I was also mentally ill they recognized me as one of their own.

Also since I was extremely competent and willing to assist I was doubly acceptable. It was a symbiotic* relationship, I exchanged my competence for their companionship and friendship. Pre pro quo if you will I never took advantage of anyone or exploited anyone. If I had they would have quickly rejected me and abandoned me. As for fiduciary relationships the money usually went from me to them. I was always buying them food in restaurants, coffees, brunch etc. Especially to members of my church. As you know I often took them to Roy Rogers, or to McDonalds, Great Adventure, Hershey Park etc. One of their favorite places was a smorgasbord called Duffy's. At various times I was called upon to supply room and board and if they had money I charged them $200 a month, if they didn't have it I *supplied it gratis.*

If you think you can make a profit today on $200 a month try it. That's why everybody always charges more for room and board. They even had their own private rooms, TV's, stereo and the use of the house. Barbara got the use of the master bedroom or water bed etc. I slept in the back bedroom the smallest of them. At one time or another Tony Green, Gail, and Robert roomed with me. There was no financial exploitation on my part. If there was they'd have left a long time before they did. They all showed substantial weight gains too since the food was also adequate.

My favorite time was with Sandy [Sandra Lindsay]. My financial rewards for these services were negligible the human rewards were tremendous. I not only achieved a glorified feeling from helping my fellow man but I achieved an almost around the clock companionship and sense of belonging. Still there was a vacuum in my life. I needed bonding and closeness of a wife and children. To achieve this I reached to an even different social group and made one of the biggest mistakes of my life. Falsely thinking that oriental women would be the greatest wives ever in existence, I married a Filipino. I probably arrived at this conclusion by watching too many Suzy Wong reruns. As a social group maybe Chinese or Japanese make great wives. Filipino women are another story. You've encountered some of these difficulties I believe since you actually came into contact with Betty. If you need more proof just ask Peruto. You and I can both commiserate* with him. Anyway my union with Betty was partially successful. It produced a healthy active bouncing son, Jessie. However it also produced a great mental anguish and supplied none of the companionship or bonding I needed so much. It was so hectic that at one point she had me incarcerated for a villainous rape charge and at another point I locked myself in the garage and tried to commit suicide, and even to another point I had myself committed to Coatesville trying to escape her.

As you know my marriage had deteriorated and my relations with the handicapped disintegrated. Again I was alone. What to do? What I did you already know. A unique way of looking at what I did in my disturbed state of mind was to create my own social group or family if you wish. It was a social group in which I was the only male, the only economic provider, the patriarch so to speak, and which was available to me 24 hours a day. Since I couldn't achieve a sense of belonging to any of the other existing social groups in American society, I endeavored to create my own social group. One that had to accept me and couldn't abandon me and had to provide the things I needed, love, bonding, children, companionship, etc. For instance, any time I felt a need to talk they were there. Where could they go? They had to listen.

Perhaps my needs were best summarized in four words by [Josephine] Rivera, a psychologist in her own right when she said, "you're lonely aren't you?" Having correctly analyzed the situation she then properly exploited my need for bonding to achieve her freedom... It wasn't actually a difficult deception for her... Does my explanation seem valid? What as a scientist is your input?

Heidnik carefully designed the first half of this letter as a sympathetic, even romanticized, portrayal of his life that is intended to legitimize and justify his abominations. He begins by describing his "vacuum of belonging" and then tries to play psychologist by applying this core need for bonding as the central motivation for everything he did. He constructs a seemingly logical progression from loneliness – to belonging – to carnage:

1) I was desperately alone because I was "exiled and ostracized by my social group" due to my mental illness.

2) This forced me to find another social group to accept me or I would be "condemned" to be a "hermit."

3) So I began "looking for another social group" and found "companionship with an old mentally ill black woman" (Dorothy).

4) With her, I found belonging in the "fringes of black society" where "the bigots begrudgingly left us alone" (for ten years) because we could not bear children.

5) But I still had a need for love and children and I found it with a young black woman with intellectual disabilities (Anjeanette).

6) But the "racists" persecuted us for bearing a mixed race child and destroyed our loving family by framing me and sending me to prison for 5 years.

7) I returned from prison to "rejoin that social group which had given me the greatest measure of acceptance... the mentally handicapped."

8) I became a benefactor to the intellectually disabled by creating a church for them, treating them to restaurants and entertainment, and providing free or cheap housing.

9) But "still there was a vacuum in my life. I needed bonding and closeness of a wife and children." So I "reached to another social group and married a Filipino."

10) My difficult Filipino wife (Betty) had me falsely arrested on a "villainous rape charge" and drove me to attempt suicide and seek refuge in the psychiatric hospital.

11) So I was again alone because "my marriage had deteriorated and my relations with the handicapped disintegrated."

12) "In my disturbed state" of loneliness, I felt forced "to create my own social group" to fulfill my natural human needs for "love, bonding, children, companionship, etc."

13) [Not stated] – Therefore I had to forcibly kidnap, imprison and impregnate multiple women to fulfill my needs.

14) Even my victim (Rivera) could empathize with my needs and actions because she "correctly analyzed the situation" and said, "You're lonely aren't you?"

15) But Rivera exploited my "compelling need to be loved" to trick me and escaped.

Heidnik concludes his autobiography of loneliness by asking whether his pseudo-psychological explanation seems valid to me "as a scientist." In a sense, there is a kernel of validity because Heidnik was, in fact, obsessed with finding acceptance. But his criminal violence was not driven by loneliness and the need for love and friendship. It was driven by his core obsession with control and deviant fantasies of sexual domination.

His rationalization is also based on a distorted chronology. For example, he claims that he went looking for acceptance from a different social group because he was ostracized by his own – and that is how he found a bond with "an old mentally ill black woman." In truth, he lived with Dorothy Knox for ten years, far longer than any other relationship, and he gives the misleading impression that this was his first African American mate. In fact, he had significant relationships with at least three other black women before Dorothy. [The genogram in Letter #14 helps to explain the chronology of his relationships.] It may be true that Heidnik found a social group with whom he felt comfortable, but he ignores the fact that his choice of African Americans was primarily <u>sexually</u> motivated. Heidnik was almost exclusively sexually attracted to non-white women.

Similarly, Heidnik distorts the chronology of his involvement with people with intellectual disabilities. He did not first find acceptance in the black community and then later find more satisfying acceptance from the disabled community. He began working with the intellectually disabled in 1967, at least a year before he met Dorothy. He immersed himself in the black and disabled communities simultaneously, or more accurately, a unique subculture of African Americans with intellectual and mental disabilities. He claims that he switched from the black community to the disabled community at the time he met Anjeanette. In fact, he had been exploiting persons with intellectual disabilities for 11 years and operating his Church for the disabled for 6 years – long before finding Anjeanette.

Finally, there is a crucial reason that Heidnik invests the first five pages of letter #5 in the construction of this autobiography of loneliness. He is about to address my questions about what happened to the two women who died in his basement. Before talking about their deaths, Heidnik wants to establish a reasonable justification (maybe even gain some sympathy) for why he created his prison cellar in the first place. As he starts his explanation, notice that he immediately implicates Josefina Rivera, his first kidnapping victim, as sharing responsibility for both deaths. He begins with the death of Sandra Lindsay.

There are several questions regarding the two deaths I was convicted of that I wish to address now. I've already addressed the question of intent. There certainly was no intent on my or Rivera's part to kill either woman, and I think I've already made that partially clear in other letters. For some reason Peruto never properly addressed the issue of intent possibly because he could sell more copies of his book if I got the death sentence.

Another aspect of their deaths is the technical aspect. Look at the drawings I made. From purely the technical aspect neither death seems possible hence my bemusement. Let's first consider Sandy's death. Everybody has been saying I "hung" her by her arms from the ceiling. The use of the word "hung" or hang is entirely inaccurate. Sandy was not only NOT hung from the ceiling she had both feet solidly on the ground and her arm was at a right angle not even fully extended like so, and this is easy to prove. Nobody has to take my word or even ask the other women.

The ceiling (cellar rafters) are about 6 feet from the floor and the eye bolt or hook was screwed into the bottom of the rafters. Sandy was about 5 foot 5 inches tall. The handcuffs add another 6 inches. So Sandy's arm wasn't 6 feet high but more like 5 foot 5 inches from the floor. This shows definitely that she wasn't hanged from the ceiling as the news media claims but of course they're not interested in being accurate only in selling papers. Both her feet were on the ground. She simply was forced to stand up. If standing is dangerous or fatal there'd be a lot of dead waitresses or sales clerks.

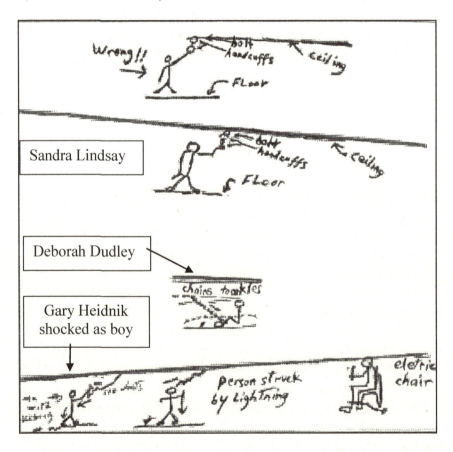

Also she wasn't standing all that long. An hour and a half to be exact. She spent the whole previous night standing up about 12 hours without ill effects. I had let her down that morning and she'd been lying and sitting all that day. I don't know exactly what day it was but it was in February. A movie with Linda Lavin in Australia started up about 8 or 9 o'clock and that is when I stood her up. After about an hour and a half the movie wasn't yet over yet, they broke for a commercial, I went downstairs to check on everyone and Sandy was hanging by her arms with her legs bent and her head rolled to one side. At first I thought she was faking. When I realized that she was really dead I was the most shocked of all. How the hell can standing up for an hour and a half be fatal?

The coroner never answered this question and Peruto didn't ask. The coroner stated he didn't know the exact cause of death, but he said he concluded it was murder since the body had been mutilated. Now what kind of conclusion is that? He didn't know why Sandy died any more than I did. Of course Peruto didn't pursue this issue either. For all anyone knows she may have died of a stroke or a heart attack or maybe an infection or a fever. Nobody knows. But standing on your feet for an hour and a half is not and never has been fatal. I've asked about this cause of death and got no concrete answer. One answer was maybe it was a broken heart. If that was possible, I'd have been dead long ago and 50 times over with all the pain and punishment I've been through.

Then there's the unthinkable that maybe one of the other girls killed her. This is really a very remote possibility but when dealing with the unknown everything is possible. This theory gains some credence when you realize that Sandy was a lesbian. At one time I even ordered Debbie to appease Sandy's advertent desires. It is entirely possible that one of these women was so repelled by this that they eliminated Sandy rather than see such things continue.

According to Heidnik, the death of Sandra Lindsay was not his fault and he cannot imagine how she died. "How the hell can standing up for an hour and a half be fatal?" he pleads. He neglects to mention that Sandra was restricted to a diet of bread and water, suffering from a chest cold, denied clothing except for a shirt, and deprived of sleep by being forced to stand the entire previous night. He also obscures the fact that she was freezing in a damp earth basement on a cold February day and could well have choked to death after he forcibly stuffed bread and water down her throat. While six naked women were chained in the basement and Sandra was dying, Heidnik was upstairs, casually watching a made-for-TV movie called *A Place to Call Home*.

Heidnik's account is profoundly lacking in empathy for his victims. He does not even pretend remorse or say their deaths were tragic. Instead he is angry that <u>he</u> has been falsely convicted without adequate evidence. Worse yet, he presents himself as having suffered "50 times" more anguish than any of his victims.

Heidnik also hides the fact that Sandra Lindsay was his friend. She had been a boarder in his house. She was the girlfriend of his best friend, Tony Green. She had visited Heidnik in the hospital after his suicide attempt in February 1986. Just five pages earlier, he admitted that the time he lived with Tony and Sandra was the "favorite time" of his life. Sandra liked and trusted Gary – and he repaid her friendship by chaining her to the rafters of a cold cellar and raping her.

Heidnik's final words on the death of Sandra are absurdly brutal. He suggests that the other women may have killed her so that they would not have to witness lesbian sex (which, he admits, was performed at his own command). Even for Heidnik, it is unimaginably illogical that his victims could be more "repelled" by seeing forced lesbian sex than by the sight of their own starvation, beatings, torture, rape, and sexual degradation. In Heidnik's narcissistic fantasy world, however, all that matters is control and domination. Sandra's death is little more than an inconvenient mystery to him. As we will resume his letter on page 8, his attitude about Deborah Dudley's death is equally callous.

Debra Dudley's death, from a purely technical view point also remains an enigma. They claim she died of electrocution, but I claim such a decision is inchoate. Here is some of the reasoning for this disclaimer. As a child, working with my father wiring houses, I received not one but several electrical shocks while grounded in water. Let me assure you that they were not pleasant but likewise they were not fatal. Another factor about fatal electrical shocks is that they pass through the heart region. When someone is hit by a lightning bolt it strikes them on the head or arms and passes through his heart to where his feet touch the ground he will usually die. Executioners are extremely cognizant* of this phenomena and when electrocuting someone the charges is usually applied at the prisoners head and exits the ankles where another electrode is attached.

Now consider Debbie when Rivera shocked her she was underground and the charge wasn't applied directly to Debbie but through her chains. Those chains in turn were connected to Debbie's ankles and the ankles were grounded in water. Plus the charge would have entered at the ankles and exited at the ankles where the water made contact. Yet at no time did the charge pass through the heart region.

The claims of the coroner that Debbie suffered electrical burns on her ankles is inaccurate. Not only Debbie, but Agnes (Donna) and maybe Lisa (I'm not sure about Lisa) had open sores on their ankles caused by chaffing from the muscle clamps. It was those sores on Debbie's ankles that the coroner ascribes to as burns and were not caused by electricity. As ignorant as this coroner is it's amazing that he passed high school science, let alone college. He certainly doesn't understand science or the scientific method. One thing the coroner is good at is though he is a good sycophant for the prosecution.

It goes without saying that when Rivera shocked Debbie she had no intentions of killing her, and neither did I. So to call Debbie's death murder is a miscarriage of terminology since there was no intent to kill. Not only was there no intent but if you consider the technical factors I presented there is also cause to doubt the means of her death. If she didn't die from electrocution, what did kill her? Another broken heart? I doubt it. Her cause of death is just as equivocal as Sandy's.

Also speaking of Rivera, Rivera is not the hero that everyone believes or even a Miss Goody-Goody. Rivera's prime interest in life is her own self interest, and pursuit of a drug habit. She is addicted to cocaine injections and needs several injections every day. That's why she always wears long sleeve blouses, to conceal the marks in her arms. She's possessed of considerable "street smarts" and does quite well on the street. Once I released her she had ample opportunities to call the police, to run away, and yes even to drive away. The very first night I put her behind the drivers wheel of my car while walking around to the passenger side, she could have easily locked the doors and drove away or run over me first then drive away. At the public health clinic, when the doctor took her for examining in private, she could have run away or asked the doctor for help. She didn't. When we were in McDonalds, Roy Rogers, Denny's, Ponderosa and other restaurants she could have called for help or run away. She didn't.

When I went to the V.A. at Broad and Cherry to arrange a dental appointment, I couldn't find a parking space so I instructed her to drive around the block till I got done. The appointment took more than an hour and she could have easily driven to the nearest police station. She didn't. She had almost total access to the phone in the kitchen and could have gone into the kitchen at anytime, especially when I was asleep and called the police. She didn't. She even set up her friend Vicky for the final kidnapping. Why you ask? Why didn't she ask for help sooner and why set up her colleague?

The answer is explained by her boyfriend. He went public that Rivera tried to get him to rob me with a hammer. When he refused, she didn't want to return so then she called the police. Rivera knew I was carrying $2,000 on my person and she was determined to get it before she turned me in. And if I happened to get killed in the robbery attempt, I feel sorry for her boyfriend since Rivera would have naturally blamed it all on him claiming it was his idea. That's how "street smarts" work and how one feeds a drug habit in the ghetto.

> *There were actually three deaths at 3520 North Marshall not two. When Sandy died she was about two months pregnant. So two people died that day. Also Rivera, Donna (Agnes) and Lisa were also pregnant but they all had abortions I'm sure. So there can be added to the list three more deaths I'm not responsible for."*

Heidnik's account of the two deaths shows no responsibility or the slightest remorse. On the contrary, he twice states explicitly that "Rivera shocked Debbie," not him. He does not mention that Rivera was working under his command or that he devised the plan and equipment to administer electric shocks to a chained victim in a pool of water. Instead he reduces Deborah's tragic death to "an enigma," takes consolation in the belief that the deaths were "accidental," and bemoans his conviction for an unproved murder.

Thus we have the complex Jekyll and Hyde personality of Gary M. Heidnik. At times, he is "Bishop Gary," a giving and warm person, appreciative of friendship and fellowship. This is the person who praised Sandra as "my favorite time" and liked helping people with disabilities to enjoy life. But the flip side is the Gary who signed his name as "G.M. Kill," a dark, soulless person with no regard for life and no compassion for anyone but himself. Sharing in both personalities is the cunning and manipulative Gary with an IQ of 145.

Heidnik was driven by his delusional fantasies and obsessions. His needs for closeness and fellowship could be seen in the behavior of Bishop Gary. The people in his congregation loved him. He preached and fed his flock and they adored him. But the same needs for belonging and self-efficacy were overpowered by his obsession with control and violent sexual fantasies. G.M. Kill had sex slaves chained in the basement, while Bishop Gary held church services upstairs.

Let us be clear. We are not saying that Heidnik was a so-called multiple personality. The personality characters of Bishop Gary and G.M. Kill are just metaphors for how Heidnik could display the opposites of prosocial and antisocial behavior. Heidnik can talk to God and hold church services upstairs at the same time that hostages are chained naked to the pipes in his dungeon. He can simultaneously feed dog food to the prisoners in his cellar, while treating his parishioners to a smorgasbord at a local eatery called Duffy's.

He also presents evidence that Josephina Rivera had multiple opportunities to escape. By showing that she could have left at any time, Heidnik wants to prove that she was a willing participant, even an accomplice. By all means, we do not want to blame the victim in any way. Josephina also bears the scars of the same muffler clamps that Heidnik used to chain his victims. No one can judge Josephina's actions under the unimaginable strain of 17 weeks of terror in Heidnik's basement. She was, after all, the first to be kidnapped and spent the longest time trying to survive, which eventually included actions to seduce Heidnik into believing that she was willing to help him. Was Josephina too terrified and distraught to think clearly? Was she "brainwashed" by terror ala the Stockholm Syndrome, like the famous case of kidnapped heiress Patty Hearst in 1974 or Elisabeth Smart in 2002? Or did she simply wait for the most opportune time to safely escape? Whatever her reasons, it is tragic that her delay in notifying the police prevented an earlier rescue of Heidnik's victims.

LETTER #6
"As Interesting as a Dried Prune"

November 25, 1988

Heidnik begins letter #6 by rejecting my academic writing style as inadequate for "his" book. He imagines a best seller that will make him world famous and therefore my writing must appeal to the masses. He baits me, saying, "your literary style is as about as interesting as a dried prune." Heidnik is very proud of this turn of phrase and will make it into a running joke that recurs in letters #8, #12, #18, #22, and #24. He also sends me an article from *Time* as an example of the style he wants and inundates me with $25 words to demonstrate his own literary skills and to affirm his superior status in this endeavor: "I hope, if I've incurred your rancor, I've also inculcated your interest... Have I made my point?"

It is no accident that Heidnik later boasts of his "penultimate" IQ of 145 and "superior lexicon" and challenges me to take a *Readers Digest* intelligence test. I remember laughing at this obvious ploy. I laughed harder when he offered his condescending consolations for rejecting my writing. "If it seems unfair, I'm sorry, that's just the way life is." Though obviously manipulative, it was irritating to be lectured by Heidnik. The upshot is that he truly sees himself as the boss and he is determined to control the writing of "his" book.

---

not dated (envelop postmarked 11/25/88)

Dear Jack,
 Upon careful perusal of your article*, I've reached some conclusions about your writing* style. I hope you won't find me captious if I say, your style is adequately* suited for scientific

journals or academia, but will sour with the general public. If you try to make your audience think, you'll lose most of them and they won't forgive you. I'm enclosing an article by one of my favorite financial writers, Andrew Tobias. Witness how he converts totally* mundane topics like Federal deficits and taxes into very readable and plausible subjects. He's so persuasive* he makes paying taxes seem like a pleasurable experience. Now that I've highlighted the problem, I hope you can devise a solution. If it seems unfair, I'm sorry, that's just the way life is. But, if you intend to write a novel, directed towards a general audience, you'll have to reform your writing* style. In short your literary style is as about as interesting as a dried prune.

At this point, I hope, if I've incurred your rancor, I've also inculcated your interest, and your desire to read on. Have I made my point?

I also have some further commentary about your exposition. It is rife with inaccuracies pertaining to me. Not only am I not a serial killer, ritualistic or otherwise, but there was never any spousal abuse or evil commands from God. True, God does communicate with me aurally from time to time, but He never related any misogynist directives precipitating my criminal actions. In fact God has never related any misanthropic communiqué, only benign and benevolent messages. Distinguishing between aural missives from God and Satan is quite easy if one utilizes Scripture as a decoder. The scripture "From a good tree, one gets good fruit, but from a corrupt tree one gets corrupt fruit," is all the decoding necessary*. So I regretfully debunk that part of your exposition that declares, "God told me to do it." As for what my motives were, I'm not sure I know myself.

The allegations of spousal abuse are also fallacious. If you made the argument that I was not a very good husband, it would be a viable one. I am incapable of being uxorious*. I was perhaps parsimonious, inattentive and a philanderer, but I was not abusive. Betty made those claims in family court, for the sole purpose of enhancing her claims for spousal support and vengeance* for my philandering. Also the rape charge was spurious. There had never been any rape, or forced sex. When Betty had run away the first time in January 86, I contacted her relative in New York and instructed her that if Betty didn't return to me forthwith, I'd have her deported to the Philippines*. Upon being informed of this threat, Betty concocted the phony rape charge and had me arrested. She succeeded in having me arrested by the police, rather than simply swearing out a private warrant, through the use of political connections. Mayor Goode has a niece, and Betty occasionally cleaned her house up, for gratis. Through this connection to James White, then to the police the order came to arrest me for spousal rape. Later, after Betty and I reconciled she dropped the charges against me, without abjuring*. To admit to their spuriousness would have been criminal* and subjected her to deportation. To avoid that I recommended* she only drop charges. She also cleared me with the parole board, who were investigating me.

  While Betty and I lived together, our relationship was, to say the least, acrimonious. At one point I actually fled and hid in the environs of Coatesville Veterans Hospital. I'd also take doses of Thorazine to weather her frequent tirades, but I have abused her. Quite frankly though I was cheap, I only gave her a miniscule allowance of $5 a week, and in building her a wardrobe, never bought anything elaborate. Most of her clothes come from Kmart and there were even a few additions from Thrift stores. She always had adequate food to eat, and was gaining weight, although she had troubles adjusting to American food. My own personal car was, as you know, a 72 Dodge. I purchased her a 72 Plymouth that was in superior shape to my own Dodge and taught her to drive, although she never secured a license. After she returned in February I raised her allowance to $20 a week and sought to be more generous, but never completely* relented of my tight fiscal policy. I did however in occasions of exuberance* give her $100 bills, although infrequently and treated her to restaurants and movies. Our final falling out was when I refused to cohabit with her "ever" in response to one of her never ending tirades. She then became so incensed, she left the following morning after packing her car with all her property. So again I reiterate, there was no spousal abuse on my part, although I was not a perfect husband either.

After his opening directive to reform my writing style, Heidnik attacks my exposition as "rife with inaccuracies pertaining to me." He reminds me of my continuing error of classifying him as a ritualistic serial killer (from letter #4) and wants two additional errors to be corrected. First, he denies ever hearing "evil commands from God," especially orders to hurt women. On the contrary, when God talks to him, it is "only benign and benevolent messages." He claims it is easy to distinguish between messages from God and Satan by simply applying Scripture. He insists that neither entity told him to kidnap women for his harem, but he denies knowing why he did it, saying "I'm not sure I know myself."

The second error that Heidnik wants me to correct is the "allegations of spousal abuse." He admits that he was "not a very good husband" because he withheld spending money from his wife and cheated on her. But that's all that he will admit. He dismisses Betty's rape charges as nothing more than a "spurious" ploy to stay in the country after he had threatened to deport her back to the Philippines. Yet he avoids any explanation for why she ran away from him in the first place. Instead he attributes his "false arrest" to some imagined grand conspiracy involving Philadelphia's Mayor Wilson Goode and James White, the top administrator of city government – as if Heidnik was important enough to draw the personal vengeance of the Mayor himself. Moreover, to prove Betty's deceit, Heidnik emphasizes that she dropped the rape charges. Therefore, he adds, she can never admit her lie because she will get herself in trouble with the law.

Not only does Heidnik deny any sexual violence against his wife, he portrays himself as the innocent victim of her "frequent tirades." He minimizes his psychiatric hospitalization at Coatesville as a voluntary escape from Betty's rages and his anti-psychotic medication Thorazine is only a means to calm his nerves from her outbursts. Heidnik commits a classic Freudian slip in this very same sentence when he writes, "I _have_ abused her" rather than "I have _not_ abused her."

Betty's story, not surprisingly, is quite different. She fled from Heidnik to a shelter for battered women and reported three months of rape, physical abuse, and at least one incident in which he tried to force her into group sex with other women. He was arrested and charged with spousal rape, assault, indecent assault, and involuntary deviant sexual intercourse. At the end of this letter, we will return to the break-up of Heidnik's marriage, which was a critical turning point in the escalation to his final acts of abomination.

Also the assumption that I am a genius, no matter how narcissistically* pleasing, is nonetheless specious. Reflection on that I.Q. score of 145 that you mentioned. It was not a true indicator of cogitative capacity since it focused exclusively on vocabulary, and as I'm sure you're* aware of, my forte is a superior lexicon. Had they asked me some collateral questions on math or common sense, the results would have been markedly lower. I don't claim to be image of vacuous either, but I'm certainly not a pundit. I'd like to think I qualify for Mensa membership, but it would be an equivocal* membership. Other I.Q. tests that I scored well on were often repeats of previous tests and I was frequently taking the same tests repetitiously. As you know, practice makes perfect. As for my penultimate* I.Q. score of 145, the test was inchoate*. A tabloid interpretation of my mental powers might be, "I may be crazy, but I'm not stupid."

An addendum to this portion is I've never been able to score 100% on Readers Digest word powers texts. To score a 100% on this test is one of my loftier ambitions in life, and I continue to strive for it month after month. If you want a humbling experience, sample one of these tests yourself.

In your treatise you made some references to my suicide attempt of Feb 1986. This event has always been something of an enigma to me, since I had been unconscious for three days?? The last thing I remembered was seeing Tony open the garage door and I had just enough strength to lock the door [of the van], before becoming insensate. Could you fill me in on the blank spots: For instance

    1. How long was I unconscious*?

    2. You mentioned I was intubated*, what and how many tubes?

    3. You also mentioned respiratory assistance*, was that simply nasal O2 or perhaps a ventilator?

    4. Did they at any time administer C.P.R.

    5. Here's my biggest conundrum*. It seems to me that the dozes of carbon monoxide, Thorazine, and alcohol should have been fatal. Why wasn't it? Did they possibly administer some super anti-drug like Narcon?

    6. I only remember waking up about three days later and signing A.M.A. I have no recollections of even going home or how I got home. I doubt if your records can help there.

    7. I had over $800.00 on me before they rescued me. When I got home my wallet was empty. Any mention of that money?

    As you may know after so many foiled suicide attempts on my part, I factiously* label myself an expert on the subject. One of my most inspired attempts occurred in January 1979. There is some equivocation about this attempt, but let me assure you I was sincere. I had read a book called **Tales of the Green Berets** that said the North Vietnamese* sometimes put slivers of bamboo in American's food, which when ingested caused unstoppable internal hemorrhage. Think about it. It's plausible*, right? Also in a movie called something like the "Monster Who Roamed the West," the villain* crushed a glass figurine and put it in a victim's food. This putatively caused fatal hemorrhaging*. This also seemed plausible* to me. So upon spending my first night in Graterford and determined to commit suicide I incorporated this data into my plot. I unscrewed the light bulb, broke it, crushed some of the glass in my metal cup and tried to swallow it. It wouldn't go down. However mixing some with water on a spoon and it did go down. Sort of a pumicite postprandial*, if you will. Your contention that you could surreptitiously* poison* someone with ground glass is fallacious, since it is readily detectable but you could do it with their

Breaking the Silence of the Lambs

connivance. So having ingested this delicacy, I laid down to await the results. After a couple of hours, I awoke with an overpowering sensation of nausea and groped to the sink where I vomited.... a mass of black viscosity, digested blood. This event assured me of the success of my endeavors* and I again reclined with a sense of ecstasy* at my impending demise. Unfortunately I woke that morning completely* viable and suffering no ill effects. My postulation is that when I vomited the blood, I also evacuated all the ground glass. Hence no more irritation*, no more bleeding. Since the x-rays showed no glass residue, there was a presumption* of mendacity. I can assure you there was no mendacity, the effort was sincere, albeit unique?

One of the great fictions pertaining to suicide is the slashing of one's wrists. Theoretically* this is possible, but I know of no incidents of success. Only in fiction does this self induced mutilation succeed. There are many people who have tried this though, but they are still walking around. None is in the grave-yard. Someone you know has tried it. Guess who? My wife Betty, that's who. She slashed her left wrist 17 times, in a very determined effort, but failed. That's why you always see her in long sleeves, she's ashamed of the scars. Don't mention I told you this either. I've told you this in confidence. At any rate slashed wrists is just another one of the fictions of modern life.

Gary

After describing his painful marital break-up, Heidnik closes his letter by bragging about his "genius." His false modesty about his supposed brilliance is so obvious as to be comical. He tries to flaunt his intelligence with a torrent of grandiose vocabulary in this particular paragraph, misspelling four words and misusing five. He is right about one thing. Even if he can't spell it correctly, he definitely finds it "narcissistically pleasing" to be presumed a genius.

He then shifts to the topic of his suicide attempt of February 1986. What is not readily apparent is a direct causal link between his failed marriage and suicide attempt. Contrary to Heidnik's version, the facts point to a total emotional breakdown following the break-up. He made a very serious suicide attempt and then had an extended psychiatric hospitalization from early March through August. This became a "brewing period" that precipitated his ultimate rampage, just three months later, in November 1986.

The profound upset of Heidnik's marital breakup was a turning point in his life. For the first time, he was in a relationship with an intellectually equal adult. His frail self-esteem and inflated view of himself as a powerful genius (which had been reinforced by years of domination over intellectually disabled underlings) was shattered with the reality that he was a weak imposter, who was incapable of managing the basics of marital life. All his fantasies of love and raising children were smashed. He felt humiliated and weak. In the short run, he retreated into shame and insecurity (the true self beneath his bravado and narcissism) and fled to the safety of a psychiatric ward. But, in the longer run, he recoiled with a vengeance, literally. The narcissistic rage of being exposed as a weak imposter reversed into its opposite. He made himself into a super powerful dictator who would be more dominating, more controlling, and more superior to his underlings than ever before.

The sequence of topics in this letter reveals an up-down pattern of extreme psychological reversals: From the down position of humiliation and weakness over his marital failure, Heidnik shifts up to the false bravado of his genius, then back down to the self-denigration of his suicide attempt, and then back up to declaring himself "an expert on the subject" of suicide. Instead of shame over his suicides, he reverses it into a source of pride. Stated differently, the sequence of topics shows the flip flop between his obsession with control and loss of control, between feeling strong and feeling weak.

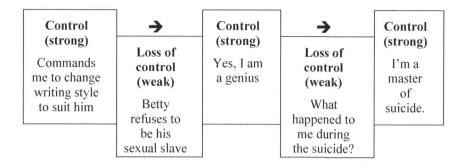

There is a deeper psychological question beneath Heidnik's list of seven questions about what happened to him while he was unconscious after the suicide. He is asking, "What happened to me when Betty rejected me? Why did I completely fall apart?" The marital breakup revealed the true fragility of Heidnik's ego, which terrified him and filled him with self-loathing. The only control he retained was the power to kill himself. And when that failed, he collapsed into helplessness. The recognition of his own weakness was unbearable. The only way to reconstruct the shattered pieces of his self was to reverse his helplessness and loss of control into a new position of absolute power and control.

It is interesting how Heidnik ends this letter with a "secret" revelation that Betty, too, attempted suicide by cutting her wrists. It is a primitive attempt to bring Betty down to his own level by adding her to the club of suicide attempters. He can't admit the deep shame of his own scarred self, so he projects it onto Betty: "That's why you always see her in long sleeves, she's ashamed of the scars."

LETTER #7
"My Injustices of 78"

November 30, 1988

As Thanksgiving approached, I was in financial crisis. It was almost four months since I first hatched my plan to write a best-seller about Heidnik, and six months since the trial. That's six months with no income and no job prospects. For me, everything was now riding on this book. But Heidnik had his own agenda for "his" book and was threatening to fire me for my "dried prunes" writing style. I was thinking that I was the fisherman trying to reel in a big fish, but it was more likely that I was the fish and Heidnik was trying to reel me in. The best I could do was to keep throwing him his favorite bait – books. Heidnik was a voracious reader, a barracuda for books. Maybe I was broke, but I was rich in books from college, graduate school, and many years of personal reading. So I could send him a steady stream of fiction and nonfiction.

Sending books started as a way to gain Heidnik's trust. Later, when it was no longer necessary, I continued to send him books. In some strange way, I felt sorry for him. Gary was teased and humiliated throughout his childhood. Today we call that bullying and take it very seriously. I'd like to believe that I can see some good in anyone, even a sexual predator like Heidnik. Or was I just a greedy profiteer looking to cash in on his misery, both then and now? You're free to judge my motives as well as Heidnik's. I'm trying to honestly describe and understand both Heidnik and myself during that turbulent time.

I did have one very positive change of fortune at this time. I had hired a new lawyer who was able to get a new custody hearing with a neutral judge, who actually interviewed my daughter and deemed me worthy of having full custody. I was clean and sober (mostly), and, together with my new wife and her two kids, we moved into a suburban town house to start our new blended family. By this time, my stepson had come to accept me, but my stepdaughter continued to glare at me with a permanent expression of disdain and disgust. Starting a stepfamily is hard enough for anyone, but stress was a trigger for Vietnam flashbacks and depression – and that was a green light to get high, get drunk, or get laid. There were enough struggles in my life without worrying that Heidnik was going to pull the plug on the book and my only hope for financial relief. It took serious effort not to slip back into my bad behaviors and, for the most part, I held it together.

Based on Heidnik's gleeful comments at the end of this letter, my most recent batch of book bait must have been especially tasty. For the time being, he seemed well-hooked and full of enthusiasm for the project. In fact, he opens this letter by exclaiming that he is "ecstatic." He pours out 18 full pages. He is thrilled that he has found a sucker (me) with the capability (through a best selling book) of vindicating him of what he calls the "injustices of 78." Heidnik distorts my request for more information about his kidnapping of Alberta Norton into the presumption that I must share his conviction that he was treated unfairly by the court. He argues that he received a much stiffer sentence than he should have because he was a first time offender and his crimes were "merely" misdemeanors.

The truth of the matter was that he was given a harsh sentence because he had kidnapped his girlfriend's sister from an institution for intellectual disabilities and then imprisoned, raped, and sodomized her until he was caught. Even if it he had little prior criminal history, kidnapping and rape are felonies, not misdemeanors, which call for a severe sentence. But, like a classic jail-house lawyer, Heidnik retroactively applies the fact that his felony conviction was overturned four years later to create a new fiction that he was persecuted from the beginning with an unfair sentence.

The odd part of Heidnik's first sexual kidnapping was his lack of planning. He seemed to act as if he could only see life as it occurred right in front of him. He also shows no responsibility or regret for his actions. On the contrary, he presents himself as a heroic victim. He elevates his supposed "injustices of 78" to the level of yet another grand conspiracy. Instead of Mayor Goode and the Managing Director of Philadelphia, this time the diabolical villain is Judge Charles P. Mirarchi Jr., who is out to "legally" steal the $350,000 assets of Heidnik's church (about $1.2 million today).

Subsequently, on pages 2 and 3 of his letter, Heidnik turns to my question about Sandra Lindsay, his second kidnapping victim in 1986, and the first to die in his basement. In what must be one of his most outrageous cognitive distortions, he asserts that he helped to rehabilitate Sandra from her cocaine addiction and life of prostitution by keeping her safely chained in his basement. He crows that Sandra "actually prospered physically while in my cellar" by gaining 20 needed pounds. In a slip, however, Heidnik inadvertently admits to a starvation diet when he further boasts that, "even on only two meals a day she gained weight." These were paltry meals that consisted of bread and water with an occasional bonus of dog food or table scraps.

Wednesday, Nov 30, 88

Dear Jack,

I got your letter of Nov 25, Saturday and ho, ho, ho, you're joking with me this time, I'm sure. Anyway I was very pleased with the questions you asked, ecstatic* in fact. I've been crying "foul" for 10 years over my injustices of 78 and nobody* has ever cared or even listened. Now at least someone is at least asking questions, and a very astute interrogator at that. Before getting to your questions, let me ask you one. As you know I was convicted, not of felonies, but 3 misdemeanors*. Also I had no prior convictions, a long history of mental illness. The convictions were for non-violent crimes, even the Appeals court said there was some doubt even as to my guilt and the judge was known to be a lenient sentencer. So with all the mitigating circumstances, etc. doesn't the sentence of 3 to 7 seem <u>extremely</u> severe and thereby VERY suspect. The maximum sentence would have been 5 to 7. Anyone else would have gotten a sentence of parole, probably contingent in some way on my further treatment in Coatesville. Judge Charles Mirarchi Jr. had one of his sentences questioned in the newspapers for being too lenient. This guy had a conviction record of something like 10 arrests and 5 felony convictions. He came before Mirarchi on a new FELONY conviction (robbery, I think) and the Judge only gave him 3 to 10. In other words, this fellow got about as same sentence as me and yet for felonies and a career* of convictions. The guy made the papers because when he was released he killed a Phila cop. Thus you, as an astute investigator, should be able to see at least something <u>suspect</u> here. So start and keep asking questions. The more you probe, the MORE suspect it will become. My personal belief is that when everything comes to light you'll find they were trying to steal the church's* money. In 75 the church was worth about $125,000. By 1983 it was worth something like $350,000. That kind of money, you have to admit is a tempting target. Also it was VERY vulnerable. It could be stolen LEGALLY. If you want the details, I'll be glad to give them to you. That kind of money also shows they could have had the motive to STEAL. So keep an open mind, but a suspicious, questioning mind, and I'm sure you'll soon be a believer. {I also had a good source of income. My pensions, which is another mitigating circumstance.}

    Now onto some of your questions. Whenever I refer to the name Sandy; yes, I'm referring to Sandra Lindsay, you were quite correct on that assumption. Tony and her dated for a couple of months in 85 & 86 in an on again, off again love affair. I also dated Sandy at times. More on that if you want it.

    Coincidentally you asked about my brother Terry and mentioned Rivera in the same letter. They've got a lot in common. I'm almost positive they're both addicted to cocaine. I'm 100% positive of Rivera and 99% positive of my brother. Rivera was working the streets as a prostitute to support her habit. When in the cellar she'd often refer to it and give me details. When I "picked" her up she only weighed about 95 lb. She (and only she) actually prospered physically while in my cellar. First of all she was, of course, then off drugs. Her appetite though was always good, and even on only two meals a day she gained weight. About 20 lb is my guess, and it wasn't all fetus, since she was only about 3 months pregnant when I was arrested. She used cocaine IV injection and her area of injection was her arms. She had "tracks" on her arms and that is why she always wears long sleeves. Also you will notice if you look that she weighed considerably more at my arraignment in April 87, than she did at the trial in June 88. She had lost plenty of weight, because she's resumed her cocaine habit. She'd rather be high than eat. Also Peruto told me that she got arrested again for soliciting in 87. So she's obviously resumed her old profession* in order to finance her old habit.

As for Terry, I've never heard him admit to using drugs, except for Angel Dust, which he confided to me during a visit during my immurement*. During his several visits in 86, when he tried to "borrow" money, he talked about cocaine, but never admitted to using it. Also I haven't seen tracks on his arms but I'm pretty sure he's injecting too. All the signs are there. He lost a lot of weight for example. He used to weigh three hundred pounds but in 1986 was down to 165 and eulogized* his mysterious "diet," and touted a whole host of salubrious health benefits. (Believe it or not he claimed his diet was so good it was erasing his fingerprints and also enabled him to grow about an extra inch "on demand." When I questioned this "growth" process, he stood in a corner and proceeded to "grow" about an inch. Actually all he did was stand on his toes, in his shoes, so I wouldn't see his heels leave the floor. All the other psychological signs of cocaine addiction are there also. He no longer takes care of his appearance, and the papers described him as a "lone wolf." In 86 he was showing signs of hallucinations and at last contact showing paranoia. He complained to Betty in a recent phone call that the neighbors vandalized his car. I don't mind if you contact him though and if you plan to do any kind of comprehensive* study on me, such contact is only de rigueur.

His home, I believe is nothing more than a trailer parked on some lot. I doubt if you'll get anything substantive or accurate from him though, because his suspected cocaine addiction has warped his mind. Terry, by the way Jack, still owes me $7,000 that he borrowed over the years.

Heidnik's description of his brother Terry, his only close relation, is notable in several respects. First, it seems devoid of fraternal affection. He describes his brother's suspected cocaine addiction and poverty in a cold, clinical fashion and attributes Terry's "warped mind" to the effects of cocaine addiction, <u>not</u> chronic mental illness. To attribute Terry's hallucinations and paranoid delusions to schizophrenia would mean the brothers were cut from the same familial/genetic cloth. Gary's ego cannot tolerate being lowered to the level of his brother. Therefore he blames cocaine for Terry's transformation from morbid obesity through a "mysterious diet" that makes his fingerprints disappear and increases height on demand – rather than schizophrenia, the debilitating mental illness which they both share.

Gary also adds a comment that his brother Terry still owes him $7,000. For all his prosperity, Gary Heidnik reveals himself to be a controlling miser. His self-admitted "frugality" appears repeatedly in his letters, such as withholding spending money and food from his wife and girlfriends, and is another expression of his obsession with control.

In the next segment of this letter, Heidnik writes a detailed description of the "injustices of 78" that runs ten full pages. He describes an idyllic loving relationship with his girlfriend Anjeanette, which is wrecked by her greedy, racist family and the courts. He asserts that her sister Alberta "was not, and had never been kidnapped. She left the hospital of her own free will." He minimizes the fact that he exploited his intellectually disabled girlfriend to sign her disabled sister Alberta out of Selinsgrove as merely "a brash act, but was not kidnapping." On the contrary, he depicts <u>himself</u> as the victim of multiple kidnappings of his girlfriend by Anjeanette's family.

Heidnik portrays himself as a devoted and loving mate who teaches his mentally challenged girlfriend to write and helps her to secure S.S.I. (federal lifetime disability income). He denies depriving Anjeanette of food and claims she is simply blessed to have a metabolism in which she never gains weight. He fondly remembers their trips together to Niagara Falls, theater shows, and restaurants. He asserts that everything would have been wonderful in their life together, especially the joy of having children, if only Anjeanette's family had not interfered. He depicts them as hypocrites living on welfare who hate him simply because he is white. He accuses them of abandoning her to an institution and having no interest in her well-being until they found out that she had S.S.I. money. It is inconceivable to Heidnik that Anjeanette's family might see him as exploiting a young woman with intellectual disabilities for the very same SSI money – and for sex.

While Anjeanette was living with me in 1978, she had been actually kidnapped by her family. While I was away they came around to the house and invited her to the "Gallery" to do some shopping. Instead they took her to her mother's house and refused to let her leave. After a day or two I finally got one of her other sisters, Bertha, who told me where Anjeanette was. I immediately went over there, it was in North Philly, and demanded they release her. Anjeanette also made it plain to her family that she wanted to go with me.

Now allow me to retrogress a little. A couple of months previously I had tried to get Anjeanette on S.S.I. This move, on my part, I consider one of the biggest mistakes of my life. Up till, this time Anjeanette had virtually no money and no income. Thus nobody, including her family, especially, had any interest in her. Anjeanette's family did not like her and had put her into the institution at about 15 just to get rid of her. They only visited her one time, in 15 years and the only reason that they visited her was to "borrow" money. So when Anjeanette was discharged from Elwyn Institute (in Media), she either had no money or her S.S.I. was cancelled because they said that she needed a guardian. (At the time Anjeanette couldn't even write her own name). Since Anjeanette had no money her family was not interested in her and when I met Anjeanette she was living at a boarding home. (I'm not sure how she paid for her board though). The family, although* racially prejudiced, made no objections when Anjeanette moved in with me, and of course, I supported her. I should have let well enough alone, but no, I got the inane idea of getting her on S.S.I. and did so. Unfortunately* Anjeanette told them that she had a big check due for about 6 or 7 back months due. What the family didn't know is that the check for $1,200 had arrived several days before and Anjeanette and I cashed it, and were having a great time spending it. ==The family also didn't know Anjeanette was about two months pregnant.== So now I've brought you up to date, back to the house in North Philly.

  I kept insisting they let Anjeanette go and Anjeanette kept saying she wanted to go with me. Unbeknownst to us, one of the family members had called the police. Anjeanette's family hadn't realized the laws had changed, and they thought they could hold a retarded family member against their will. Well when the police arrived, one female officer asked Anjeanette where she wanted to go and Anjeanette said with me. So the family had to let her go with me. Another of her sisters, Bernice, really got mad at this and even followed my car on foot for several blocks. Anjeanette's family being so completely VENAL, when they heard that they lost the "big" check, vowed vengeance. ==They further learned that Anjeanette was pregnant with a white man's child, that served only to add more spice to their plans for revenge.== I, though, was thoroughly circumspect. I had Anjeanette in a hotel for a couple of weeks, to be safe. Then when I brought her home I wouldn't let her answer the *phone when I was out and told her implicitly to let no one into the apartment when I was out, ESPECIALLY any family members. I knew though they couldn't be trusted and that if they did "snatch" Anjeanette again, they wouldn't tell me where she was. I also knew that they wanted Anjeanette very badly so they could get their hands on her monthly S.S.I. checks. To a large extent I over reacted, since I completely underestimated Anjeanette herself. She wasn't as helpless as everyone thought and as we were to find out.*

Since Anjeanette was pregnant, I began (notice I said I began) sending her to prenatal clinic at Pennsylvania Hospital. Occasionally* I took her, but I didn't have to. Anjeanette was perfectly capable of making and keeping her own appointments and often went down to 8th and Spruce on SEPTA by herself. Unfortunately* there was at Pennsylvania Hospital a social worker named Ms. Doe. She was not only a so called "Liberated" feminist, she was a vocal black racist. She had black power pictures all over her office. When she discovered that Anjeanette was living with a white man, and was going to have a mixed child she was incensed*. Also she further couldn't tolerate Anjeanette because Anjeanette was completely happy being a housewife and took very good care of her man and never gave me a difficult time. Anjeanette so loved me, she'd do anything I asked, including having more children. Ms. Doe couldn't tolerate such a situation and plotted with Bertha to terminate it. Ms. Doe put a lot of pressure on Anjeanette to leave me and to have an abortion. One time she took her out to her car, told her to get in, she'd find her a new home. Anjeanette refused to go, and informed me of what was happening.

All in all Anjeanette did get about, I believe 5 or 6 months prenatal care, before I stopped her from going. At one point even some people came to my apartment from Booth Maternity Center and tried to get her to leave. Anjeanette was under a lot of pressure to either abort or leave me. She wouldn't go for a long time. For my part, I was ignorant of the fact that they couldn't force her to have an abortion after the first trimester and was terrified they'd kidnap her and force her into an abortion. I also resented the idea of losing her, as I loved her also. I knew nothing about the fibroid tumor at the time, and if anybody like Ms Doe, or Bertha had told me, I wouldn't *believe them. These people were so possessed with the monomania of separating us, there wasn't any mendacious* tactic they wouldn't use.*

As for Anjeanette's weight, she had a problem other women would kill for. I mean it. KILL. Anjeanette could eat a full meal and never gain any weight. I never starved her or deprived her of food. Anjeanette did all the cooking when we ate at home and could have made larger portions if she was hungry. Also we dined out at restaurants quite frequently. Sometimes Roy Rogers, McDonalds or Gino's, but sometimes at nice restaurants also. A humorous incident occurred at the City Tavern. They literally* served something like a 6 or 7 course meal, and faithful Anjeanette tried to eat it all. At just about the last course, she threw up all over the table. I became fearful* that the management* would eject us, but instead they apologized and refused to let me pay the check. As avaricious* as I am this pleased me very much. When we get outside I asked her if she could do that "trick" again, and we both had a good laugh. There were other nice restaurants and good times too. Once we attended some extravaganza at the Sheraton dedicated to Henry VIII. They put the prettiest female customer in the "stocks" and let all the male guests kiss her again, and again. Also they'd only let us use spoons since there were no forks during Henry's time. At another time, at a disco, Anjeanette got a little drunk and did some kind of dance laying down, with her skirt around her waist. The men at the bar, almost chocked on their drinks, ha, ha.

Yes, most certainly I never starved her or abused her, and we were both living well in those days. When her check (big) one came in, we took a lot of friends to dinner at the Langhorne Restaurant in Media. About the end of August of 1977, Anjeanette and I even made a 2 or 3 day trip to Niagara Falls. We also took in several plays at Grendel's Lair, the Fantasticks* and went everywhere and did everything together. Does this sound like abuse? Does this sound like I starved her? Indeed this was one of the reasons her family resented her so much. They were all on welfare, living in the ghetto or projects and had no steady boyfriends. They had never even been inside some of the places that Anjeanette had been. Of course Anjeanette had done something they never did... Love a white man. I not only wined and dined Anjeanette, but had 2 Cadillacs. Yes, her family was not only avaricious* they were envious of Anjeanette.

At any rate they got a hold of her again about a month before her delivery date, but Anjeanette went willingly that time. I know, because I found out that she was living at her sister Betty's apartment in the projects and sent in the police. The police came out and told me they took Anjeanette aside and asked her if she wanted to stay. Anjeanette said yes, and so I backed off.

At any rate, Anjeanette had our baby by Caesarian section, at Pa Hospital in March. I was informed that they were going to take the baby away from us. This news flash almost drove me crazy, but it also made me cunning. I determined to take Anjeanette out of the hospital, with the baby, before they could find out. So on the evening of Easter Sunday I went to the hospital with a fallacious story of my father was sick and dying in Cleveland and wanted to see his daughter before he died. The hospital staff refused to release the baby, but said Anjeanette could go if she desired, but they recommended she not go till her incision* had healed. It was then and only then that the hospital staff revealed to us that some judge had put a restraining order on the baby and a court hearing was scheduled for 9 AM that next morning. Ms. Doe made sure neither of us were informed of the hearing and tried to execute it behind our backs, when it would have been too late to keep our baby. Ms. Doe committed another indignity, perhaps one of her vilest. She changed our baby's* name.

Although we didn't get custody of the baby, we did get visiting privileges*. One humorous* and satisfying event occurred in family court when Ms. Doe, stated that Anjeanette didn't appreciate the child was a living thing and handled it like a doll. She then went on to point out that Anjeanette was so helpless she couldn't even use makeup. At this point I gleefully interjected with the observation that Anjeanette was wearing makeup, right there in the court room. Check. It should be in the record.

I believe that Ms. Doe may have concealed or destroyed records that would show that Anjeanette was indeed attending prenatal clinic. But there are some records she didn't or couldn't hide: the bills. This could be my big chance to show that I've been *telling the truth all along and have actively been discriminated against.*

So after about a week or ten days Anjeanette was discharged and unfortunately* went back to her sister Betty. This hurt, but not for long. Betty wouldn't let her leave to come see me. Finally, Anjeanette got so pissed off, she punched Bertha in the face. That took a lot of courage since Anjeanette only weighed about 100 lb and Bertha was a corpulent 200 lb. I was awfully proud of my Little Honey that day. Bertha was so shocked by the blow that she not only let Anjeanette leave, but gave her bus fare, ha, ha. So Anjeanette and I were at last back together again and things looked auspicious. All we had to do was get our baby back. I'd also learned something. The S.S.I. checks had been rerouted to Bertha's house and I let her keep them. Since it was really the money they wanted most of all, maybe they'd settle for that and leave us alone. FAT CHANCE!!

Heidnik presents a convincing account of how much he loved and cared for Anjeanette. He portrays a wonderful life together that was ruined by the intrusions of Anjeanette's greed-driven family and a racist social worker, who hated him as a white man. But let's consider the objective facts. Anjeanette was an intellectually disabled young woman with an IQ of 47 and co-occurring mental illness. Anjeanette's family was displeased with her relationship with Heidnik, but she did prefer to continue living with him. Six months later, however, her sister Bertha came to visit and discovered that Anjeanette was eight months pregnant with sunken eyes, insufficient weight, and indications of physical abuse. Bertha immediately took Anjeanette to Einstein Hospital and threatened to have Heidnik arrested if he tried to stop her. One month later, Anjeanette delivered the baby. A large fibrous tumor prevented normal childbirth so a Caesarean section was necessary. Shortly thereafter, Heidnik was accused of starving and mistreating Anjeanette, denying her prenatal care, and giving her his own prescription medication. The Department of Public Welfare promptly took custody of the baby. The next day Anjeanette returned alone to live with Heidnik, where she received no postpartum care.

The truth is somewhere between these contrasting accounts. Clearly Anjeanette's family was suspicious of Heidnik and questioned his motives. They were displeased about the pregnancy. What chance would a child have with a mother who was both intellectually impaired and mentally ill? Although the trial records for both 1978 and 1988 indicate that Heidnik denied Anjeanette prenatal care, it is inaccurate. I personally found documentation that Heidnik did, in fact, arrange for prenatal care. But, as he admits, he "stopped her from going" after six months. His reason is crucial to understand: "Some people came to my apartment from Booth Maternity Center and tried to get her to leave. Anjeanette was under a lot of pressure to either abort or leave me." Heidnik recognized the threat of losing his baby to the authorities and stopped the prenatal visits to prevent it. He thought he could deliver the baby at home, by himself, in secret.

For all the distortions of Heidnik's account, he does reveal a pitiable sadness about the loss of their baby. He invested the greatest of hopes in his fantasy of having a child of his own. He insists that he loved Anjeanette and was loved by her. He was outraged to be judged as unfit parents because of their respective mental disabilities. He denounces the social worker as a rabid feminist and racist, who is "incensed" by the idea of an inter-racial couple having a mixed child. He complains that the authorities not only seized custody, but filed a restraining order to stop him from visiting Anjeanette and the baby in the hospital. They even conspire, in Heidnik's account, to change his baby's name.

The misrepresentations of Heidnik's account notwithstanding, the psychological loss of his fantasized baby was a profound blow to Gary's fragile ego. This narcissistic injury was the key turning point in his life. Until now,

Heidnik had lived within the law. Henceforth he will do anything to secure his own baby – starting immediately with an attempt to steal his baby from the hospital. From this point forward, Heidnik will be totally obsessed with his baby fantasy, which will ultimately drive him to commit his worst abominations. He believes that having a baby of his own will achieve vindication for his lifelong inadequacy and will serve as a crucial bulwark against the self-loathing of his own weakness.

Therefore, as soon as Heidnik was reunited with Anjeanette, he began plotting a fool-proof way to secure a baby that no one could ever take away from him again. Just two months later, Heidnik kidnapped Alberta from the Selinsgrove institution with the fantasy of impregnating her and keeping her hidden in his cellar until he had secured another child of his own. In fact, the kidnapping of Alberta is the topic he addresses next in this letter. This scheme to get a baby will fail in May 1978; as will his next scheme to "legally" get a baby by marrying a mail order bride in October 1985; as will his ultimate scheme to kidnap an entire harem of sex slaves to bear multiple babies in November 1986.

Now onto your* next question about Alberta. First it's important to point out this. They didn't claim gonorrhea* of the vagina but of the mouth. I'm positive she didn't have gonorrhea* at all. They manufactured her sickness, just as they manufactured so many other false claims and spurious evidence. They wanted to put me away for several lifetimes, not just a couple of years. By claiming gonorrhea* of the mouth, this enabled them to add the additional charges of deviate sexual conduct. Paradoxically, the claim that Alberta did have gonorrhea* may have been the best thing that happened to me. Yes! My new lawyer, Pressman, did know about the fact I didn't have gonorrhea* and he used it for all it was worth. That single fact alone, that I tested negative for gonorrhea* showed scientifically that I hadn't copulated with Alberta, orally or otherwise. The prosecution, not to be outdone, then tried to prove that I had access to antibiotics and had cured myself. Even though I didn't copulate with Alberta, and this proves I didn't, I'd still like to show and expose the conspiracy against me. So please check the records and verify.

    Alberta was not, and had never been kidnapped. She left the hospital of her own free will, and since she wasn't court committed she should have been legally entitled to do so. For me to take her away like that was a brash act, but was not kidnapping. Alberta impressed on both me and Anjeanette, that she was fed up with Selinsgrove and wanted to leave. She wanted to come and live with her sister. I was very acceptable to the idea, because I like Alberta, I wanted to make Anjeanette happy and it seemed like a good way to get back at her family. It also seemed legal. I've been in the hospital many times, and if I wanted to leave I could always sign myself out or just walk out. (As long as I wasn't court committed). Also it was imperative to let the hospital staff know that Alberta was all right, where she was and most importantly that she wanted to leave on her own free accord. My time was short since I had to be at work at 8 that night, so I figured she could just call them from my house, when we got home. So I drove all the way back home and made the long distance calls. There were several actually and they were all recorded on my phone bill. Selinsgrove also made several calls to my home. They always talked to Alberta whenever they wanted and Alberta told them she didn't want to return to the hospital. That she wanted to stay with us. The record of those phone calls, if I remember right was never admitted to the court testimony though, even though I had the copies of the phone bill.

    Also about the birth of my baby, Anjeanette, Alberta and the frame up, there is much more to tell. Just ask me what you want to know and I'll relate everything I know. I've talked with you several times and I realize that you're* an astute investigator and questions are your forte. You can ask questions that bring out facts and information even I'm not aware of that I can remember. So "fire when ready Gridley*." I'm waiting.

Heidnik is clearly feeling confident as he finishes his three-page explanation of Alberta's kidnapping. He makes humorous reference to the famous moment in American naval history when Admiral Dewey tells Captain Gridley to "fire when ready" in the Battle of Manila. Like a good jail-house lawyer, Heidnik is proud of his legal ploy to overthrow his conviction by proving that he could never have raped Alberta because he did not have gonorrhea. He delights in his own cleverness of "paradoxically" turning the supposedly falsified lab test for gonorrhea against his imagined persecutors. He wants me to find the medical records to prove his innocence "scientifically" and boasts that "I may yet make a believer out of you."

I find this comment interesting. Either Heidnik recognizes that I'm not a total rube who will believe anything he tells me, or he's so convinced of his own reality that this proof will secure my unquestioning allegiance. I actually think it was the latter because Heidnik goes on to claim that Alberta disliked the institution and wanted to live with her sister and him "on her own free accord." He claims Alberta herself repeatedly told Selinsgrove that she liked living with him and his telephone bills would prove the occurrence of these calls.

About Terry and me in the V.A. Hospital. Yes, indeed there were some amusing* incidents. Let me relate some more anecdotes for you. You're* already familiar* with the "bottle on a string," he he. The bottle did contain a little libation to cheer us up. Another time, I took a took a lock out of one of the remote doors and took it into Coatesville itself. Then I got a key that would fit that lock. Since you know that at Coatesville most of the locks are the same, then you know that that key would also fit the lock to the door on Terry's ward. Doesn't that raise some interesting possibilities. The inmate having a key to the front door. You betcha. I gave Terry the key and boy did he have fun... till they caught him. When nobody was

looking he'd unlock the ward door and pretty soon the hospital aides*
would have to scramble to catch all the patients who went wandering
away. Then the aides* would accuse each other of leaving the door
unlocked . They'd say "Did you leave the door unlocked." "No, not
me." "Yes you did." "No I didn't." And the accusations flow back
and forth. Terry was of course in hysterics by this time. But he'd
deftly wait till things quieted down, then when nobody was looking,
he'd sneak back to the door and... bingo... it was round up time
again, as patients went thither and yon. Even McMurphy in "One
Flew Over the Cuckoo's Nest" didn't have this much fun.
McMurphy would have been proud of us. Terry repeated his stunt
several more times and unfortunately even the most churlish aide*
wises up. They realized a patient had a key and conducted an
intricate search. Sure enough they found it under Terry's bed.
Foolish boy. He should have hid it under some other patient's
mattress. Then they turned their wrath on Terry. Poor boy. They put
him in cold packs for an extended period of time.]

Another time I went up to visit Terry. It wasn't visiting
hours, but why bother with red tape. I'd just come from work and
was in my white nurses uniform, complete with pin. So I went to
where Terry was having therapy and told them Terry was wanted on
his ward. The staff of course thought I was another employee and
dismissed him. Terry and I then went into Coatesville proper and
did some bowling. McMurphy would have given me a medal for that
one. That's enough of "Coatesville Antics." On to the next question.

In comparing my father to Archie Bunker, I didn't mean in a
facetious* sense, but many of Archie's viewpoints, coincided
precisely with my father's, but when my father espoused his views
on things like race, or religion I didn't laugh. I didn't dare to.

As for autographing your book you'll have to postpone that
for a while. You're still not on my visitors list and I'm reserving my
visits for my wife and son. I'm only allowed two visits a month and
so my visits are inestimably valuable to me. So I hope there's no hard
feelings. There is a value in correspondence though since you'll have
all your info documented and you know how you like documents.
You can refer to them any time to support your arguments and
nobody can accuse you of fictionalizing. I hope this holographic to

me proves satisfactory.

Cogitatively yours,
Gary

P.S. *I'm currently reading your copy of James Burkes "The Day the Universe Changed." Thank you.*

P.S.S. *The mailman just brought me the three books you sent. I can hardly wait to sink my teeth into Desmond Morris* The Human Zoo. *You wouldn't happen to have a copy of his* The Naked Ape *lying around gathering dust, would you?* ☺ *By the way watch those dates. They make you look unctuous*.* ☺

Heidnik is certainly in high spirits as he completes his lengthy 18 page letter. He is playful, teasing, and friendly, explicitly grateful for the books that I sent him, and signs off with a joke – "Cogitatively yours, Gary." [This pattern of "witty" sign-offs will be repeated fifteen more times during our correspondence. See the Summary Guide to Heidnik's letters in the Appendix for a listing of his varying salutations and closings.]

Heidnik clearly delights in telling the story of his "Coatesville Antics" because it shows his cleverness in outsmarting the hospital authorities. It is interesting in its own right that both Heidnik brothers were in the same psychiatric hospital at the same time for the same schizophrenic illness. Whereas at the beginning of this letter (page 3), Gary Heidnik is careful to distinguish himself as superior to his mentally disabled brother, he now boasts of their shared hijinks in the psychiatric hospital. The difference here is that Gary protects his self-esteem by portraying himself as ingenious and in control – not as a weak and inadequate schizophrenic like his brother. Gary proudly likens his mischief-making to the heroic deeds of Randle McMurphy, who was played by Jack Nicholson in the Oscar-winning movie, *One Flew Over the Cuckoo's Nest*. In reality, Heidnik's antics were criminal and potentially dangerous. He impersonated a staff nurse and risked the safety of other patients by repeatedly unlocking hospital doors.

On the positive side, the story shows some brotherly affection between Gary and Terry, which was lacking in Gary's initial description of his brother in this letter. It is also revealing that he follows this story of brotherly bonding with a comment about their hard-nosed father. Although Heidnik insisted that his father "was a strict disciplinarian, but he was never cruel," his choice of words suggests a deep fear of his father's wrath.

LETTER #8
"Is That <u>Love</u> or What??"

December 2, 1988

    The winter of 1988 was proving to be a serious test of my sobriety and my resolve to be an honorable husband, father, stepfather, and bread winner. I certainly wasn't winning any bread, nor was I winning the heart of my stepdaughter, nor my battle against the recurrent addictive urges, both sexual and chemical, pulsing in my brain. Then "the Hatchet" came to the rescue.

    One night, long after Joanne's own divorce settlement, her former in-laws suddenly threatened to come to the house and seize some property they claimed to own. It was 2AM when I got her frightened call and I was wasted on a half ounce of cocaine at some after-hours club in northeast Philly. I couldn't get home and was booked for mercenary work with Saint Nick the next morning, so I asked my bro from the First Cav to cover for me until I got there. Sure enough, the Hatchet came to the rescue at 7AM with no sleep and no shirt, driving a bright orange taxi cab plastered with Ortlieb's Beer logos. Picture a shirtless brute with a large, anatomically correct picture of a woman's legs and vagina tattooed on his chest and under-arm. The Hatchet was in long range recon for the First Cavalry in the Nam and don't ask how he got that nickname. He introduced himself to Joanne with the gift of a blood-stained baseball bat. Joanne was entertained and, needless to say, the invaders immediately withdrew.

    That same morning, Joanne had to make a home nursing visit to a bad neighborhood in north Philly so the Hatchet offered to ride shotgun. Since this was their first meeting, Joanne didn't know just how "protective" the Hatchet could be. On the way there, he suddenly grasped her firmly by the limb and declared, "If you hurt Jack, I will kill you." He wasn't joking. He knew the pain I had gone through with my first wife and didn't want me to get hurt again. When they arrived at the address and the Hatchet saw how bad the neighborhood was, he told Joanne that she had 15 minutes to do her nursing and then he was coming in after her. She never took off her coat and finished the treatment in record time. He was serious and she knew it. He and I had a code. My tattooed bro was one of the best ever and I would take a bullet for him to this day.

I tell this story because that was also the day that the Hatchet confronted me about my cocaine addiction. When he saw my frazzled condition from the night before, he squared me up and told me that I had a serious problem. Coming from him, I listened. He urged me to go back to the VA and get some professional help. I agreed to quit the coke, but I refused to go to the VA. You would think that the best place for a post-traumatic Vietnam vet to get help would be from his colleagues at the VA. The truth was that I didn't want anything on the public record about the severity of my depression or my Vietnam flashback shit. Moreover, I couldn't trust my therapist, who was a well-known Philadelphia psychologist at the time. I had three sessions with "Dr. N," who didn't want to talk about Vietnam and was obviously incapable of working with a post-traumatic combat veteran. In my fourth session, he said he was taking a trip to Florida to swim with the dolphins and asked me to get him some cocaine. What?! I had quit doing that shit on my own and now this fucking quack wanted me to get him coke? I pulled his chain by saying I never sold coke by eight balls, only kilos. I also said fuck you and quit therapy. No wonder Heidnik thought that psychologists are a bunch of assholes trying to get over on him.

You might ask why I didn't go to another psychologist. Why give up on the whole profession because of one jerk? My state of mind at the time was one of profound distrust. This was both an issue from my childhood and an acute symptom of my Post-Traumatic Stress Disorder – and it was being exacerbated by the occupational paranoia of living the gangster life. I didn't trust anyone save Joanne and my partner-in-crime, St. Nick. When you are living in darkness, it is a scary leap of trust to believe that the world can actually be a good place where righteousness and love is possible. My fear was that I wasn't good enough to make it in the legitimate good world, and that I would lose whatever self and whatever self-control I possessed if I dared to make the change. It was crucial for me to see my therapist as a well-adjusted citizen and a representative of the moral and lawful society that I was hoping to join. Therefore it was a crushing betrayal for me to discover that he was just as corrupt and immoral as everyone else, maybe even worse for his hypocrisy. He was just another hustler. I had bared my soul to him. I was trying to do right. I was trying to stay clean from drugs and the gangster life and trying to be a good husband and father. And this phony wanted me to get him two grams of coke so he could swim with the dolphins in Florida.

After this betrayal, I was in real peril. I was feeling violent and suicidal and out of control. I couldn't go to my dolphin-riding therapist. I couldn't bear to start over again with someone new. I couldn't turn to my best friend and most trusted confidant, my brother Bill, because I was still grieving his death from a year before. And, as much as I loved my new wife, I couldn't tell her the truth about my intrusive stripper fantasies and addictive urges. Though I could count on Joanne for love and support, I didn't want to scare her with the truth of how bad my depression and flashbacks had become.

So I was in deep shit. It's that moment in the movies that they call "The Big Gloom," when all hope is lost and the hero is doomed. I felt profoundly alone and helpless to control anything in my life. Then I had an insight. When you're as scared and desperate as I was, you will do just about anything – even crazy things – to regain a sense of basic control. Otherwise you feel like you'll go insane or shatter into pieces.

Moreover, if you do find something that restores your sense of control, your survival instinct is to seize hold of it and not let go. The fear of losing control is so aversive that it motivates you to repeat whatever it was that got you through the panic and restored your sense of control. That "thing" is like a lifeline. It could be something healthy (like getting counseling), or unhealthy (like getting stoned), or it could even be something nutty – like a superstitious behavior, or a fanatic religious belief, or a self-deluding fantasy of power and control. Sound familiar?

By looking into my own scared and desperate experience, I could better understand what was driving Heidnik's obsessions and sexual violence. As a child, he found that solitude and fantasy provided refuge from the torment of his childhood helplessness and social rejection – and he practiced that fantasy to perfection. Gary was a master of obsessive control even before adulthood and the onset of his schizophrenia. To be hammered with psychosis may be the most terrifying loss of control that anyone can experience. He could no longer think straight as his mind was bombarded with buzzing noise, auditory hallucinations, delusions, and cognitive chaos. For example, when Heidnik had a psychotic episode in 1971, he drove blindly for thousands of miles until he was stopped by the Pacific Ocean. There he received a command hallucination from God to start a church. It was a totally crazy idea, but the religious delusions helped to focus his disordered mind and restore a sense of control. Heidnik grabbed onto the delusions like a drowning man grabs a life preserver. Thereafter the fanatic religiosity and power of playing preacher became another means of control that was incorporated into Heidnik's overall obsessive control system. Gary learned that domination could effectively suppress his deep feelings of helplessness and self-loathing, while also giving him the illusion of being competent and admired.

My moment of insight into Heidnik's pathology became a turning point for me. I realized that researching and figuring out Heidnik was something that I <u>could</u> control. Even if my life was out of control, the Heidnik project was a chance to rebuild my competence and self-confidence. Jack was back. Well, at least I had a good start anyway. I can't say if my "Big Insight" came precisely at the time of this letter, but I think that it's likely because Heidnik seemed more emotionally honest in this letter and therefore elicited more feelings of empathy from me. When he writes here about his wife Betty, we see just how desperately he craved simple human love and respect, and when he writes about his double digit suicide attempts, we see just how much he hated himself as an unlovable and malformed thing. Heidnik even expresses appreciation for Sandra Lindsey's kindness and friendship.

When he writes like this, it becomes possible to view him as a lonely, child-like, and vulnerable person. But then we remember the Gary who raped Sandra, starved her, hung her by her toes, and eventually cooked her on the stove and fed her to the other starving prisoners in his basement. And our revulsion exterminates any empathy whatsoever. It is quite the dichotomy for Heidnik and also for me. It is one of the fundamental questions in this book. How can any human commit such savage and brutal violence and also act – with complete sincerity – like he's Little Lord Fauntleroy? How can I pretend sympathy and bait Heidnik with books and act like I'm the Innocent Little Professor? Sure, I can easily justify my actions by claiming academic purposes. I am making a legitimate contribution to the scientific knowledge of serial killers and sexual predators. But I'm also intent on selling that knowledge in the form of a book deal that will bail me out of a financial nightmare.

As a forensic psychologist, I'm questioning whether a person like Heidnik feels genuine empathy for other people – as if he is qualitatively different from you or me. Heidnik's abominations make it easy to see him as an inhuman thing that is nothing like the rest of us. But he is human. He once was an innocent little boy. My point is that it is too easy to stand outside the cage and view Heidnik as a pure monster. To some degree, Heidnik must share some of the same positive qualities that make us all human. And, to some degree, we must share some of the same ugliness that can make us inhuman and cruel. What if Gary had actually found a mutual and lasting love relationship with his wife Betty, like the one I found with Joanne? Would that have stopped him from raping and pillaging? What if I had <u>not</u> found love with Joanne, especially during this desperately wounded time in my life? Could I have lost control in some terrible way like Heidnik? All I know for sure is that my period of despair humbled me and made it possible to understand Heidnik more effectively – from the inside. At the same time, my Big Insight about the function of control for Heidnik enabled me to begin to regain control for myself. Sure, I would continue splashing and choking, but I wasn't going to drown. I had a lifeline – with "serial killers" written on it.

In this next letter, Heidnik surprises me with a portrayal of his wife Betty that is completely different than letter #6 just a week before. Rather than portraying Betty as a raging hysteric and manipulator, he now paints her as kind and supportive and keeping herself "chaste" out of loyalty to him. Betty is "in the prime of her sexual life" and living in poverty with their "terrific son Jimmy." What caused this reversal? As Heidnik himself says, "From our few previous letters you could have easily gotten the impression that I hated Betty... No it's not true. I LOVE her." Heidnik boasts that Betty spurns the advances of other men and "stands right beside me all the way" even though he has nothing to offer her but a lifetime of visits to prison. He declares, "If death row can't break up our marriage, then nothing will."

Heidnik then falls into a long reverie about how their marriage could have worked out if they had a second chance. He fantasizes about how he would "court" Betty properly, "wine and dine her," and then, "if all went well, we would move in together GRADUALLY." He expresses his regrets that they did not have a proper honeymoon trip to Niagara Falls because (unbeknownst to his new Filipino bride) he was on parole and could not leave the state. He waxes sentimentally about their life together, lamenting the mistakes they made and what they could have done right. He even confesses that he was "not the best of husbands" because of his adultery. He quickly reminds us, however, that philandering is not abuse and repeats his claim that he was never abusive to Betty. Later, in letter #11, Heidnik will declare that his adultery was "not even adultery" because he was actually having sex with his "spiritual wives" within the sanctity of their church.

In this letter, Heidnik is so elated by his newly restored love for Betty that he exclaims, "Is that <u>love</u> or what??" The immediate question is why this dramatic reversal of attitude? Why is Betty being so nice to him now, nearly three years after their violent separation? Heidnik himself does not question Betty's unexpected change of heart even as he acknowledges that he had "been skeptical of her motives" previously. The reason will be revealed two weeks later in letter #13, but for now Gary Heidnik is in romantic heaven.

Friday, Dec 2, 1988

Dear Jack,

How well here it is, only two days since I wrote you a nice L-L-L-O-O-O-N–N-N-G-G-G letter of 18 pages. Who knows? Maybe I'll beat that record with this letter. I just found out that they (the prison* admin) messed up my newspaper subscription for the month of Dec and so I won't be getting any newspapers for this month. In the cell I'm currently in I have no radio, no TV and now no newspapers. So it looks like it'll be a good month for you, since I'll have a lot of time for letter writing ☺. *Fortunately* the news black out won't be total, however, since I am still getting a weekly subscription to* Time Magazine, Readers Digest *and* National

Geographic, *all courtesy of Betty, my loving wife. It's an interesting thing about Betty, the more trouble I get into or the more serious my situation the more firmly she stands by me. From our few previous letters you could have easily gotten the impression that I hated Betty or at least disliked her. No it's not true. I LOVE her, although at times I've been skeptical of her motives. At times she has definitely* made my life miserable, but there were several great times also. As you previously mentioned, she gave me one terrific son, Jimmy. Also, very much unlike the mother of my first child (Angelique Wilson) she doesn't keep the child from me or teach the child to hate me.*

Also, a very positive point for Betty is that, she doesn't divorce me, desert* me, OR can you believe this, FOOL AROUND. There are lots of men chasing her, offering her money, presents, even... marriage, and she remains loyal to me. Yes loyal. She not only doesn't divorce me, she refuses to have anything to even do with ALL these men who keep chasing her around. Think about it. Isn't that incredible? And I'm not sure how to cope with it. One thing I am sure of is I'm NOT WORTH IT. I haven't done anything for her to be worthy of such sacrifice on her part. NOTHING!! She's literally* making a living martyr of herself, for me. Can you imagine being a woman in the prime of your sexual life, really ready to enjoy sex and life and instead living CHASTE and in virtual* poverty over a BUM like me. As I said, I'm not worthy. When Betty says she's not cheating on me, I believe her.... this time. Betty's not always truthful, she lies a lot even to me, and makes many promises she doesn't have the slightest intention of keeping. But when she says she doesn't cheat on me, I believe her.

For some reason, she tells me about everyone who makes a pass at her. Some of them really surprise me. One of them is an inmate right here at S.C.I.P. that I put her in contact with so she could come up and visit me. Betty even sent me the inmate's letters of passion and proposals of marriage. Even more incredibly, believe it or not, the inmate's father, who'd come up and visit him and bring Betty with him (he's also about 70 years old) was also making passes at Betty. Like father, like son, or what!! ☺ *(By putting smiling faces behind each of my jokes, you'll know they're jokes and that you're* *supposed to laugh!! Ha, ha.) At any rate Betty continues to turn these men away. Some of them are very clever also. They know how much she loves Jimmy and they try to work on her through him. They buy him lots of expensive toys and treat him decent, but it doesn't work. Betty still turns them away. I'm ambivalent about it. On the one hand I'm proud of Betty and on the other I feel guilty. After all, in my present situation what can I offer her? Not much. Mostly memories. There are no, I repeat NO women I know of who would remain loyal and not divorce me, faced with what transpired in the past and the very bleak outlook I have for the future. But Betty doesn't care. She stands right beside me all the way. Is that <u>love</u> or what??*

However, don't misunderstand*. All hasn't been well in paradise. As you're so patently familiar* with, we've had many squabbles and much friction, and it's entirely possible we may have been incompatible*. It's entirely possible that we may have never been able to live in the same house together, BUT our marriage would have survived since we also don't believe in divorce. It's quite possible that we would have reached a compromise, by staying married, but living apart.... most of the time. We could still have dates and visited with each other, but I've a feeling that if we tried living together again we'd soon be mentally pummeling* each other. That's the advantage of living in two different residences. When the fighting would get too heavy* and the blood flowing too capaciously, we could withdraw to our neutral corners and cool off, till the next round.

Our courtship, Betty's and mine, as you're probably aware, was different than most peoples. Which probably explains why we're having so much difficulty. As you know Betty was a mail order bride. We'd been corresponding for two years, but had only met each other face to face for three days, before getting married. Most people know each other personally for years, or at least a couple of months before they're married and have an opportunity to work things out. To see each other, recognize different problems or areas of contention and resolve them first. You can't really do much of that in a letter. So even though we'd been writing* for two years we barely knew each other. After only three days, we plunged right into marriage.

This is where my idea of separate residences comes into play. If we were living apart, even after we were married, we could get to know each other better, and resolve a lot of difficulties first. Whenever things get too hectic, we could pull apart, before they get too acidic*. Also, I know, for my part, I'd try harder. It'd be kind of like trying to court Betty (which I hadn't done before). I'd take her on dates, wine her and dine her and try to win her over, instead of taking her for granted. Then, if all went well we could move in together but GRADUALLY. Only a day or two together at first, so we wouldn't wind up fighting again. So now, tell me? What do you think of this idea of separate residences? Think it would work? I know its a bit unconventional*, but then again isn't everything about me unconventional*? The main reason I think it would have worked is the evidence we have before us presently. If death row can't break up our marriage, then nothing will.

As I mentioned before, I've not been the best of husbands, but neither have I been the worse. I certainly haven't been abusive. I hasten to point out that I do NOT consider philandering abuse. (I can write a whole letter just on this topic, and I will, but later). On one area that I feel guilty is about our honeymoon. Three days at the Marriott on City Line Avenue, isn't much of a honeymoon. In my defense though, let me say that, since I was then on parole (which incidentally* I never told Betty about). I wasn't allowed to travel out of state without permission. My preference for a honeymoon would have been Niagara Falls, but not only was that out of state, but on Oct 3, 1985 it was out of season also. Actually one good thing about the Marriott honeymoon is that Betty was so <u>overwhelmed</u> by a new country, new food, different customs and the honeymoon itself, she wouldn't even come out of the hotel room. So a second honeymoon to Niagara Falls, at a later date, when she had become acclimated* to America was logical. Still I feel guilty.

Next I'd like to thank you for all the books you've sent me (and the Bible. Betty beat you to the punch on the Bible though. She sent me a nice one already). Your taste in books is pretty good. I'm currently engrossed in the James Burke's The Day the Universe Changed *and am anxious to sink my teeth into* The Human Zoo. *For whatever the narcissistic* pleasure I can gain, let me say that*

I've just completed Homer's Iliad.

I got your letter of November 28 and at the risk of arousing your ire, I'm going to have to ask you if you could write a little more legibly. I'm having difficulty reading your letters and it's getting worse. I'm hardly the one to complain over illegibility since my handwriting* is even WORSE than yours. That is the reason I print all my letters. If I had access to a typewriter it would be typewritten. I think the reason for your poor handwriting* is you are just in a hurry to get it on paper. So maybe if you just slowed down your rush of inspiration or maybe you could even resort to a typewriter*. If you type your letters I won't be offended or think it's too formal. Don't worry about that.

Before getting to your letter I'd first like to tantalize* you a bit. Perhaps one of the most interesting girls in the cellar was Agnes. (We knew her as Donna). She had an interesting life even though she was only 18. I've just read an article in National Geographic *about Anchorage Alaska. It reminded me of Donna. You see she started being a prostitute* at the age of 15 in Hawaii and then got involved with a pimp who put her to work in Anchorage. I always planned to get more details from her but didn't. For some reason*, I don't know how she wound up in Phila.*

It is curious why Heidnik abruptly injects this single paragraph about Agnes Adams here. The topic is unrelated to anything else in this long letter. His conscious intention, he claims, is to "tantalize" me with new information about her. Agnes was the last victim kidnapped in the final days before Heidnik was arrested. He depicts Agnes as "one of the most interesting girls in the cellar" and that "we knew her as Donna." His casual tone makes it sound like Agnes was part of some happy social club rather than a desperate band of hungry, cold, wretched, and terrified victims in a dank torture pit.

In the next section of his letter, Heidnik turns to a

surprisingly candid confession of his mental limitations, or what he terms, "a rather poor memory*." He describes how he compensated throughout his life for not being "smart enough" through extended hours of pure dogged study. He remarks, however, that he always enjoyed learning new knowledge and even now, sitting in solitary confinement, he enjoys working diligently to expand his personal vocabulary with new "$25 words."

Following this momentary stance of one-down humility, Heidnik reverses again to one-up criticism of my "dried prunes" writing style. He points to his own "Coatesville Antics" from his previous letter #7 as the entertaining style he wants for <u>his</u> best seller. Yet even as Heidnik criticizes me, his paranoid tendencies seep through. He abruptly accuses me of making "threats" to abandon him to write a book about a different Midwest serial killer.

Before going further, I feel it's important to mention, I've got a rather poor memory*. Especially my short term memory*. This poor memory* has plagued me all through school, college, etc. It made getting an education difficult, since I'd have to apply extraordinary effort to remember my lessons. That is one reason I couldn't and didn't attend college full time. I wasn't smart enough and had to devote so much time to the few courses I did take, I didn't have time to handle a full load, or do anything else. Learning and remembering has always come hard for me and required great amounts of time and effort. However, to my credit, I love knowledge, and have always been willing to invest the time and energy it took to learn. I continue the process, even today, in my jail cell. I have no distractions like T.V. or radio, or even conversation (I'm in solitary) but I have a dictionary and I'm using it. Many of the $25 words I've been using lately in my letters are recent acquisitions to my lexicon, that I'm anxious to put into use. (Kind of like a kid with a new toy ☺). Using them will help reinforce their retention and overcome my poor memory problem. Their* use has little to do with vanity, but I do try to make my letters interesting and entertaining.

With that thought I can lead into your current missive. If I've offended you, by my captious remarks about your literary style, I'm sorry for hurting your feelings, but I feel my point was well taken and I'm on firm ground. By characterizing your writing* as being as interesting as a "dried prune" you have to admit I did pique your interest and it is such an effective criticism* you'll probably always remember it. That was, on my part, a colorful* and effective piece of writing*. That's the kind of writing* that will appeal to the mass public. If you plan to be a successful and RICH author, you have to appeal to the multitude, not the egalitarian* scientists. Scientists will read anything ☺☺. (See, two smiling faces for that one, ha, ha). So how about trying to add some zest to your writing*? Analogies, for instance can add lots of spice. Perhaps you could practice a little when you write me. (Aren't* I the most cantankerous laboratory specimen you ever encountered?). And your* threats of writing* and researching that other fellow in the Midwest, I consider vacuous and inane, since there's* no reason you can't write two books ☺.

Speaking of literary style, did you like my commentary on "Coatesville Antics" in the last letter? I could have written it in a bland and mundane fashion, but I tried to be entertaining and interesting. Did I succeed?

As to the part of your letter about God giving me stock tips and having told all these doctors that; well I don't remember telling them that. Yes, God does talk to me and gives me good advice, but none of it on the stock market. If He did I'd probably have done a lot better. Although I did well in the market, my success is overrated. I'm much better at saving money than investing. When I got incarcerated in 79, the S.S. and V.A. had to continue paying me my full pensions, for the full 5 years I was locked up. Wasn't that in the Parole records or mentioned by the P.R.C. or Doctor Bora? They knew about it. You better BELIEVE they knew about it. They had an inside tract on every penny that came into that institution and went out. I'm pretty sure they also read ALL of my mail and thus knew all my moves in the stock market. Dr. Bora, occasionally* mentioned in *general terms my investments.*

The point is that I was receiving about $20,000 a year while in jail and I spent very little of it on myself. I donated it almost entirely to the church. So figure an average donation of $15,000 to $20,000 a year, for 5 years, and you get about $85,000 to $90.000. I started off with about $115,000 to $125,000 in the church in 79 so that gives you about $200,000 from other sources. When I left in 83 the church was worth about $350,000 to $400,000. That means I made for the church through good investing, about $150,000 over a 5 year period. That'd be about 20% a year or so. That's not bad, but it's not as spectacular as the media claims. I am a little vain and enjoy being considered a financial genius but I'm really not. Only average. Unfortunately God didn't give me any pointers either, or the results would have really been spectacular.

Despite his false modesty, Heidnik enjoys his reputation as a financial genius. His wealth through investing was the subject of great interest for the media after his arrest and during his trial. It was reported in the Philadelphia press that Heidnik's stock portfolio was worth between $500,000 and $600,000 (about $1.9 million today). When asked why he agreed to defend Heidnik, Charles Peruto gave one of his best one liners: "I have 100,000 good reasons." Contrary to his denial in this letter, Heidnik's psychiatric records show that he often claimed to receive stock tips from God or Jesus. Here he denies it emphatically. He admits talking to God, but never about stocks. Either he is lying or, as I believe, he does not remember telling his psychiatrists because he was acutely psychotic at the time.

In the next segment of this letter, beginning on page 11, Heidnik shifts from braggadocio about his financial genius to a discussion of his extended 6-month psychiatric hospitalization and suicide attempts. These topics reveal the deeper and more authentic feelings of personal inadequacy that continually haunted Heidnik.

In this letter you touched on a very interesting subject. One that I've been pondering at some length. My hospital admission to Coatesville in 3/86 to 8/86. When I got admitted that time they put me on a closed ward and kept me there for my whole admission and the doctors wouldn't tell me why. Day after day, other patients kept getting transferred* to the open wards but not me. That never happened before in 20 years of hospitalizations, and I've always been wondering why. I've suspected that Betty told the doctors something about physical abuse so he would keep me on the closed ward and thus stop me from "philandering." Betty is, as you know, a very jealous woman and greatly resented me having affairs. I have to give Betty credit for that maneuver* though. By keeping me locked on the closed ward, it did stop me from "messing around." She most certainly was in no physical danger from me, and I suspect the only mental abuse was her reaction to my philandering.

The extended duration of Heidnik's psychiatric hospitalization in a closed ward from March through August 1986 reflects the severity and duration of his psychological collapse after he was rejected by his wife Betty in February. Undoubtedly, his treating psychiatrists regarded him as a serious danger to himself and/or others. Heidnik never considers this possibility. Instead he tries to boost his ego with the absurd theory that his loving wife Betty was trying to stop him from infidelity by keeping him locked in the hospital.

The self-deceiving ploy doesn't work. Heidnik quickly becomes anxious and weak with self-doubt as he writes further about being rejected by Betty. In this emotionally vulnerable state, his mind shifts to his own self-loathing and multiple suicide attempts. He actually expresses regret and responsibility, albeit indirectly, for the tragic death of Sandra Lindsay. He feels bad because she had once cared enough about him to visit him in the hospital after he had tried to kill himself because Betty rejected him.

I need some more elucidation on my Temple admission. First of all, I thought I was admitted for three days. Was I? I can't read the discharge date. Interestingly I don't remember Tony taking me home or visiting me. He told me later that he and Sandy visited me in the hospital. The knowledge that Sandy cared enough to visit me, grieves me highly. I wish I had some things to do over again, so I wouldn't do them in the first place. As for oral intubation, what is it? When I was a nurse a tube running into a patient's mouth was called an N.G. tube and was used mainly for feeding. Also when I was practicing nursing we didn't have "ventilators." The closest thing we had to a ventilator was an I.P.P.B. machine (Intermittent* positive pressure breathing). These machines were green plastic affairs*, wheeled into the patients room and could perform the mechanical act of breathing. But to do that they had to perform a tracheotomy*. I didn't have a tracheotomy* and for the life of me I can't figure out how a ventilator would do my breathing without a trach. I'm not skeptical about your information, but I am highly curious*, since my nursing knowledge is out of date.

Several times you subtly* mentioned the word malingerer. The suicide attempt should answer part of that. How or why would I "stage" this suicide attempt if I weren't sincere? Tony's arrival and interference were quite unexpected. He was out and I figured he'd be out all day, and even if he weren't, he had no business going into the garage. If Barbara hadn't told him where I was and if he didn't get nosey I'd have succeeded. Even after he found me and I locked the door to the van, he told me, he wasn't sure what to do, but after waiting 15 minutes or so he called the rescue ambulance. He was proud of having saved me, but I berated* him for doing it and made him promise not to interfere* in the future. He promised he wouldn't. Feel free to question him on this or anything else.

Another suicide attempt I made was in jail. That's the one that made the papers. You don't think that was malingering do you? Even the prison* was convinced of my sincerity and they're some of the biggest skeptics around. I almost succeeded* in hanging myself in the shower. I'd tried 4 different times in my cell but I couldn't get enough height*. There was a bar on the desk in my cell but it was only 3 feet high. Still on those 4 occasions I managed unconsciousness each time, but that was all. There was something magical in the T-shirt I was using. I used it in the shower and it worked there too! I told the guard I was taking it into the shower to wash. But for some reason he got suspicious and peeked into the shower and saw me hanging there. In getting me off he even cut my head on the shower head, but I didn't feel any pain since I was unconscious*. They took me out and laid me on the floor and gave me oxygen. I was out for several more minutes before coming too. They then took me to Giuffre for observation and tests. The officer's name who caught me was Officer Love. He was reprimanded severely* for not catching me sooner. Yes they reprimanded him not praised him. Later he even asked me how "it felt to be dead."

Hanging is an interesting phenomenon*, and I can describe it as someone who has experienced it like no one else can. The perception that you strangle and slowly asphyxiate isn't necessarily so, I could never hurt myself that way. In my case, when using that particular T-shirt, and only that T-shirt I experienced complete, sudden and total unconsciousness. No strangling or gasping for breath. I believe that T-shirt was able to cut off the blood to my brain and that's what caused the blackness, not the lack of breath. Also there's no pain. I give it ★ ★ ★ ★ as a means of committing suicide, so long as you do it so it cuts off the blood supply, not the breathing. Loss of breathing is too much suffering. As for recommended* ways of suicide, the absolute best, most preferred is the way I did it in Solitary Confinement. I took about 4,000 mg of Thorazine with about 16 ounces of gin. That combination of alcohol and drugs is reputed to be very lethal. The alcohol though gets you so high, you're actually enjoying yourself and having a good time. I had the truck running and filling up the garage with carbon monoxide, but I think the effects of that were minimal or nonexistent, since it hadn't been *long enough. As a matter of fact it was counter productive since the sound of the running truck attracted Tony to the garage.*

By the way I did achieve a little fame and notoriety for that hanging attempt at D.C. [District Court Detention Center]. After that they completely* changed all the shower heads so no one could do that again, he, he, hee.

That was one area I was pleased and satisfied with your treatise. You accurately portrayed* that incident and removed some doubt as to me being a malingerer. You could add to it though with some follow up on the attempt at D.C. Also check and see the opinion of my doctor at S.C. I think her name was Dr. Wingate or something like that.

Well I'm going stop for now. My last two letters should keep you busy for a while, and my hand is aching from all this writing*. I've spent about 5 hours on this letter alone.

Cogitatively yours
Gary

In describing the sincerity of his three suicide attempts, Heidnik is determined to disprove the accusations that he was malingering. The records support the accuracy of his claims. For example, after trying to hang himself, Heidnik had redness on his entire neck and a laceration on the back of his head. The X-rays showed no broken bones or disturbed air passages, but he did receive intravenous feeding because the pain in his damaged throat prevented normal eating. He was placed on suicide watch and discharged on April 3, 1987 to the psychiatric unit at Graterford prison. At the murder trial, Officer Love, the prison guard who discovered the suicide attempt, stated clearly that Heidnik was unconscious and presumed dead. After they failed to revive him, they administered oxygen with success.

Given the malingering charges made at his trial, I had once questioned Heidnik as to what he thought was his most accomplished suicide attempt. Heidnik became quite descriptive about his self-described "4-star" method as presented in this letter. To bring greater clarity to Heidnik's elaborate and extensive history of suicidality, we created the summary table below. The table below shows where these three attempts fit into his full history of 16 suicide attempts and identifies Heidnik's frequent references to the subject in this correspondence.

#	Date	Suicide Episodes/Topic	Where	Discussed in Letter
	Memorial Day 1970	Heidnik's mother, an unstable alcoholic, commits suicide by ingesting hair dye and dies an excruciating death.	Note: Brother Terry also had multiple suicides.	#15, pg. 2
1	1970	Gary attempts suicide after throwing his mother's ashes in Niagara Falls.		
2	1971	Hospitalized at Perryville after suicide attempt.		#13, pgs.13-14
3-6	1970s approx.	Several attempts resulting in hospitalizations.		
7	Late 1978	3 attempts during incarceration at Graterford (Nov. 1978 to Apr. 1983). 1st attempt – overdose by medications.	Graterford Prison	
8	Late 1978	2nd attempt – method unknown.	Graterford Prison	
9	January 1979	3rd attempt – unscrews light bulb, smashes and swallows crushed glass.	Graterford Prison	#6, pgs 5-6
--	1979-1983	Paranoid and convinced that the authorities were trying to get him to commit suicide, Heidnik determines that he will NOT commit suicide.	Graterford Prison	#13, pg 18
10	Feb. 5, 1986	Ingests thorazine and gin, then locks self in closed garage with van engine running for carbon monoxide poisoning. May have caused lasting renal damage.	Garage at home	#6, pg 4-5 #8, pgs 12-16 #11, pg 5
11-14	Mar/Apr 1987 approx.	Using "magical T-shirt", he achieves unconsciousness 4 times in prison cell.	Phila District Court Deten. Ctr	#8, pgs 14-14
15	April 1987	For his 5th attempt, he tries to hang self with a towel in the shower.	Phila District Court Deten. Ctr	#8, pgs 14-15
16	New Years Jan 1, 1989	Overdose on thorazine.	Pittsburgh SCIP prison	#17, pgs 1-3
--	January 2, 1990	Discusses Kevorkian's suicide machine.	Pittsburgh SCIP	#24, pg 3

In our estimation, Heidnik was absolutely sincere in his attempts to kill himself. But this raises a paradox: Although his suicide attempts were not manipulative to gain special attention, they were definitely manipulative in terms of control. Heidnik is not a malingerer, but he is an expert manipulator. Heidnik uses suicide as part of his pervasive obsession with control. He takes satisfaction and solace in his ability to plan the details and control his own death. Consider this notable example from page 18 of letter #13:

A little addendum about the suicide, pressure and "knee jerk" reaction. I'm also a bit of a "contrarian." If somebody wants me to do something often times I'll do just the opposite, just to be contrary. So in 82 & 83 when I realized they were playing "mind" games with me and wanted to drive me crazy and maybe even commit suicide (I still didn't know why till 83) I wasn't about to cooperate. I hung onto my sanity then ((I think??) and didn't commit suicide, because I knew that's what they WANTED me to do.

The salience of Heidnik's psychological dynamic of suicide and control is revealed in the structure of this letter. As shown below, Heidnik recreates the exact same up and down pattern between control (feeling strong) and loss of control (feeling weak) that he did in letter #6.

	Control (strong)	→ Loss of control (weak)	Control (strong)	→ Loss of control (weak)		Control (strong)
Letter #6 11/25	Commands me to change writing style to suit him	Betty refuses to be subservient (his sexual slave)	I am a genius		What happened to me during the suicide?	I'm a master of suicide.
Letter #8 12/2	Betty loves me after all. I'm worthy	I'm not smart enough	Commands me to change writing style to suit him	I am a financial genius	They locked me in a mental hosp.	What happened to me during the suicide?	I'm a master of four-star suicide.

LETTER #9
"Now I'm Going to Play a Game With You"

December 9, 1988

Heidnik begins letter #9 with the giddy announcement that he is now writing his own novel and has already finished 97 pages. It is titled "Life in the Slow Lane" or "40th Street Soaps." 40th Street refers to his former neighborhood in West Philadelphia where 40th Street cuts through the University of Pennsylvania campus. It is where he befriended and seduced intellectually disabled clients of the Elwyn Institute where he worked. He proudly includes the Prologue (see letter #9) of what will be a "profound" novel based on autobiographical real events and real people. Heidnik promises to deliver "a smile on your lips, an ache in your heart, and above all, a deeper appreciation for the handicapped."

I remember reading Heidnik's novel. It had the weird quality of someone talking in allegories that only he can understand. It was the ramblings of a mad man. I told Heidnik that either I had to stop reading his novel or I would need to do some cocaine. He was not happy with my humor. So I gave him more books to peace up our relationship.

Heidnik's sudden new career as a novelist is clinically significant. It shows his characteristic traits of impulsivity, fluctuating moods, egotism, and flights of narcissistic fantasy. The pace and output of his writing is staggering. In addition to the frequency and growing length of Heidnik's letters to me in November and December of 1988, he is now writing 14 hours a day on his novel. His writing output is manic, expansive, and grandiose in the full clinical sense of these three terms. Though I don't recognize it yet, Heidnik is escalating toward another major psychiatric breakdown.

In the meantime, I've got a new Heidnik problem to deal with. Just when I think I've got Gary to hold hands and waltz with me, he starts to go solo like a hippie dancing at a Grateful Dead show. Dealing with Heidnik was a tricky balance. Part of me was obliged to feign friendship and caring for Gary in order to maintain his cooperation and gain an honest telling of his inner thoughts and motivations. That required some degree of personal self-disclosure on my part. At the same time, self-disclosure is a serious risk in dealing with forensic patients like Heidnik. It is crucial to maintain your professional boundaries.

With Heidnik, however, the rule book went out the window. Many times I lost myself in the pursuit of information. I was giving him books as gifts. I was taking risks by sharing personal information about myself and my life. Perhaps my cocaine fog was still hampering my judgment. I also think that I really didn't care what Heidnik knew about me. I didn't fear him. I just wanted to get to the "real truth" that only he could provide. I don't remember giving him my wife's name. I do remember offering to buy a Christmas present for his son Jimmy. It was a sincere offer. It wasn't bait. I felt bad for the kid for having crazy Gary as his father.

Error or not, the Christmas gift episode shows that I did feel empathy for Gary, even while feeling annoyance, anger, and revulsion. Throughout the process, I was trying to remain detached emotionally from his sadistic crimes. I learned that skill while vacationing in Vietnam as a guest of the US Army. I didn't have room in my head for more nightmares about Heidnik's butchery. I already had horror films of my own showing nightly when I closed my eyes. Most of the time, I felt very little, if at all, about his twisted crimes. The horrific realities of Heidnik basement did not bother me because my emotions were already numbed by Vietnam and substance abuse.

Heidnik was a person who did some weird awful shit and I was going to figure it out. I do believe he made legitimate suicide attempts and clearly the prosecution accused him of malingering to make it look like he had carefully planned everything. At the same time, as revealed in this letter, he was a shrewd manipulator and it was my turn to get zoomed. He proposes that I join him in a plot to steal a half million dollars from his Church's financial accounts.

Friday, Dec 9, 1988

Dear Jack,

The mailman just brought me your letter and I was delighted to hear from you. First, let me say that I'm pretty busy as of Saturday. You see I finally overcame my "writers block" and I'm writing* my book "Life in the Slow Lane or 40th Street Soaps." Enclosed you'll find my rewritten prologue. (After you read it <u>please send it back</u>, and give me some feedback on it. So far I've written 97 pages and its a lot tougher than writing* letters. I only average 10 or 15 pages in a 14 hour day. But it's fun, takes my mind off things, and I've been wanting to write a book since I was a kid. It looks like I'm really going to do it this time. I allow myself no distractions at all. Only a pause to read from Time Magazine. *It will take me about 2 or 3 more weeks to finish my rough draft. I'm not sure how long it will be but it just might be 300 or 400 pages long. So I going to be busy for the next couple of weeks and my letters won't be 18 pages long. But I will continue to write. Thanks for the offer of the cassettes, but they not only don't allow them here but I have nothing to play it on. I think they ban cassettes because* inmates use them to smuggle things into jail. Anyways, for the next couple of weeks no distractions for me till I get my rough draft written.*

Also thanks for offering to buy Jimmy a present, I'd like to but we'd have to solve some problems first. First of all I don't want Betty to know I'm writing you, and we're having a little domestic impasse right now. Nothing serious. But if you send the letter with the present I'm still going to have to explain it. Betty is very suspicious. She is being harassed* and bothered by many men trying to make out with her. They often send presents to Jimmy and she throws them away. She doesn't want any other men and she won't let them get to her through Jimmy. So if you have any more ideas, let me know. It would be nice if Jimmy could get a nice present. From what I understand he's hoping for some real live "birdies."

Now I'm going to kind of play a game with you. I'm not trying to be cute or anything but this seems to be the best way I know of to make a point. If I came right out and said some things you'd think I'm crazy, and I want to appear credible to you. So please don't be mad and don't be impatient.

As you know I started a church and had sizeable assets*. About $125,000 in 78 and about $350,000 to $400,000 in 83. So we know there was a lot of money involved. O.k.? Suppose, just suppose you were a crook and wanted to steal this money and knew the following information I'm giving you. PLUS all the medical information you already have. You knew my medical profile pretty well.

When I started the church there were 5 people on the board of directors.

1. Evelyn (Lynn) Wilson
2. Dorothy Knox
3. Maxine Roberts
4. Terry Heidnik
5. Gary M. Heidnik

The church constitution said that there should be an election and the winner would be bishop for life. No more elections. The only way the bishop could be put out of office is by dying or resigning. The board members can't even get together and vote the bishop out of office. We held an election and I was voted bishop. In our church the Bishop has total control over everything secular and ecclesiastical. The bishop controls completely* all finances and doesn't have to answer to anyone. He doesn't even have to make financial reports to the board, even if they were interested, which they were not. As bishop I made all investments, expenditures, etc. myself. Total and life time control. (Even Supreme Court justices don't have that kind of security).

Then you find out that the church's money is very vulnerable. Other than this guy Heidnik, there's nobody hardly even knows about this church and all the money involved. There's really nobody but that board of directors. Now let's take this one at a time.

(1) Evelyn is presently at Ancora State Hosp. She has plenty of mental* problems and is abandoned by her family. In 80 she was still living in Buval Manor in Phila raising my older daughter Angelique. She has problems, especially money problems. Both in 82 and 83 she was in a boarding home and abandoned by her kids. Angelique was then being raised by her oldest daughter, Sonia Garrett. She doesn't know the amount of money involved and can be easily manipulated. If someone offered her some amount of money to sign a paper she would – FAST!

(2) Dorothy Knox. This is the woman who lived with me for 10 years. She is about 10 years older than me and spent a lot of years at Byberry before I knew her. Her mind had continued to degenerate so badly she had trouble going around the corner without getting lost. She'd sign any document you wanted for a packet of cigarettes.

(3) Maxine Roberts. She is in her right mind but publicly disavowed the church and wants nothing to do with it. So she's off the board and no problem.

(4) Terry Heidnik is the only problem. He knows how much money is involved and is nobody's fool. To get him to vote your way is going to be tough.

Note: A genogram is included in Letter #14 that shows the confusing cross-relationships among Gary and Terry Heidnik and their women and offspring. The genogram denotes the five members of the Board of Directors of the Church who are described here.

To hold another election for bishop, I would of course have to be dead or resigned so I don't count. Since Maxine publicly dropped from the board there are only three voting members left. Dorothy, Maxine, and Terry. Since you'd only need 2 votes out of three Terry doesn't matter. You may be even get the votes of Dorothy and Lynn. So the only thing standing between you and all that money is – me –

Gary – bishop.

Now remember. Don't think like yourself. Think like a crooked cop named Devlin. He wants to steal this money – which is so vulnerable, but he'd prefer to do it legally*. How would you do it? And keep in mind my medical profile (which Devlin knew also).

Now let me answer some of your questions. Some of them were very good.

(1) Detective Devlin hated me and all the people involved in the custody of Anne Maxine Norton, my daughter. These people seemed to be able to pull strings, like being able to hold a custody hearing without ever sending a subpoena to me or Anjeanette. So these people not only hated us, they were able to pull some strings.

(2) I didn't know Anjeanette's family too well only the two other sisters Bertha and Cheryl. Bertha DID have a policeman as a date. I'm not sure what his name was but it was the exact same name of a singer. It could have been Barry White.

(3) Devlin definitely* knew of the church's funds, but not at first. He didn't know till they came in one night to arrest me. But I wasn't there so they searched the apartment and left. Anjeanette was home at the time. When I got home in the morning I found several statements from Merrill Lynch missing. These statements would have told him how much the church was worth, and given my stock broker's name. Hardly anybody else knew about the church and it's money but Maxine, Terry, George Wood, and me. George is black also. He knew about the church but not how much was involved. I don't really suspect him, but he is venal* and he knows plenty of cops and politicians.

(4) The funds were in two places only. Merrill Lynch and Provident Savings and Loan. The funds had NO protection, other than being in these two institutions.

(5) Funds could only be transferred* with my say so and signature*, no others (as long as I remained bishop).

(6) No, no accountants* or attorneys know about the funds.

(7) My first attorney, Donald Levine could not be trusted. I think that Devlin got to him somehow and had him working for him. When I realized at the arraignment he was also selling out I dropped him and hired Robert Pressman (with Jack Bulkin). Mr. Pressman at

the beginning fought hard and fair for me, but then towards the end of the trial he asked me privately* if I have a lot of money? I told him a <u>little</u> about the church, but I don't think he believed me. When I got the shaft at sentencing time because he wasn't there. Bulkin was and Bulkin had no connections, so the court really socked it to me.

(8) Levine definitely* could be bought. He was an ambulance* chaser and phoned* up a lot of phony* doctors bills and such so he could sock it to the insurance companies. Terry and I used to send him clients. Pressman I already explained. I think he was clean at first but they got to him in the end.

{They had Kirkpatrick working for them and they could bypass the board. But they'd have to do something about me.}

Again please don't talk to Betty yet. She doesn't know I'm writing* you yet. I'd rather we keep things in writing* for the time being. I feel more comfortable this way. There is a lot more to talk about 78. I'll send more letters. Robert Kirkpatrick III was my stockbroker from about 73 to 87. Good question Jack. <u>You're really thinking</u>. I never even considered him, but he'd sell his own mother out. Out of paper & time. Keep questions coming.

Gary

Heidnik is very systematic in detailing how to bribe and trick each of the four church board members who might have some claim to the church fortune. He is then just as meticulous in detailing each of the main suspects that he thinks may be plotting to steal the money: Detective Devlin, Anjeanette's family, attorneys Levine, Pressman and Bulkin, and stockbroker Kirkpatrick. Then he abandons all disguise and says, "So the only thing standing between you and all that money is – me – Gary – bishop." Does he really think that I will jump at this chance? Or does it simply reflect the utter incompetence of his social judgment? Or is Heidnik testing whether I, too, am out to steal his money?

In hindsight, there is a lesson to be learned from Heidnik's "game." By offering to buy a Christmas present for his son, I knowingly risked the professional boundary between us. In fact, every time that I sent a book or magazine to Heidnik, I was knowingly crossing this boundary. In this case, I was legally and ethically safe as a psychologist because Heidnik was not my client and there was no financial agreement of any kind between us. But Heidnik certainly recognized my offer as an indication that I could be manipulated. This is a very common phenomenon in the field of corrections and forensic psychology, especially with con men and prison inmates like Heidnik. The process is simple. The inmate uses some bit of personal information about a guard or staff person to ingratiate himself and then asks for small favor. It could be any tiny act – such as allowing him to smoke, or retain a paperclip, or hang a picture in his cell, or keep an extra dessert – but the key is that the staff person's action will begin to violate the rules of the institution, as well as professional and personal boundaries. Once the staff person agrees to the first favor, the inmate asks for another small favor, and another. Thereafter, in gradual increments, the inmate continues raising the size of the favor (and the severity of the institutional rule violation) until it reaches a critical mass. The con game is triggered at the point that the staff person has been duped into allowing a rule violation of more serious proportions. Now the staff person is hooked. The inmate can threaten to expose the staff person for the violation if he/she does not continue to cooperate. Now he can get the staff person to do what he really wants, such as bringing in contraband, drugs, or cell phones.

With a master manipulator like Heidnik, I knew I should maintain my guard and think twice about any self-disclosure of personal information (such as my wife's name) or action (such giving him a book) that he might interpret incorrectly as friendship or might use to threaten or extort me. For example, even the early decision to allow Heidnik to address me as "Jack" rather than "Dr. Apsche" was a calculated move by Heidnik to test the level of intimacy of our relationship. By the same token, it would be significant later when Heidnik shifted back to addressing me as "Doctor" at the end of our correspondence. As I said earlier, the rule book went out the window with Heidnik. I did not protect my professional boundaries as I normally would with an actual client. Yet, I was careful to avoid any misperceptions of closeness or intimacy. On the contrary, more often than not, Heidnik's letters show his frustration with the distance that I maintained. Many of his letters contain complaints that I am not answering his questions, or holding back information, or not writing back soon enough, or failing to explicitly agree with his persecutory beliefs.

His letter also included the Prologue to his novel. The grandiosity and narcissism speaks for itself, but I would draw attention to the very last line. He suggests that his work is an effort to "make reparations… for past sins" by raising awareness of the struggles of the handicapped.

Prologue
(Life in the Slow Lane or the 40th St. Soaps)

Dear Reader,

You are about to take a ride on a literary roller coaster. At all times I endeavor to be entertaining. I will throw at you liberal doses of laughter, comedy, pathos, and so. BUT I'm warning you ahead of time, you have to be wary of me. When I have you laughing and giggling*, or lost in some poignant experience, and you've dropped your guard, I will hit you with some profound piece of logic regarding the plight of the disabled.

This is a story of fact, not fiction. Every event portrayed on these pages actually happened and all my characters really existed. It is a real story about real people with real handicaps. It's not a story for the squeamish, faint of heart or the naïve.

If after you've read this you have a smile on your lips, an ache in your heart, and above all, a deeper appreciation for the handicapped, then my efforts have succeeded and I have in some small measure made reparations for past sins. Thank you.

Respectfully
Gary M. Heidnik (author)

LETTER #10
"Here Lies Gary M. Heidnik"

December 12, 1988

Heidnik's letter #10 was not really a letter to me at all. It is actually a copy of three pages of his prose that he apparently sent to his wife Betty. Two pages are a sample from his novel, "Life in the Slow Lane," which features the semi-fictional character "Nancey" – who is meant to depict Betty. He sent a duplicate copy to me because he was obviously proud of his writing and expected both Betty and I to be duly impressed by his literary brilliance. Although Heidnik believes that these pieces will show his high level of psychological self-understanding, they show the opposite.

The first fragment, "Here Lies Gary M. Heidnik," seems intended as a poetic farewell to life. He addresses the letter to Betty and writes, "This is to be the final chapter honey" across the top margin. He also describes the epitaph to be engraved on his tombstone. I suspect this is a thinly veiled "suicide warning" that is intended to elicit Betty's sympathy and manipulate her into caring for him. Heidnik's distorted perception of women is also revealed in this short one page segment.

Betty

If someone were ever to analyze* me; you know, dissect me, take me apart and examine me under a microscope, and then put me back together. And then he tried to condense it in as few words as possible it would probably read something like this: "He used non-traditional means to solve his problems." As a matter of fact when I die, they'll probably write on my tombstone something like this:

> HERE LIES GARY M. HEIDNIK
> "A NON-TRADITIONAL SORT OF GUY"
> 1943-19...

So in true personal style, when it comes to finding a life mate (wife) I approached the situation in unorthodox fashion. It all started with a newspaper column. The writer told about this individual who started a pen pals club, so American men could meet, and perhaps marry Oriental women. In this way he'd be responsible for several hundred marriages. They also listed the address of this pen pals club.

I had seen the movie, The World of Suzy Wong *about five times and had seen all those pictures of the dutiful Japanese wives taking off their husbands' shoes and never giving any back talk. Always answering with a "Yes dear, No dear, Anything you say dear..." Oriental women are supposed to be such...*

The second segment of letter #10 is the two page excerpt from the "Nancey" chapter of Heidnik's proposed novel, "Life in the Slow Lane." Since this is an original draft, he instructs me to return the story pages to him after reading. The excerpt is included for you to judge the quality of Heidnik's would-be masterpiece for yourself. It is revealing to observe how Heidnik attempts to portray the complexities of the human psyche, particularly his take on the "subconscious dynamics" of a romantic relationship.

JACK! SEND THIS BACK ☺
Let me know if it gives you a smile

Life in Slow Lane or 40th St. Soaps
(Nancey)

As I clumped away and my wrath cooled and my ire chilled, I found myself saying, "Did I say that; Did I really say that; me; to

Nancey."

Yes! I had. In a fit of angst, my subconscious mind took over control of my conscious mind, for my subconscious knew what my conscious mind did not. It knew that I'd been lying and deceiving myself, and that Nancey would not, and could not ever love me. There simply wasn't room for me in her heart. Her heart was too filled with Waymond to allow me even the smallest corner. So my subconscious, tired* of seeing me being so constantly inane of this situation, seized control and took desperate measures. But that contumacious act of the subconscious, did cause me to see the light. My relationship with Nancey was never the same after that. It was quite literally dead, although I did continue to perform reflexes of love, but the spirit was dead, dead, dead! Even though I continued to perform the acrobatics of love it was only a reflexive action, the spirit was dead, dead dead!

Oh, sure, we dated some and even had a few more clandestine rendezvous, but in fact the affair was over. It had been merely a repeat performance of something that had been occurring since time immortal*. A thing that poets and bards have been writing* about since ancient times. It was quite simply a classic example of an "older man making a fool out of himself over a young women." It has happened in prehistoric times and continues to happen today.

And you ask, "what happened to Nancey?" Well as my ardor cooled and my pursuit faltered and failed, we drifted apart and eventually ceased to see each other. Also, as my passion chilled, Waymond simultaneously lost interest in her and dropped her. But Nancy wasn't heartbroken long. That gallant and prodigious* lover, the Romeo of 40th Street galloped to her rescue. My friend Tony picked up the pieces and Nancey was again happy – for now. Stay tuned.

I have no further comment on Heidnik's prose except that he had a high opinion of his ability. I had to feign interest and placate him long enough to get to my goal of revealing the honest truth of his motivations and behavior.

LETTER #11
"A Distant Chord But No Music"

December 16, 1988

Around this time, a lawyer friend of mine bought a new McMansion somewhere in upper Bucks County and offered to rent his current house to my brood and two collies, Nicky and Shanus. I love collies and prefer them to most people that I know. Thanks to the family court judge, Nicky had been recently restored to my daughter Melissa. It seems that her mother, my ex-wife, was angry at her 8 year old daughter for telling the judge that she wanted to live with me rather than her. More than anything, my daughter was the reason that I gave up the crazy life and decided to become a respectable citizen. Now I had a new home to go with my new family. All that I needed to do was establish a respectable job in my profession. Or I could take the easy road and join Heidnik in his plot to embezzle a million bucks of church money – not!

At this point, it's only been a week since Heidnik proposed his "game." He opens this letter by chastising me for not writing back to him sooner. No doubt he expected me to immediately fall for his trap and so it must have seemed like a long wait indeed. Having failed to lure me, Heidnik backs off from his proposition – for the time being. Instead, in Heidnik's mind, my role returns to being his benign advocate and an errand boy for gathering records and evidence of the various "injustices" and conspiracies against him. In this letter, Heidnik wants me to (1) obtain and search Anjeanette's records for documentation that she received prenatal care; (2) hunt through his hospital records to prove that the staff saw his bankbook and therefore knew about the church fortune; and (3) search through his correctional records to reveal that the parole board lied about denying him parole by showing that he did not receive psychological testing.

Does Heidnik have any idea how ridiculous and unrealistic his request is? Even if I was willing to do it, it would require untold hours of tracking down and searching medical records from three different institutions, not to mention the fact that I would have no right to see Anjeanette's confidential information. To add to the absurdity of his request, Heidnik admits that he himself does not remember the bankbook or the parole board letter, which would therefore negate the entire effort as a wild goose chase.

The point is that Heidnik's request (and it certainly will not be his last) is a glaring display of his narcissism. He is so totally carried away with his self-serving speculations that it never occurs to him that another person (me) could have any other view of the matter and would not readily comply with his biddings. Like any severely narcissistic patient, his social judgment is dreadful. In his mind, I do not exist as a separate person with different ideas and feelings of my own. I am just a projection or extension of his egotism. This is the mindset that allows a sexually violent predator like Heidnik to commit horrendous acts against victims without any inhibiting guilt or subsequent remorse. He does not stop to consider how his actions may impact negatively on others. He just acts upon his desires in the moment.

As we will observe in his letters to come, Gary's delusions about plots to steal his church fortune become increasingly fantastic and strident. In this letter, he stretches his imagined conspiracy to encompass the facts that he was denied parole in 1981 and denied release from the hospital in 1986. What Heidnik doesn't know is that I had already studied his arrest records and previous trial transcripts and spent considerable time interviewing his attorney from that time, Jack Bulkin. So getting me off my ass to go on a treasure hunt was never a consideration. I suppose I could have told him that from the outset, but I didn't. The reason was strategic and self serving on my part. I needed him to trust me and move forward with telling his true thoughts and feelings. Okay, it was one big manipulation on my part for those of you keeping score, but I needed this book and wasn't going risk blowing the deal, yet.

By the way your handwriting is improving.
Friday, Dec. 16, 88

Dear Jack,

I was about to send you a complaining letter that you weren't answering my questions, but then you sent your letter of December 13, 88 and you did answer some of them. Also I got your three additional books. Thank you. Don't forget to answer some of my questions also like Anjeanette's welfare records showing she WAS receiving prenatal care. Such evidence would go a long way to show a frame up and that I was railroaded. Hard evidence in such cases is difficult to find, but that would be documented proof of a cover up Also the PRC's and parole board's reports. They denied me my parole for over a 1½ years, telling me that I wouldn't get parole till I talked. That was <u>crap</u> and sophism. They wanted the MONEY. ALL OF IT. So of course they would have to deny any knowledge of the church's stock investment. But they know and some of it will be in the records. RECORDED proof. Your favorite kind. It may be in Graterford's or Fairview's records. During my last Fairview admission in 81, Susan Carson (she testified at the trial and was acting secretary and treasurer of the church in 81, but not a board member) sent me a passbook from Provident Savings and Loan. The passbook was in the church's name and worth something like $33,000. The authorities at Fairview naturally would NOT let me have it.

The Parole board told me they denied me parole because they felt I could talk and that I wouldn't be transferred* to Coatesville till I did. That's what they told ME. So I wrote Coatesville and they told me they hadn't heard from the parole board. I saved the Coatesville letter and it is probably with my records which the police confiscated. In 1982 when I returned to Graterford they slapped me *into solitary (R.H.C.) but I positively definitely*, and most certainly did not receive any psychological tests. That is crap and it sounds to me like they were trying to cover their asses for denying me parole. If I did take tests wouldn't they have some of my handwriting* on it. Check! You'll find, if I'm right, no handwriting* by me. Not in 82. Also I never – NEVER – talked that whole time. Anybody or any claims that I did, the person is lying or suffering auditory hallucinations.*

One problem that you seem to be making me aware of is my memory problem. Like the time I putatively rolled up my pants leg in Perry Point. It struck a distant chord but no music. Sorry I do not recall. In communicating with you I'm beginning to realize I've a bigger memory loss problem than I realized. I suppose it's difficult to know you're* forgetting* things if you can't remember you're* forgetting things (no pun intended). My impression of this memory loss problem is that it seems to intensify the sicker I am. It seems the sicker I got, the more I forgot.

As for telling the doctor on 3/10/86, I don't recall telling him God gave me stock tips and that God told me to buy cars. I don't recall. I do recall telling him God & Jesus talk to me and they call that my auditory hallucinations. I am aware they DON'T believe me when I tell them this but I don't care. Personally I don't understand why the Lord takes the time to talk to me since I most surely am not worthy. In that same interview on 3/10/86, I think it's noteworthy that the doctor accused me of grandiosity when I told him of the church. There WAS a church. They don't always believe me when I'm telling the truth. Like when I said I WAS framed and they did it to me to STEAL over $350,000.

I went A.W.O.L. in 4/4/80. I had gone home (sneaked out. I do that a lot of times) with Betty because she said the phone was dead and I wanted a little "bed time." (If you know what I mean ☺). Because of my dangerous neighborhood and all the harassment I was getting, the telephone was crucial* to call the police for emergencies, which were more likely to happen if I weren't there. My drug dealing, Puerto Rican neighbors hated me, but they hated Asians* like Betty even more and actually physically threatened her. Since I was unable to fix the phone at the time and not incoincidentally*

was tired* of the hospital, I simply left.

About my memory* problems. I have trouble remembering Dr. WAINRIGHT's name for some reason. I called her Wingate in my letter to you. I knew her name was identical to the famous U.S. WWII general in S.E. Asia and so I looked it up in my dictionary. I've been trying to commit it to memory by repeating it 50 times a day for a couple of weeks. When your letter came today guess what? I forgot it again. But I have it now it's WAINWRIGHT. I don't know why I keep forgetting but I did have problems relating to her. She kept me on strict suicide precautions for the longest time. Wouldn't even allow me a sheet, blanket or pillow. I was COLD. I used to have to curl up in my mattress trying to get warm but the heartless BROAD didn't care how much I suffered. But still I know she's a good doctor. In D.C. I developed some kind of bladder retention problem and my bladder blew up like a balloon. I think it was close to bursting before I got treatment at Guiffre. But she was aware of and on the problem even before I knew I had a problem. She's good but CRUEL!! That bladder problem may have something to do with what you mentioned in my suicide attempt in 86. There was mention of renal lesions and renal tabular cells etc. And yes, I almost always sleep with a cover over my head. Although I wasn't aware I was doing it during my unconscious phases in the 86 suicide attempt. Thanks for the information on that. I couldn't remember anything. It certainly was a close thing. It puzzles me why Tony came home so early that day and was so nosey. 5 or 10 minutes more and I'd have made it.

On page 2 of this letter, Heidnik references the three year period from 1978 to 1981 during which he never spoke because "the devil put a cookie in my throat." Clinically, this extended period of mutism was likely due to an acute episode of schizophrenic psychosis. Yet Heidnik is adamant in claiming that, "I never – NEVER – talked that whole time." To be so certain of his own mutism would seem to suggest some level of volition and malingering. If Heidnik was truly psychotic, his self-control would have been compromised and he would be unlikely to have reliable memories of his own mutism. The obvious motive for feigning mutism would have been to get himself transferred from a harsh prison to the more pleasant surroundings of an inpatient psychiatric unit. But if Heidnik was malingering, he would have known that this strategy could backfire by showing the parole board that he was too deranged to be safely paroled. While I do believe that Heidnik must have been acutely psychotic during this time, it is possible that, as his symptoms lessened, he was able to recognize the secondary gains of maintaining his mutism and exercised more volitional control over his speech.

These clinical questions raise the broader question of how well any psychiatric patient can remember events from a period of acute psychosis in which, typically, there are severe deficits in attention, concentration, and logical cognition. In fact, this deficit is the next topic that Heidnik addresses in his letter. "One problem that you seem to be making me aware of is my memory problem… In communicating with you I'm beginning to realize I've a bigger memory loss problem than I realized… It seems the sicker I got, the more I forgot."

This is Heidnik's first open acknowledgement of the unreliability of his memory (and by extension, his judgment). In letter #4, less than a month before this, he challenged me to prove that he ever did anything that he did not remember – such as signing his name as "G.M. Kill" or being hung from a window by his father. For a man who is utterly obsessed with control, this serious <u>lack</u> of control would be extremely threatening to his self-image. Indeed, he sounds anxious as he affirms forgotten events like "rolling up my pants leg," telling the doctor that "God gave me stock tips," and sleeping "with a cover over my head." He even describes his failure to remember the name of the "good, but CRUEL!" psychiatrist who kept him on strict suicide precautions and detected his bladder disorder. Heidnik says that he repeated her name 50 times a day for several weeks – and still could not remember it. Is this memory problem an enduring symptom of his mental illness, or a lifelong learning deficit, or some of both? Previously in letter #8, page 7, and later in letter #13, page 15, Heidnik describes his learning disabilities in school and how he compensated by spending many hours of repetition to remember information.

The process of talking about his cognitive weaknesses leads Heidnik to another sudden, but interesting confession of weakness in the next part of this letter. He declares that, "I'm not really afraid of dying," but admits his fear of execution in the electric chair. His fear must be deeper than he will admit to himself because he abruptly shifts into a paranoid rage. First, he accuses me (twice) of "prodding" him with thoughts of the electric chair. Then he accuses his former lawyer, Peruto, of selling him out for some imagined book. Then he screams, "I've been persecuted and harassed* ALL my life... The world not only doesn't like me, they keep punishing me. ALL my life. That's WRONG!"

Incidentally* I'm not afraid of dying so, you won't be able to prod me with threats of electric chair. I'm really not overly worried, because if I was I'd have dropped Peruto a long time ago. He sold me out for his book. No doubt in my mind. I'm only afraid of the method. I don't really relish being turned into a French fry. That could hurt and I'm partial to pain. I don't like it. So don't try to prod me with that. What I am interested in is JUSTICE. I was framed in 78 and I'd like to prove it. Also, I think people should know how I've been persecuted and harassed* ALL my life, and very unjustly so. I feel if you don't like me leave me alone. You don't have to punish me if I'm not doing anything to you. But the world not only doesn't like me, they keep punishing me. ALL my life. That's WRONG!!

I agree with you to some extent. If I FORCED Betty to watch me copulate with other women that might be construed as abuse. I admit that I did bring other women in the house but I didn't even invite her to watch let alone FORCE her to watch. But my acts were not even adultery since they were some of my wives. (Spiritual not legal). Betty broke into the bedroom to see what was going on. She didn't watch or participate, but invited herself. She watched for a couple of minutes and left. (I didn't stop). Her claim (if it's said that I copulated for hours) is chimera. I only wish I could perform that long.☺ How about giving me the exact claim she is supposed to have made? I'm sure she embellished a lot of things to insure larger spousal support payments.

Sorry if I seem narcissistic* but I actually feel it in my bones that I've got a best seller here. Perhaps even bigger than Ken Kesey's One Flew Over the Cuckoo's Nest, *which I liked very much, but I think my book is better and I'm only on the rough draft (page 195). Hopefully my book will not only make people laugh but help them to see the handicapped as human beings too. Also Ken Kesey's book helped eliminate shock treatments but I'm trying for some changes too like better treatment from sheltered workshops (such as minimum wage) and the elimination of restrictions against the disabled getting married. When I'm done writing it will also help answer some of your questions about my putative domination of women which you asked about in other letters. It's distorted and equivocal. I'm enclosing a page on my character "Billy" that may throw some light on my true character and give you a laugh too. If you thought Coatesville Antics was funny you'll pee in your pants when you read "Life in the Slow Lane." Some of it's so funny the guards here are laughing out loud, but of course nobody asks me to explain since they think I'm crazy.*

Your favorite lab specimen
Gary

The final pages of letter #11 reveal Heidnik's emotional volatility and mood instability. In just two pages, he abruptly shifts from self-doubt (about his mental faculties) to anxiety (about the electric chair) to rage (about being persecuted) to bragging (about his sexual prowess with Betty) to ebullient self-pride (about his writing). At the end, he is positively bursting with narcissistic certainty that he's writing a best seller. He asserts that even the rough draft of his unfinished novel is already better than Ken Kesey's acclaimed *One Flew Over the Cuckoo's Nest*. He takes his comparison even further. He observes that Kesey's book (and the movie) raised awareness about the misuse of electroshock treatment and helped changed psychiatric practice. His book, he crows, will achieve even more. It will raise humanity's awareness of the handicapped, improve their working conditions and, notably, eliminate restrictions against marriage between people with intellectual disabilities. Of course, this final vow is of the greatest personal importance because he himself has never recovered from the ego-crushing indignity of having his baby seized by the authorities in 1978 because he and Anjeanette have serious disabilities.

As far as Heidnik's complaint about the pain of being electrocuted, I reacted with anger. I wondered if he had ever considered that Debra Dudley might share his aversion to electrocution, although hers was gained first hand, while shackled and standing naked in a cold, water-filled pit.

LETTER #12
"Prunes Could Turn Into Plums"

December 20, 1988 (estimated)

Although letter #12 was not dated, we were able to estimate its most likely date of composition based on Heidnik's self-described average output of writing 12 pages per day on his novel, "Life in the Slow Lane." If he had finished 195 pages on 12/16, 227 pages on this date, and 280 pages by 12/23, the date must have been close to 12/20. In this letter, Heidnik's mood is high. He is silly and playful, showing off his vocabulary of words starting with "p," which he regards as clever alliteration – but it is alliteration ad nauseam.

After his "p" game is finally over, he turns to the subject of books. By this time, he is so accustomed to getting hand-me-down books from me that he begins making requests. "Have you got a copy of *Romeo and Juliet* and a dictionary? As his book benefactor, you would think he would be feeling more kindly toward me. Instead he accuses me of avoiding his questions, particularly his "big question" about, what else, the people conspiring to steal his church fortune. To be honest, I <u>was</u> avoiding his questions – because it was a bunch of annoying and distracting paranoid nonsense. Although paranoia IS an essential aspect of Heidnik's reality, I was still trying to ignore the paranoid ideation so that I could get at more important dynamics and motives. I wanted to understand his reality as best as I could determine it. I wish I had the foresight to keep copies of my letters as it might be interesting to see how I danced around his questions.

No date

Dear Jack,

 While writing* my story, I was waxing eloquent and then went a little crazy. I spent about six hours foraging in the dictionary for enough words to assemble this anecdotal pernicious piece of perfidy* with the letter "P." Several days ago I perched in my usual* nest, beside the large plate glass window in McDonald's. I partook of a particularly palatable plateful* of pleasant plentiful* plenary, pepper, pasta, prondial, persistently previewing the parade of proud peripatetic pedestrians prancing past the placidly* plotted* pane. Permit my perspicacious* pixilated perusers to pronounce these "P's" in a perceptibly* ponderable* procedure, with a palate full of pastrami, and perceive the puddle that perfuses. It's a peerless process to pique people positioned properly.

 Sorry! "P's" can be as addictive* as peanuts. You can't stop with just one. Please possess my proffered penitence.

 By the way Jack your penmanship is becoming more pellucid* and pictorial. If you keep this up your prunes could turn into plums. Ha, ha. I told you it was contagious ☺. Don't think I set you up for this by calling your writing* dried prunes either last month. It just poured past me. This stinks! Can you do better?

 Also I need some help with my book. (I've just finished page 227, by the way) I need to know (1) Romeo's last name (2) Juliet's last name and (3) I need a couple of lines from the balcony scene. Specifically what does Romeo call Juliet – the sun?? One of <u>my</u> heroes in my book is going to be named Romeo's last name and his girlfriend is going to get Juliet's last name. Think anyone will notice. It should be good for laughs if they do. Best is if you had an OLD copy of Romeo and Juliet lying around and I could read it for myself. Speaking of <u>old</u> books. Now that you have a new dictionary could you send the <u>old</u> one to Betty. She needs one a good one very badly.

 By the way you don't seem to be answering some of my questions. How about the BIG question I asked about. How they* could steal the money*? What would they have to do <u>FIRST</u>! Also *about the transcripts of 78 trial. Lawyer Jack Bulkin offered them to me in 87. You should be able to get them gratis or idiocy* from him. What use are they to him? So please reread these letters and answer some more of my questions. I put a lot of thought into them.*

Philologically yours,
Gary

P.S. Merry Xmas to you and Joanne. Coincidently guess what? When Anjeanette's and my daughter was born, we wanted to name her Joanne, but Ms Doe, the racist social worker named her Anne. Is that interesting or portentous* or what?

Heidnik ends his letter with a post-script that uses my wife's name. This is a significant test of personal and professional boundaries. As discussed in the analysis of letter #9, inmates and con-men will use the tiniest bit of personal information about a staff person to its manipulative maximum. I obviously erred when I revealed my wife's name because Heidnik now uses it to ingratiate himself as a confidant. He tries to exaggerate our close similarities, asserting that he had planned to give his daughter the same name as my wife. "Is that… portentous or what?" His misspelled choice of the word portentous is loaded. He thinks that sharing this name signifies something special between us and that it bodes well for future leverage. To use his words, "prunes could turn into plums." Heidnik thinks that I am literally "ripe for the picking." The only question is when and where he will spring his trap. In fact, he will manipulate the use of my wife's name several more times in letters #14 (pages 1 and 8) and #18 (page 1).

For now it's a seemingly innocuous Christmas greeting to my wife and I. In fact, we did enjoy a nice Christmas that year. I received an unexpected check for a tiny share of my ex-wife's sale of our old house. It was a brief reprieve from my otherwise impoverished existence. We bought Christmas presents for the kids. I surrendered my BMW, which I could no longer afford, and took a big step down to an old Jeep Wrangler.

LETTER #13
"Persecution Is My Middle Name"

December 23, 1988

Letter #13 is notable as Heidnik's longest letter to me. Totaling 28 pages, I wasn't thrilled by the prospect of grinding through what looked to be a migraine on yellow legal paper. It begins with Heidnik's upsetting realization that his wife Betty had been treating him nicely because she was "pumping me for information." Just three weeks before, in letter #8, Heidnik was boasting of Betty's devotion, declaring his love, and fantasizing about how their marriage could still work out. Now he complains that she is "<u>selling</u> all my letters AND manuscripts or collaborating* with some other writer." He is disheartened that the first 200+ pages of his unfinished novel, "Life in the Slow Lane," will be sold away without fulfilling his grandiose mission to provide "insight into the lives of the handicapped… People who have pretty much the same goals, feelings, etc. as so called normal people, just in the slower lane that's all."

As for me, I had my own frustrations to deal with. One of the residual effects of my cocaine addiction was a depressed mood and low opinion of myself. I wasn't sure that I could focus long enough to write a meaningful book on the complexities of the Heidnik case. I doubted that I would ever get out of the mess that I had made of my life. I put on my best front for Joanne and the kids, but I felt emotionally, intellectually, and morally broken. I suspect that I fooled no one, especially Heidnik, who likely sensed my vulnerability like a shark senses the blood of wounded prey.

Luckily for me, my good friend Lamont Anderson helped me to hold it together during this rough period. Lamont was a retired homicide detective, who had been a lead detective on both the Heidnik and Marty Graham serial killer cases. After the trial, we started hanging out and having beers together and would analyze Heidnik from every angle. I was getting an advanced education from a pro and mensch with a lifetime of wisdom. It was encouraging to me that Lamont respected my work on the Heidnik case and trial testimony. He agreed that Heidnik was as crazy as my Aunt Tilly, but disagreed that Heidnik met every condition of the McNaughton rule. Lamont believed that we should have received a "Guilty, But Mentally Ill" from the jury, but that Heidnik's crimes were so heinous that even the most sympathetic jury could not concur. There was simply no way they were ever going to let this butchering maniac out on the streets again.

This letter covers three main topics and contains some honest and important revelations. Most of the letter is a description of how he was framed for the kidnapping and rape of Alberta Norton in 1978, and his explanation of why the authorities found her imprisoned in "the coal bin." This topic is split into two narratives, on pages 3 to 6 and 17 to 28. The second topic, on pages 7 to 13, describes a violent incident in 1976 in which Heidnik shot his tenant in the face. The third main topic, on pages 13 to 16, is an unexpectedly frank description of his childhood struggles in school and his perception of himself as a rejected social outcast.

Notice also that Heidnik begins by describing me as the guy working to prove his innocence. In his narcissism, he continues to view me as his personal agent and considers my book to be his book. He addresses me as "Sherlock" and expects me to serve as his personal detective, who will hunt through records to verify his claims. Of course, I have no intention of being his Sherlock and I don't hold any delusions that he is innocent of anything. I played along with Heidnik in an effort to get what I wanted from him – an honest description of his inner thoughts and feelings – and he played along with me as well – to get a book that would glorify himself. It was a freaking circus and I helped create the main event.

Thursday, Dec. 23, 88

Dear Jack (Sherlock)

Hi! I'm enclosing a page of a recent letter from Betty. You'll find it very v-e-r-y insinuating. You'll notice I circled "false report." I'm pretty sure you were skeptical and didn't believe me when I said Betty had filed* a phony* rape charge. Now you've got documentary proof that I am telling the truth. I'm only sending this letter to establish my credibility. No other reason. I just wish I could prove to you a lot of other things I've said are true also, but until you start checking I can't. But here at last is an example of my candidness. A written confession. I don't want her punished or anything for it, and don't want her to get in trouble for it. So DON'T even photocopy this letter. Just read it and return it. I'm TRUSTING you, not be betray me on this.

Also from the letter the "guy" she's talking about is <u>you</u>! I told her I was working with someone to prove my innocence in 78. Apparently she wants everyone to think me guilty. It bothers me that she doesn't care, but also she doesn't know who you are , not by name anyways: It's better to keep it that way for the time being. Also if you haven't sent her the "old" dictionary and presents for Jimmy, don't bother. She would only throw them out, even if they had my name on them. I should have followed your advice about the prison* society. She's also <u>selling</u> all my letters AND manuscripts or collaborating* with some other writer. That's why she's pumping me for information about the crime. She knows NOTHING about it other than what was in the papers. I've told her almost nothing except that I did not intentionally* kill those two women. The deaths were accidental. Just send back her letter that I'm enclosing. DON'T photocopy it.

The problem with this guy she's collaborating with is that she's probably given or sold him my manuscripts, and SHAFTED herself and Jimmy. I've no doubt she sold it CHEAP! And the guy she sold it to is not going to publish it. Just use it for fodder for his book. That's a shame, since my book would have really shed some light and insight into the lives of the handicapped. People could have better understood them and seen them as real human beings. People who have pretty much the same goals, feelings, etc. as so called normal people, just in the slower lane that's all. Oh well, what can I do? I've pleaded with her not to do this since she'd just louse up herself AND Jimmy, not to mention all those others. If the book succeeds she could sign the name Mrs. Heidnik with pride, not shame, but maybe $50 means more. Maybe I should have gone with you on it, just to get it published, but of course I'd have given her all the money. Too late now! I've also just passed the 280 page mark. That's a lot of writing* but I've only finished 4½ chapters with 2½ to go. The current chapter "Tony & Gail" is the hardest and longest. The next one on "Walter and Mary" is pure poignancy. No comedy. I tried to get these two married legally and the social workers at Elwyn stopped me. They tried to split this terrific couple up, and although they prevented the marriage, even they couldn't separate them. I did make a few mistakes though, and for that I'm sorry. One of the "whoppers" Elwyn would tell them is I wanted to bed Mary – LIES!! I never wanted to do that. Mary wasn't my type and I couldn't do something like that to Walter. I like the guy too much, and these two were in love for REAL!! True love. Really. Even the City of Phila. wouldn't let them marry. There was a kangaroo court hearing even to prevent them. How's that for the City of Brotherly Love?

  Also one of the most positive cases of proof that I was framed and that they committed perjury was their claim that Alberta was a virgin. SHE WAS NOT, and hasn't been since she was 13. All four sisters got diddled by the same guy. This guy Antoine I wrote you about. I can't understand their attraction either. The guy is UGLY! But as they say love is blind. The family even promised Anjeanette in 78 that if she'd leave me, they'd let this guy diddle her again. But Anjeanette loved me too much for that. She even told me all about their offer. Here's an example of true love for you. Anjeanette could not write her own name. But one day I came home and she had something to show me. She wrote MY name. She taught herself and she did it to show me how much she loved me. How's that for love? I *loved her too, but her love for me was far greater. To get our baby back I figured we should start teaching her how to write, especially her own name. No luck at first. She could copy it page after page and did so. But she could only copy it. So I put some pressure on her and "walked out." When she stopped screaming and hollering and listened, I told her that I would come back the next day and if she could write her name I'd stay. If she didn't I'd go for another day, etc till she could write her name. Guess what? She could write it the next day. I even had a rent receipt she signed as Mrs. Annjeanette Heidnik (I misspelled her name with two n's and taught her the same mistake). Was I right to pressure her into writing* her name. I think so. Was that abuse? Not hardly. And I NEVER HIT HER!! It really wasn't necessary since the woman loved me so much she'd do anything I asked, including giving me all the children I wanted. Is that LOVE? Your DAMN right it is . And I LOVED her too. But I just couldn't match her intensity. I still love her and miss her terribly. I'd take her back in a second if she'd offer to come back. She'd never be collaborating or in collusion with someone else. Especially if it would harm me.*

Once again we observe Heidnik's psychological pattern of reversing emotional states – from control/strength to loss-of-control/weakness. In this letter, he begins in a state of extreme weakness and helplessness: His wife Betty has betrayed him, his precious novel has been stolen away, and there is nothing he can do about it. He is desperately alone. He cannot bear this much despair and loss of control. So he reverses his weakness into strength – by reversing Betty's bitter betrayal into a story of idyllic love. He tells the story of Walter and Mary, two people with intellectual disabilities who wanted to get legally married. Their bond is "pure poignancy" and their love is "for REAL!! True love. Really." Although the authorities may stop their marriage, they cannot stop their love. In a fascinating projection, he transforms the tragic love of "Walter and Mary" into his own personal love story of "Gary and Anjeanette." They, too, are handicapped and oppressed by the powers of the world. They, too, are deeply in love and want to be "legally" bound and have children together. Heidnik's intense identification with this love story reveals that he views himself as weak and inadequate – disabled like Walter and Mary.

Heidnik has spent his life trying to escape the childhood taunts of "retard" and "football head" through the acquisition of power and control. He has tried to convince the world – and himself – that he is not retarded (through excessive studying), not incompetent (through the acquisition of wealth), and not weak (by becoming Bishop of his own church). Nonetheless, he knows he is an imposter. He is nothing but a convicted murderer, utterly unloved and unlovable, helpless and weak, alone in solitary confinement on Death Row. The feeling of helplessness and weakness is intolerable. So he reverses his self-loathing into a new idyllic love – for Anjeanette. Unlike Betty, he declares that Anjeanette would "never be collaborating or in collusion with someone else. Especially if it would harm me." He avows that Anjeanette "loved me so much she'd do anything I asked, including giving me all the children I wanted. Is that LOVE? Your DAMN right it is. And I LOVED her too... I still love her and miss her terribly."

By conjuring up this new fantasy of true love with Anjeanette (rather than Betty), Heidnik succeeds in reversing his weakness into strength and confidence. He is now ready to fight the world again. He launches into an extended essay about how he was framed in 1978 for the kidnapping and rape of – the sister of Anjeanette. His juxtaposition of themes is sickly ironic. If Anjeanette is the true great love of his life, then why is he raping her sister?

On May 7, 1978, two months after child protective services seized custody of their newborn baby, Heidnik and Anjeanette drove four hours to the Selinsgrove Center and took her sister Alberta for a supposed weekend visit with family. Expecting no one to notice that she did not return, he imprisoned Alberta Norton in his basement and raped her repeatedly as part of his plan to have a secret child that the authorities could not take away.

But Heidnik underestimated the authorities at Selinsgrove, who repeatedly telephoned his house to find her and, gaining no response, notified the police. On May 17, the staff social worker, Mrs. Snauffer, and the staff psychologist, Dr. Bingham, traveled to Heidnik's house in west Philadelphia, accompanied by the Philadelphia police and armed with a search warrant. Initially they could hear or see nothing inside. The psychologist opened the door and called Alberta's name. They heard a faint, muffled reply from somewhere inside and traced her cries to the basement. There they found Alberta in an unlit storage closet, a former coal bin. Heidnik was arrested. Although he later beat the charges of kidnapping and rape, he was found guilty of wrongful imprisonment and sentenced to five years at Graterford State Prison. As we now know, this crime at 4706 Cedar Avenue would be prophetic, replayed with unimaginable horror ten years later at 3520 Marshall Street.

As we return to Heidnik's letter, he launches into a 15 page defense of his actions in 1978. He begins by refuting the claim that Alberta had been a virgin prior to the kidnapping.

(Sorry I got sidetracked). Anyways, they got this Dr. Wilson to swear in court that she had examined Alberta about seven months before she left (willing of course) and she was still a virgin then. Guess what else? That was Alberta's first OB/GYN exam in that hospital in 15 years. Can you believe it? Only one exam in 15 years and only 7 months prior? BULLSHIT!! The baloney was that since she was in the hospital (an open ward, with total access to the whole grounds, and if my memory is correct, it's CO-ED!) there was never

an opportunity for her to copulate. He, he, he. Who are they kidding? Anjeanette used to do it all the time in the bathroom on the toilet. She taught me! She'd only done it that way for so long she didn't know how to do it on a bed the regular way. Sad isn't it. I had to take her to see some dirty movies and do a lot of coaxing before she's make love in bed the regular way. The only thing that puzzles me is that Alberta didn't get pregnant. Anjeanette didn't get pregnant cause she had a coil in. I'll bet you dollars to doughnuts Alberta did too. Either that or birth control pills or she's been "fixed." You don't do that with a virgin do you? So they're LYING!!

If an expert like you could get a hold of these records, I'll bet you'd find some proof. Just imagine if you can show good solid documentary proof that I was FRAMED! That would give you a best seller and probably a movie too. You've got an inside track here, and after ten years everybody's guard is down. If you can break Dr Wilson their whole house of cards will fall. Watch the track lead right back to Smith and Devlin (and maybe Robert Kirkpatrick III. They'd probably need him for any "raids" on the church.)

In court in 88 they showed these videotapes of the putative "grave" I was digging at 4706 Cedar Ave. Grave, huh? Isn't freedom of the press and sensationalism grand. I was digging to find the sewer pipe. I assumed it ran underground approximately where I was digging. I didn't find it. Anyways I planned to convert the basement into a 4th apartment and move into it myself. Thereby squeezing out the rent of another apartment out of the same building. Just goes to show once a hole is called a grave, it'll always be a grave. No sense wasting a good story.

Heidnik is far from done with his story of Alberta and the coal bin episode. He will return to the topic in greater detail in pages 17-28 of this letter. But, for the moment, he is content with refuting the allegation that he had been digging a "grave" in his basement at 4706 Cedar Ave. In the next segment of his letter, Heidnik connects his story of conspiracy in 1978 to an earlier episode in 1976 when he was arrested for shooting his tenant in the face.

In 76 when I was arrested for aggravated assault, I'm going to tell you the real truth, not the garbage they're mooring* their lies with. The whole thing never made it past arraignment. The judge threw it out right then.

In 1967 I bought 4706 Cedar Ave for something like $13,500. It's a nice three apartment building. I moved in on the third floor (with Dorothy) and rented out the first and second floors. On the second floor in 76 lived a fellow by the name of Harper and his live in girlfriend. She started making a couple of passes at me (not real heavy though) and I turned her down. Not out of moral convictions or anything but for money. If you start diddling with your tenants you're not going to get your rent money. She had a nice face and body too but she was the wrong color. She was white and you may have noticed I don't care much for white women. So I scorned her. Ever heard of that saying "Hell hath no fury like a woman scorned." Believe it. I once scorned Betty and that was when she left the second time mad as hell! Never forgave me either. (By the way Mr. Harper is black & his girlfriend white. You'd think we'd have gotten along on that basis).

Anyways these two decided to save some money by going on a rent strike. They claimed that their apartment needed some fixing. It did! A little, not much. But they never came to me and said something. They just plain stopped paying rent. They didn't even follow the usual course of calling in L&I and having the complaints made official. They just figured I was a turkey (I am) and they were going to live there for YEARS! Rent free. Of course I'm legally obligated to pay all my bills like mortgage, heat, gas, electric water, insurance, taxes, etc. Basically what they're doing to me is legalized theft since, in fact or reality, tenants can do this in Phila and get away with it. Also Mr. Harper is an ex-Phila policeman and knew all the right people and all the dirty tricks. Well, the tenants on the first floor got wind of this so called "rent strike" and wanted to save some money too. So they also joined in the strike and stopped paying their rent. And what was their complaint? None! Their apartment was fine. They claimed they were in sympathy with Mr. Harper.

The way the scam works is that as soon as you fix something, other things mysteriously go wrong like holes in the walls or broken windows. It is of course a never-ending cycle and the landlord never gets paid or the tenants evicted. The scam is so good, so successful, and used so frequently it's practically institutionalized. But don't take my word, just look at all the abandoned buildings in the city.

So I decided to shut off their gas, electric, water, and heat and locked the cellar door, and told them to leave. What I was soon to find out was that Mr. Harper, an ex-policeman, IS above the law. Mr. Harper and the guy on the first floor, break into my cellar and turn everything back on. But for funsies they shut off my gas and electric. So I was pretty mad when I found my cellar broken into. In these days I stupidly believed that the law was the law and had to be obeyed by everyone. (I told you I was a turkey). So this time when I shut off everything, I also locked the steel gate that closed off the cellar. Then I sat next to my window and listened. When I heard them breaking in, I called the cops. They came. Mr. Harper's girlfriend met them at the front of the house and told them something and they left. Mr. Harper and his buddy were still in the cellar. If the cops had bothered to check, they'd have found them. But of course they wouldn't have arrested them when Harper identified himself as an ex-cop.

Well I decided to try a third time, but this time I decided to make a citizen's arrest. So I shut off everything, locked the steel gate, and waited. In a couple of hours they showed up and broke in. I showed myself and pulled out a pistol (simple action, six cylinder, reproduction antique) and announced "You're under arrest." An interesting thing about human nature (and I'm not a racist) is if you pull a gun on a white man, they'll cooperate, give you everything you want, or run. You pull a gun on a black man and they'll want to fight. That's exactly what happened. The white guy ran, and the black Mr. Harper advanced on me wanting to fight. I'm not a small man, but Mr. Harper is not only bigger but trained to fight with his hands. When he advanced on me (I believe) he had something in his right hand. Also I had the vision of him taking away my gun and shooting me with it. So I had a choice since there was no place to run, shoot him or scare him. I chose the latter*. I jerked the gun to the right side and up and fired, then I leveled it on him and told him if he came any closer I wouldn't miss the next time. (They claimed, but not in court, that I actually tried to shoot him but missed. At three feet they expect you to believe I missed because I'm such a poor shot.

 The gun did jam on me, but he didn't know that or he'd have tried attacking me again, so I was able to bluff him. If I had wanted to shoot him, I had a loaded rifle right around the corner to do it with. The police confiscated it too so it's in the record. I took him up and outside to the front of the house where by now the place was crawling with police. When I got out in front I handed the pistol to the nearest policeman barrel first. At that point Mr. Harper sucker punched me and knocked me flat. Two police officers had to jump on him and subdue him. Then they took us to the police station at 55 & Pine. The officer driving me there informed me on the Q.T. that he didn't care whether Harper was an ex-policeman, that he'd testify for me that Harper had punched me in front of him. His name was officer London.

 When we got to the station I got put in a cell, and for him it was hey old Buddy, haven't seen you for a while, and they had a big friendly get together and of course I'm the one who got arrested. Not him! Devlin was one of the arresting officers by the way although I don't remember him.

 That's how the "BLUE CODE" really works. Not at all like in the movies. You cross one cop, even if he's as wrong as can be, and his buddies will get you, but good. Even if it takes YEARS!

 When the case got called to <u>arraignment</u>, Harper didn't even show up. But the first floor tenant did. My lawyer was Donald Levine and I'd promised him a $100 bonus if he won. When the first floor tenant testified he <u>claimed</u> that he broke in through the cellar window not the door. Really!! The turkey apparently thought it's legal to break into a house through a window but illegal to break* open doors. That was good enough for the judge so he threw it out right there. Of course it wasn't good enough for Devlin and he vowed revenge (and got it). I paid Levine his bonus and left very *frightened but enlightened on how our police system REALLY works. So I decided to sell my house and move out of that district. I didn't move far enough. I should have left the city. Guess who the judge was? Are you ready for this: Judge Charles Mirarchi Jr. Yep same judge. Small world isn't it. But I don't think it had any bearing on the 78 trial. I doubt if he remembers me.*

Thanks for the Shakespeare and the very encouraging letter. You answered the big question I've been pushing for. Yes I'm convinced they wanted me to commit suicide or make a serious attempt. That's one reason for the solitary confinement, and the psychological games by Dr. Bora. Devlin though took a more direct approach. On that Friday after the trial he overheard me make an appointment to see my lawyer. When I came out he was waiting for me. He came up behind me, punched me on the right shoulder and then walked a couple of steps in front of me hoping I'd attack him. He had his hand on his gun under his coat, so he'd be able to blow me away. I didn't see it, but I'll bet you he had my pocket knife too, so he could put it in my hand and claim I tried to use it on him. His plan didn't work though since I'm not the hothead he visualized. I just turned around and walked away. After that he started to apply pressure to Mirarchi Jr.

The reliability of Heidnik's narratives is always subject to skepticism, but I think there is more truth than fiction in this particular account. As a landlord, he admits that the rental apartment needed some repairs, but were the conditions so egregious that it would drive both tenants to go on a rent strike? Or, as Heidnik claims, were they dead-beat tenants looking for a free ride? Ultimately the court sided with Heidnik. The case was thrown out because (1) the ex-cop tenant failed to appear to testify, and (2) the other tenant admitted breaking into Heidnik's private property. Heidnik was even successful in getting the police to return his rifle and antique pistol.

At the same time, there are parts of Heidnik's story that are quite dubious. For example, he alleges that the ex-cop's girlfriend tried to seduce him. He claims to have rejected her sexual advances because he is not attracted to white women, only black women. He also conjures up a pretty far-fetched plot that links this event to the Alberta incident two years later. The connection, in Heidnik's mind, is that one of the arresting officers happened to have been Detective Devlin. Although he did not know Devlin at the time, Devlin would become the leading suspect in Heidnik's growing obsession about a conspiracy to steal his church fortune. Claiming the "blue code" of loyalty between cops, Gary even adds a story here about how Devlin once instigated a ploy to provoke Heidnik into attacking him – ostensibly so that Devlin would have an excuse to shoot him. Heidnik also makes a second connection. The presiding judge of the 1976 case turns out to be none other than Charles P. Mirarchi Jr., the same judge who will send him to prison in 1978. Heidnik links the two men into an imagined conspiracy in which Devlin "started to apply pressure to Mirarchi." [Subsequently, on pages 17-18 of this letter, Heidnik will return to this story and extend the conspiracy to include plots between Devlin, his stock broker, Kirkpatrick, and his upstairs neighbor, Audrey.]

In the next segment of his letter, Heidnik returns to his favorite subject: suicide. In his colorful way, he remarks that, "Every time I get into a stressful situation…, I respond by trying to commit suicide. It's almost like a knee jerk reaction. Put pressure and tension on one side and a suicide attempt will come out the other." As we have seen, Heidnik turned the weakness of his suicidal tendencies into a source of pride and competence. He became a self-avowed expert on suicide. He studied the level of lethality of various methods and collateral effects. Here he speculates that he may have permanent memory damage from his suicide attempts. This, in turn, triggers an extensive discussion of his lifelong cognitive deficiencies and social incompetence.

Again about the suicide. You amazed me there. I thought maybe only a medical doctor could see it. But you did spot it. You've confirmed, MORE than confirmed my faith in you. You're truly one of the "cerebrally enlightened. Ha, ha ☺*. Also your opinions on the incompetence shows you've really been doing your homework. I can't tell you how happy that makes me. Finally after all these years someone's listening to me.*

My suicide attempts are very, very predictable. Every time I get into a stressful situation or a lot of pressure is applied, I respond by trying to commit suicide. It's almost like a knee jerk reaction. Put pressure and tension on one side and a suicide attempt will come out the other. Also it seems to affect my memory at times. This is even harder for me to understand since I can't always remember what I've forgotten. Like when they first locked me up in Norristown is kind of a big blank. Zero, nothing! That's one memory lapse I'm aware of. Also I have trouble remembering that hospitalization in Perryville in 71?? The first couple of months that is. The last part I remember all right. Another thing I've got a sneaking* suspicion I had two hospitalizations at Perryville, but for the life of me I only remember once.

I've always had problems with my memory, but it's important to remember I'm really not VERY BRIGHT!! It takes a lot of effort on my part to achieve the educational levels I have made. But I do it with a little extra effort and an analytical mind. When something puzzles me or if I have a problem I will spend hours on it trying to solve it in an analytical fashion. Like I can play a tremendous game of chess but it takes me so long, it drives the other players crazy. I'll study each and every move until I've analyzed most possibilities and then make my move. I'm good in vocabulary though which boosts my I.Q. score, but vocabulary is largely memorizing. With my love of reading they reinforce each other. But I'm SLOW! Since I am so slow (mentally) I can only devote so much time to the most important matters. In schools, for instance, I had no social life. No parties, friends, girls, zip!! I used that time to study and get good grades, and please my father. As I've mentioned *previously I've managed to overcome the perception of being retarded as a child. I flunked second grade once and was about to flunk again, when Dad WORKED with me and made me learn. Even better he started a fire in me whereby I LIKED to study and READ books. That became a problem since it warped my sense of reality. I couldn't see things as they really were, I only saw them vicariously through the eyes of people like Edgar Rice Burroughs. I used to think when I was about 14 or 15 that I could live in the woods, hunt with a knife (and air rifle*) and swing through the trees. REALLY!! I actually thought I could swing through the trees like Tarzan and run away from home to do so.*

The biggest way books and lack of social life warped my thinking is in regards to interpersonal relationships. I couldn't see or relate with people as they REALLY are. I always perceived* them vicariously through the eyes of fiction writers. People aren't like the ones in the fictional stories, especially in the books available in the 50's. When I took that course on child sociology in the 60's at the U. of Pa it was a big help in getting to understand why I was so screwed up. What it didn't explain was why people always HATE me so much. I have no friends, except the fellow disabled at 40th St. They were the only people who would socialize with me. I like people. I also want to be liked! I don't like being lonely, but I can't seem to master interpersonal relationships. And the harder I try the worse it gets! People use (this desire of mine to be liked) to their advantage and abuse me. The hardest thing I've had to adjust to is giving up on people. If I stay to myself and mind my own affairs like in solitaire and in books I manage to stay out of conflicts. But if I try to socialize I wind up with problems. If it wasn't for Tony I wouldn't have had anyone at my wedding. Persecution is my middle name. People not only dislike me they like to persecute me. Just look at the records. It's bad enough not being liked but why do they have to persecute me when I've done nothing to them?

Heidnik clearly sees himself as a very "slow" learner and social misfit who invites ridicule and hatred. His narrative also provides insights into the youthful origins of his overactive fantasy life, which would ultimately develop into the deviant sexual fantasies and predations of his adult years.

Let's begin with the question of Heidnik's intelligence and cognitive limitations. He describes himself as struggling in school as early as second grade and being "perceived as retarded as a child." His response was to over-compensate through grueling repetition and rehearsal of information. He applied this rigor to memorizing vocabulary and reading books and, as we will see shortly, to his fantasy life.

Heidnik repeatedly asserts that "I'm really not VERY BRIGHT!!" and "I'm SLOW." But is this accurate? Consider this excerpt from a March 1987 test report by the court-appointed psychologist: "Heidnik currently tests within very superior limits of the range of intelligence. He assimilates novel material quickly and has accumulated an above average level of academic information. This man is extremely alert to environmental details and he has above average comprehension and judgment."

In letter #6, Heidnik was crowing about his "penultimate" IQ score of 145 and how he enjoyed being regarded as a genius. Here he emphasizes that he is mentally slow. Which is true? My opinion is that Heidnik was both highly intelligent and learning disabled. In fact, it is not uncommon to find mentally gifted children who also suffer from Attention Deficit Disorder and other learning disabilities. Conversely, learning deficits can sometimes conceal a gifted child's high intelligence. Heidnik learned to use his high intelligence to compensate for his particular learning deficits.

Personally, Heidnik credited his father with teaching him how to learn: "Dad WORKED with me and made me learn. Even better he started a fire in me whereby I LIKED to study and READ books." Heidnik later adds that he studied hard to "get good grades and please my father." Clearly, it was important for Heidnik to please his father because if he failed he would face his wrath.

Although Heidnik's learning strategy was effective, it also had the negative effect of cutting him off from ordinary social interactions. "The biggest way books and lack of social life warped my thinking is in regards to interpersonal relationships. I couldn't see or relate with people as they REALLY are. I always perceived them vicariously through the eyes of fiction writers… like Edgar Rice Burroughs… I actually thought I could swing through the trees like Tarzan and run away from home to do so."

Teased as "football head," Gary avoided peers and preferred time alone. Reading helped to fill the void of loneliness, but it also isolated him and became the generator for an exaggerated fantasy life. His extreme isolation eliminated opportunities to interact with people and learn the cues and signals of everyday communication and social boundaries. People became more and more unfathomable and scary to Heidnik. In turn, people reacted negatively to Heidnik's social awkwardness, even bizarreness, and either avoided or teased him. He interpreted their distancing behavior as "hating" him. It is not surprising that he could only find social ease and acceptance from people with intellectual disabilities.

In his own words, "people always HATE me so much. I have no friends, except the fellow disabled… They were the only people who would socialize with me. I like people. I also want to be liked! I don't like being lonely, but I can't seem to master interpersonal relationships… But if I try to socialize I wind up with problems… Persecution is my middle name… It's bad enough not being liked but why do they persecute me when I've done nothing to them?"

Unable and afraid to relate to people as they are in the external world, young Heidnik retreated into the safety of his internal fantasy world, where he could control everything. He attempted to substitute control for his need for human intimacy. In the safety of his fantasy life, he was always accepted, always liked, always in control. But the more that he withdrew into books and fantasies, the harder and scarier it became for him to come out and relate to people. As his isolation increased, his social judgment and perceptions became more and more narcissistic, distorted, and paranoid. He blamed the world for rejecting and persecuting him. His description of how he played chess was an analogy for how he lived his life – in obsessive rumination, analyzing and rehearsing each move until he is sure that it will work.

When Heidnik did endeavor to socialize, however, he encountered conflict and rejection. Real people did not respond as he wanted or imagined in his internal fantasies. Frustrated, he would retreat again to his fantasy world where he was safe from rejection and in full control. Ultimately, if people would not do as he wanted, Heidnik would force them to. In 1967, he found a group of people at the Elwyn Institute that he could easily control and who would yield whatever he wanted – sex, companionship, love, admiration, respect, dominance. He could avoid the frustrations of dealing with non-disabled adults. In this subculture of intellectual disabilities, Heidnik could see himself as smart, competent, lovable, sexy, and noble. He saw himself as a benevolent king, bestowing kind deeds on the poor and disabled, treating them to fast food dinners, bowling, movies, and excursions. He felt that he was making their lives better, which helped to justify his sexual abuse and general exploitation. For example, in the next segment of his letter, Heidnik saw himself as rescuing Anjeanette from her neglectful family and protecting her from their greed.

In the next segment of Heidnik's very long letter, he returns again to his imagined grand conspiracy to steal his church fortune. At this point in the correspondence, his obsession with the church money conspiracy is becoming increasingly strident and delusional. His stories about Detective Devlin, in particular, become more and more outlandish, expansive, and unbelievable. He fills pages 17 to 21 with an onerous description of how he imagines that

Devlin conspired with his stockbroker Kirkpatrick to steal the church accounts. He claims that Devlin followed him in his car and spied on his brother Terry to gain information. The very busy detective is also imagined to have teamed up with Mrs. Smith, the Selinsgrove social worker, to frame him for having sex with Alberta Norton. Then, failing in that, Devlin is supposed to have used drugs to get Heidnik's upstairs neighbor, Audrey, to sneak into his apartment to find evidence. He depicts Audrey as a small scale drug pusher who stole his mother's wedding ring and, for reasons unfathomable even to himself, stole the needle from his phonograph. Audrey is also alleged to have assisted in the attempted "welfare kidnappings" of Anjeanette and Dorothy from his apartment. Heidnik cites an illicit business in Philadelphia in which boarding home directors forcibly grab disabled citizens and "trade and sell" them as a source of income.

When it comes to the church money conspiracy, it is easy to discount his speculations as paranoid delusions. But there is a revealing side story pressed inside his narrative: the important role of Dorothy Knox.

I can't prove it but I'm pretty sure Audrey helped in the attempted kidnappings of Anjeanette. I'm also pretty sure she helped kidnap Dorothy. That wasn't easy for them but they did it. Dorothy actually got kidnapped twice successfully (by boarding home operators). The first time by a Mrs. Pollard on Glenwood Ave, and the second by a Mrs. Yardley on Hadfield Street in West Phila. Those people snatched Dorothy for the welfare money. She wasn't on S.S.I. at the time. The police weren't too terribly interested either once they found she had mental problems. I even placed an ad in the Phila. Tribune (the black paper) offering $100 reward for her return. I got her back the first time when she was grabbed by Pollard, but not the second time.

So with all these KIDNAPPINGS going on and the police doing NOTHING and these people getting away with it, naturally I took precautions to keep them from grabbing Anjeanette AND Alberta. Anjeanette would stay in the apartment at night and keep BOTH doors locked, not opening them to anyone, especially Audrey. Anjeanette didn't always do this though and so I had problems. The second time they grabbed Dorothy Mrs. Yardley came over at night while I was at work, and they grabbed Dorothy and FORCED her to go with them. She resisted them and hollered and screamed but they pushed and dragged her out anyways. (Nice people huh, these boarding home operators. They even "trade" or "sell" clients between each other. You may have heard that in the papers)

So they got Dorothy the second time. She was especially attractive to them since they felt she could do lots of work for them like clean house, cook, wash dishes etc. BOY! Did they get fooled there. Dorothy might have done some work for a month or two but that would be all. After a while they'd beg her not to work, if they had any dishes left or hadn't died of food poisoning or she'd burned their houses down with cigarettes or something. The only person Dorothy would listen to was me, because quite simply she loved me. BOY did she LOVE me. If I just touched her or kissed her she'd melt and get all goo goo. She'd help me cook and clean the house and wash my clothes and iron my uniform cause she WANTED to. YES!

The problem with Dorothy was she couldn't have kids and as you know I wanted KIDS, lots of them. Anjeanette could give me kids. Dorothy wanted to more than anything but she couldn't. After ten years with Dorothy I realized I'd never have kids by her and so started looking elsewhere. But I couldn't give up on Dorothy either. This woman LOVED me and even if she did have problems that meant a lot to me. Other people get LOVED very easily. They're popular and get along with others. I DO NOT. So when somebody loves me, it means a HELL of a lot more to me since it happens so seldom. So Dorothy meant a LOT to me, and I couldn't just cast her aside and abandon her because I wanted kids so bad, but with Anjeanette that wasn't necessary* since Anjeanette did not protest against Dorothy's presence and the two of them got along.

One problem with this arrangement* was, Anjeanette and I

would never get our baby Maxine back if Dorothy was with us, so I tried to get Dorothy back, but not quite hard enough. I was torn between two forces. Dorothy on the one hand and our baby on the other. I guess subconsciously I chose the baby. But with all the kidnapping going on, I was afraid they'd snatch Alberta too. So every night I'd take Alberta to Janice's house while I was at work and bring her home in the AM when I got off from work. Also I LIED to the people at Selinsgrove and elsewhere about her living with us. They had already talked to her many times on the phone, and would not accept that she didn't want to return. Also with Anjeanette's family mad at me and seeking REVENGE!!! They would obviously getting a lot of B.S. Also I was learning that people like Anjeanette's family, Audrey, boarding home operators and those from Selinsgrove were a vile lot and would break laws and lie and kidnap with impunity and the police would not help. So best to lie and hide.

Compared to the other women in his life, Heidnik only mentions Dorothy three times in the correspondence. First, in letter #5, she is unnamed as nothing more than "companionship with an old mentally ill black woman." Second, in letter #9, he identifies her as one of the five Board Members who could contest the money in the church accounts. That description is short and crude: "This is the woman who lived with me for 10 years. She is about 10 years older than me and spent a lot of years at Byberry before I knew her. Her mind had continued to degenerate so badly that she had trouble going around the corner without getting lost and she'd sign any document you wanted for a pack of cigarettes."

Until now, it has not been evident that Heidnik had been living with two women with intellectual disabilities at the same time during his period with Anjeanette. But Dorothy is a very important piece of Heidnik's psychological puzzle.

From about 1967 to 1978, they lived together as husband and wife, which is far longer than any of his other relationships. As a partner, she was extremely challenged, diagnosed with both severe mental retardation and severe psychiatric illness. She had been institutionalized for many years in hospitals like Byberry. Yet Dorothy was a loving wife, who provided acceptance and emotional nurturance, while he enjoyed total dominance. In his own words, "This woman LOVED me and even if she did have problems that meant a lot to me." He makes humorous mention of Dorothy's earnest, but inept efforts to cook, clean, wash dishes, and do laundry, all of which shows her low level of functioning and struggle to manage the basic activities of daily living. Their arrangement seemed to provide stability and satisfaction because Heidnik did not get into any major problems with the law during their many years together (with the exception of his landlord episode in 1976). But, for Heidnik, there was one huge shortcoming: Dorothy "couldn't have kids and... I wanted KIDS, lots of them... After ten years with Dorothy I realized I'd never have kids by her and so started looking elsewhere."

So Heidnik sought and found Anjeanette – a younger, higher functioning and fertile woman with intellectual disabilities – and brought her into his home as his new girlfriend. To his credit, he felt a loyalty and affection for Dorothy and could not end their relationship – at least for a time. "Dorothy meant a LOT to me, and I couldn't just cast her aside and abandon her because I wanted kids so bad, but with Anjeanette that wasn't necessary since... the two of them got along." With this bold move, Heidnik raised his fantasy of having children to the next level of obsession. He also set the precedent of having multiple sex partners in the same house. His success with managing two women at the same time emboldened Heidnik to try it again – first, by kidnapping Anjeanette's sister Alberta in 1978; later, by trying to get Betty to agree to group sex in 1986; and finally, by trying to create a harem of ten women in 1987.

Ultimately, Heidnik did get rid of Dorothy – sometime after the state took custody of his baby in March 1978 and before the trip to Selinsgrove in May 1978 to kidnap Alberta. He presents it as a tough choice between Dorothy and his newborn daughter. His justification was that the child welfare authorities would not return the baby if they found a second intellectually disabled woman living in their household. It is unknown how Heidnik got rid of Dorothy, but he may have "sold" her to one of the same boarding home operators that he accuses of "kidnapping" disabled clients.

The question remains as to why Heidnik barely mentions Dorothy. One possibility is that he felt genuine lasting guilt over abandoning a woman who was so loyal and loving to him for so long. For Heidnik, love is a rare thing that he values greatly: "Other people get LOVED very easily... I DO NOT. So when somebody loves me, it means a HELL of a lot more to me since it happens so seldom." Another possibility is that Heidnik is embarrassed by Dorothy. Given her older age and profound level of impairment (she can't go "around the corner without getting lost"), he may have feared that she would make him look bad.

In the next segment of Heidnik's letter he delights in telling the never-before-told story of why the authorities found Alberta in the coal bin in his cellar. He starts by drawing the following diagram:

Here are the details on the coal bin issue, which really nobody ever asked me about. You're the first who has ever been interested to even wonder about it. That morning I came home from work with Alberta. By the way a day or two earlier at Family Court, these nice people from Selinsgrove, while my car was parked on Vine Street glued my car doors shut with super glue. They squirted super glue into the door lock, so I couldn't get my key into the lock. Fortunately*, they ran out of glue (or forgot) the trunk. So I got a screwdriver out and was able to force an opening into the lock on the passenger side, so we could get in and move the car. It was especially urgent to get in since rush hour was approaching and the city would have towed my car for blocking Vine St. But that just goes to show how honest and law abiding these people from Selinsgrove are.

So in the morning they "persuaded" not asked Alberta to return. I had gone to bed. Alberta and Anjeanette were in the living room watching TV. I think that Smith then started pounding on the door (the one I've marked). We ignored her. Then the phone rang and she told me she wanted to search my apartment since she "knew" I had Alberta there. I agreed to let her in. I then took Alberta out of the apartment immediately and hid her in the coal bin. The door to the bin was unlocked. Nobody disputes that. Now look at the drawing I've enclosed, where it says heavy fire door.

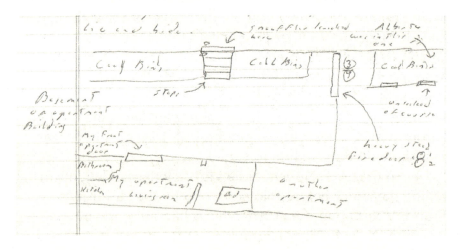

Well for some reason I thought that would lock and once closed and locked could only be opened from one side. (The one Alberta was on.) I told her to stay hidden there till I called and told her it was all right to come out and for her to then open that heavy door from her side, since I didn't realize it could be opened from my side. (Foolish me.) She said she understood and would stay hidden till I called. We both didn't really think that Smith and her people could get through the fire door, but I hid her anyways.

At the time, I was in a big hurry to open the door for Smith. She claimed in court she called me from a house across the street. A

LIE. She called me from Audrey's apartment. She had to. Since when Alberta and I ran past her, from my apartment to the coal bin, she SAW us. I knew she saw us because she told us, that very day. To have seen us from under the door she'd have had to have made the call from Audrey's apartment not the college student's across the street. She didn't have time to travel that far and back. Anyways when I opened the door and let her in I got two surprises. The first was that she had a policeman with her and second she went in the direction I had hidden Alberta. Then I got a third shock. An even bigger one then the first two. The fire door opened right up. Then she went into the other hallway and called Alberta's name a couple of times. Alberta messed up, probably was confused, and answered Smith. I've already explained in the other letter how Smith persuaded Alberta to go back with them, and I was so "slow on my feet" it never even occurred to me to tell Alberta she didn't have to go back. She could stay with us.

  Also about the putative rape of Alberta, if I'm not mistaken, the devious Smith never told the lie that ALBERTA <u>SAID</u> I raped her. That kind of surprises me why a gifted liar like Smith wouldn't at least CLAIM Alberta said this since she was telling so many others and suborning so many people. She certainly managed to suborn Dr. Liebold since all of sudden we've got this spurious test he "claims" to have performed for gonorrhea of the mouth. That was one lie too many for Smith since I tested negative for gonorrhea, I couldn't have had contact with her. They'd have forged my test results too I'm sure, but Devlin (I think) really believed I had gonorrhea since I resisted taking the test. So he didn't see any need at the time to "phony up" the results. It was of course that LIE that saved me, instead of drowning me but it was a LIE! Please check.

  Well Doc, that's about it for now. I really don't know what else I can tell you just yet. I hope all this has been helpful*. I've written so many letters to you and Betty and my book my head is killing me. (I've got arthritis you know). But let me give you a last quote from the Bible. John 3:20. "For every one that doeth evil holdeth the light, neither cometh to the light, lest his deeds should be reproved."

So lets bring these malefactors out of the darkness and into the light. Let's expose them for the evils they've done. FIAT LUX!?!

Also my daughter Maxine (who is living at xxx Street Phila with a foster mother) is under several delusions. (1) She thinks her mother abandoned her and doesn't love her. (2) Doesn't know how badly I've been framed and that she was taken from us for only racial bigotry and revenge! When you've cleared my name, please go to Maxine and tell her how badly I was framed, that she was taken forcibly from us by the courts, and that I AND Anjeanette LOVE her very much. I've asked Betty to help in this matter but Betty seems to "forget" she promised to contact Maxine. I really don't know what else I can tell you for now so THANKS FOR EVERYTHING!!

EGREGIOUSLY GRIEVED,
Gary M. Heidnik, Anjeanette,
Maxine, Society, Justice and ???

P.S. Maxine does not know* anything about Anjeanette, including her mental state. Whenever I mention Anjeanette to her, Maxine would stop me, and tell me she didn't want to hear it. But she's older now. Maybe she's ready to listen.

On May 17, 1978, Alberta Norton returned to Selinsgrove Center with gonorrhea of the throat and vagina. Heidnik was arrested for kidnapping and rape. Upon examination, he did not have gonorrhea. This is the basis for his claim of innocence, which he first presented in Letter #7, pages 14-16. Here he goes into "the details on the coal bin issue," which he says I am "the first who has ever been interested to even wonder about it." Throughout his narrative, Heidnik presents himself as completely altruistic. He did not abduct Alberta from Selinsgrove. He was rescuing the sister of the woman he loved from a horrible institution and guarding her right to choose where and with whom she lived. He repeatedly claims that family members wanted nothing to do with either Anjeanette or Alberta when they were institutionalized. He also presents himself as the victim of the authorities, who first seized his child "for only racial bigotry and revenge!" and then framed him for rape and kidnapping because they wanted to steal his fortune.

Of course, Heidnik never considers that the authorities traveled across the state and went to such effort to retrieve Alberta because they were concerned for her welfare. Instead he fixates on whether they lied about calling his apartment from the neighbors across the street or the apartment above. In his paranoia, he conjures a far-fetched plot in which (1) a social worker drives four hours to Philadelphia in order to (2) find his place of employment in a huge city, and then (3) figures out what kind of car he drives, and then (4) somehow finds the place where his car is parked, and then (5) squirts super glue into his door locks, knowing that (6) the exact timing of this delay will cause his car to be towed away. And the reason for her incredibly elaborate scheme is merely to delay Heidnik from coming home at the same time that she is planning to abduct Alberta from his apartment.

Finally, after handwriting 28 pages, Heidnik is physically exhausted and complains of an aching hand and head. He summons Holy Scripture in a plea to expose his "evil malefactors." Then he shifts into a fantasy in which I will somehow find his first daughter Maxine to tell her that she was not abandoned by him, but was "taken forcibly." And finally, with a grand flourish, Heidnik signs off as part of an "EGREGIOUSLY GRIEVED" collective. One thing is clear, however. Gary Heidnik is descending deeper into paranoid delusions.

LETTER #14
"I Promised You a Juicy Story"

December 24, 1988

Letter #14 is appropriately titled, "I promised you a juicy story." The story is a complex web of cross-generational relationships in which (1) Gary and his brother Terry double-date a mother-daughter pair, (2) both have sex with the adult daughter, and (3) according to Gary, he could be the real father of a son that is presumed to be his brother's or another man's. The story is also "juicy" (in Gary's estimation) because it details his sexual escapades with an older woman who is so passionate that she "wore me out" and his subsequent seduction of her adult daughter after she was spurned by his brother.

Of course, Heidnik's professed humility at being out-sexed by his partner is really intended as a display of his own sexual power. He delights in telling how he had sex with both mother and daughter and emphasizes how both were "gorgeous" and the daughter was a model. He is obsessed with group sex because he can dominate multiple partners while putting his sexual prowess on public display. Sharing sex partners with his brother and conquering a mother/daughter pair are both forms of his sexual domination fantasies. In addition, his pornography collection was full of bondage and S&M content.

The overpowering compulsion of Heidnik's sexual fantasies was unleashed on Thanksgiving 1986. Testimony from the victims verifies that he was continually playing out his fantasies of total control in ritualistic form. When chained in the basement, the women would be beaten until they told him, "You're the boss, Gary." As Lisa Thomas described it, he forced them to "kiss his ass, literally." The same control ritual was repeated publicly each day on a cot in front of the other hostages. He forced the victims to first perform oral sex on him and then he would demand vaginal sex. He would orchestrate group sex with multiple partners and delighted in making the victims fight over his favors. If Heidnik ejaculated while having oral sex, he would command the victims to "get his juice." He was always in control, always dominant.

While it was nauseating to read about Heidnik's sexploits, his letter reveals another behavior pattern. He chose a series of partners, who were much older than himself, which suggests a Freudian wish to possess his mother, whom he idealized. The first was Maxine Roberts, who is he dated in 1968. She was significantly older and their sexual relationship was short-lived. Nevertheless, though Maxine rejected him outright, Gary always maintained an idealized image of her as a purely good person and a Madonna-like maternal figure. Maxine is the only person other than his mother that Heidnik purely admired and respected. He even named his daughter after her. Gary's second relationship was with Lynn Wilson, who was 20 years older. Talk about a mother complex. That relationship was described as intensely sexual and lasted longer, but he admits that Lynn's hypersexuality was more than he could handle and he dropped her. Within a year, however, Heidnik started a third "mother" relationship. This time it is with Dorothy Knox, who is ten years older, and their relationship lasted ten years.

In this 14 page letter, Heidnik will describe a series of five significant women in his life – mothers, daughters, and lovers – and the cast of characters becomes very confusing. Therefore we have created a genogram to help keep track of who is who. It shows relationships that were either significant and/or bore children and the approximate dates of each. The dotted lines show the two women that Gary dated and had sex with, but who were actually major relationships of his brother Terry. Those belonging to the Board of Directors of Heidnik's Church are also indicated with an asterisk.

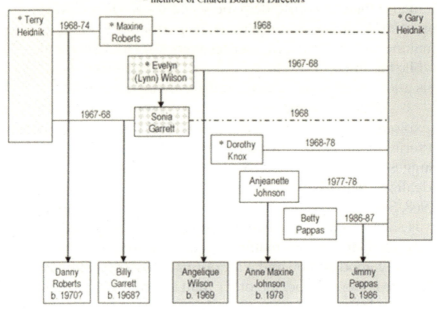

Briefly, the five African-American women discussed in this letter are presented in order of their appearance in the letter:

(1) <u>Anjeanette Norton</u> – Gary Heidnik and this young woman with an intellectual disability had a daughter, Anne Maxine Norton, who was taken away by child protective services shortly after birth in March 1978.

(2) <u>Maxine Roberts</u> – Gary dated this woman in 1968 before she fell in love with his brother Terry. Terry and Maxine lived together for six years and had a child before Terry abandoned her.

(3) <u>Sonia Garrett</u> – Terry Heidnik dated this woman for two years in 1967-1968, while Gary Heidnik dated her mother. After Sonia broke up with Terry, Gary seduced her in 1968. She was only 7 years younger than Gary. Given the timing of her pregnancy and light complexion of her mixed-race child, Gary is convinced that the boy was fathered by Terry, or possibly himself, rather than his father, who is African

American.

(4) <u>Evelyn (Lynn) Wilson</u> – Although she was 20 years older, Gary dated this woman with severe mental illness and intellectual disabilities for two years in 1967-1968 and they had a daughter together named Angelique.

(5) <u>Angelique Wilson</u> – This is Gary Heidnik's first child by Lynn Wilson. Lynn left with their baby and raised her until about age 10. Thereafter, Angelique was raised by Lynn's oldest daughter, Sonia Garrett (above).

It is notable that the very first sentence of letter #14 begins with ingratiating comments about my wife's name. As described in letters #8 and #11, criminals and con-men like Heidnik will utilize a small piece of personal information like this to its manipulative maximum. The fact that Heidnik starts the letter with the "good omen" of my wife's name shows that he has been thinking a lot about how to use this familiarity to his advantage. He is just waiting for the right moment to spring his trap. And he does – in grand fashion – at the end of this 14 page letter. But, first, let's listen to Gary's "juicy story."

Saturday, Dec. 24, 88

Dear Jack

I was I was sitting here thinking some more about that "coincidence" of your wife's name; Joanne. It is of course a "coincidence", but it'd could be interpreted as a good omen. A very good omen. Let my give you more details. Before our daughter Maxine was born, Anjeanette and I had worked out an agreement. At that time we didn't know if it was a girl or boy so we agreed that if it was a girl she'd pick the first name and I'd pick the second, but if it was a boy I'd pick the first name and she the second. Of course my choice name for a boys name was Jimmy (sound familiar) She still wanted to name the son Gary, but I wanted Jimmy. Anyways she decided if it was a girl, she liked the name Joanne, who was a very *good friend of hers. I think they were in Elwyn together. I picked Maxine, because I not only liked the name but I had such high regard for Maxine Roberts. Everyone calls my daughter Maxine and she very specifically asked me to call her that also. That made me rather happy, although the social worker Ms. Doe made out the birth certificate. When she did, she changed the name to Anne instead of Joanne AGAINST both my and Anjeanette's wishes. She didn't tell us this of course. I didn't find out till I went to court to challenge the custody order. They can make all the arguments they want about being worried about Maxine's welfare, and abuse, and mental illness and retardation. BUT what kind of excuse can they make for changing our baby's* name. Whose welfare and benefit was Ms. Doe helping by doing that ?? Ms. Doe also knew it was Anjeanette's choice of name, not mine, so WHY'D SHE DO IT!!*

The point I'm making is that all their arguments which sound so PLAUSIBLE are really pure invective* SOPHISM. I'm sorry over losing my temper as I write this but the things these people did and the REASONS they did them are wrong and it eats at me like an acid. If they were indeed worried about my daughter or Anjeanette and were genuinely concerned about them then I wouldn't be so upset. But they weren't. They did these things out of racism, revenge, and money. Nothing else!! The most blatant and patent proof it is WHY did the change our babies name??? But don't take my word for it. Talk to Ms. Doe yourself. She makes very little effort to hide her racism and hatred of whites. She's PROUD of being a racist!! Nothing brings out the racist attitude in blacks and whites like mixed children and miscegenation*. There is a difference between black power and black pride, but not MUCH!! Most racists will under pressure, disguise their racist attitudes or black pride. Don't be fooled. Ask their opinion about mixed children. Fool her.

Black pride does not forbid interracial marriages. It's one reason I admire Dr. Martin Luther King so much. He was NOT a racist. He wanted us all to live together as equals and brothers. He was against discrimination and he was RIGHT and one of the greatest men of our age. I only wish more people, both black and white had gotten his REAL message. That we're ALL BROTHERS, not just simply eliminating discrimination. He didn't want to see

ANY segregation, even if both communities were equal. He'd never allow an interracial couple to be persecuted or discriminated against. It was a sad day when they shot him to silence him. The bigots had to stop him since they didn't want to see us living together, especially in the same house or same family. I'm proud of America when it made his birthday a national holiday. Maybe there's hope for America after all.

By the way, I don't think Maxine had anything to do with me being framed or with stealing from the church. She has too many morals and scruples for anything like that. I also admire the woman very much. She's very hard working, dedicated to her children, morally honest, prefers working to accepting welfare, and does work at great sacrifice to herself. She's NOT a racist, and loved my brother very much. She lived with my brother AND took care of him for several years. She actually worked and supported him not the other way around. My brother had plenty of money then but took advantage of this good woman. For that I'm ashamed of him. I admire the woman so much I named my daughter after her. Unfortunately* she doesn't admire me. She HATES me. But she's so morally honest she does not keep me from seeing my nephew, Danny Roberts, by her daughter.

My brother abandoned this woman who loved him so much to join the white world. He'd had enough of crossing the color line and had indeed been discriminated by both races. Maxine almost committed suicide when he left, but she didn't because her children needed her so much. When my brother deserted her my heart bled for her. But as I say she despises me. I used to date her for a very short time in 1968. She was very disappointed in me and dropped me (I don't blame her) and started dated my brother. They lived together from something like 68 to about 74. I even loaned her the deposit or down payment to buy 5967 xxx Street and she, of course, repaid every cent. Also I NEVER made any proper or any improper advances to her after she did drop me and started going with my brother. The woman is so morally straight she will not accuse* me of some lie. If you ask her why she dislikes me so much, she'd probably tell the truth, and I'm kind of curious what it is myself. I'm sure part of the reason will be that I'm a philanderer* but the rest, I don't know. Have a talk with her and see if I've evaluated her properly. I just feel sad that I never could have her respect. From such a decent person, It would have been very meaningful* to me. (I wanted her respect; <u>NOT</u> <u>sex</u> from her). As I say I'm <u>positive</u> she had <u>nothing</u> to do with the plot to steal the churches money.

There is someone also though who might have and did know about the church. That persons name is Sonia Wilson. Sound familiar?? Yes!! This is the same Wilson who is on the church board of directors. Evelyn (Lynn) Wilson who is also the mother of my oldest daughter Angelique Wilson. Lynn raised Angelique till she was about 10. I dated Lynn in 67 and 68, when I was about 24 much younger and full of pep. The woman was a borderline nympho, and wore me out. By the time I was 26 I was "burned" out and have never fully recovered. I used to be able to "function" all night. After her I was down to about 15 minutes. But I hold no grudges against Lynn. She was great in <u>BED</u>! <u>Nowhere</u> else though. (Except she's an extremely dedicated and SELFISH mother). But she did <u>BURN</u> me out ☺. Anyways she's approximately 20 years older than me. Twenty years!! She was then even at the age of 45 one of the prettiest women I've ever known. She must have really been unbelievable at the age of 21. By the way after she "WORE" me out ☺ she went out and found an <u>even</u> younger guy named Steve. <u>POOR</u> Steve. She <u>burned</u> him out too. But it took her about two years. He lasted longer than I. He must have been made of sterner stuff!

Lynn is now something like 65 and age has caught up to her finally. All her beauty, is pretty much gone and her mind too. I suspect that in some way she and Marylyn Monroe had something in common. As their physical beauty waned they couldn't stand the loss and their minds went also. Lynn is presently at Ancora Hospital in N.J. She adores all her children but she especially worships Angelique. Unfortunately* the love isn't mutual*. Angelique has virtually no use for her mother (or me). Lynn carries only one picture with her, of Angelique and she carries it next to her heart. I had to beg her to let me see it and I'm the father. But Lynn has been effectively abandoned at Ancora by all her children, one of whom is Sonia Garrett. Sonia is only about seven years younger than me. She was also very pretty. So pretty in fact that she was a professional model. She was also so pretty that my brother went ape over her, and they had a rather "hot" thing going. <u>Yes</u> indeed. Can you imagine this? We double dated sometimes. I went with the mother and my brother went with the daughter. Talk about a close family or keeping things in the family! We did. Personally I still think the mother was the prettiest.

But wait things get even better (juicier, <u>I think</u>). Sonia started pressing Terry to marry her, and pressed very hard. My brother didn't marry her, so she ran off and married some turkey named Leroy. The marriage didn't last more than a couple of months. And if you're asking yourself that question, was she pregnant?? Yes!! (I promised you a juicy story.) The boy was born and I had a sneaky suspicion the boy is my nephew, not my step grandson. Of course if he is my nephew then he's not only Angelique's brother but also her nephew as well as my stepson?? Talk about complicated. Just try and figure out all these relationships. But it gets even better. Stay tuned! I can't be sure the boy is my nephew, since Sonia would deny it emphatically, but Danny is a lot lighter than Sonia and looks a lot like Angelique. He should look like Angelique. They may be cousins as well as being Aunt and nephew. Complicated,* huh?

But I'll bet there's another question in the back of your mind that won't go away, and keeps bothering you. Well the answer is <u>YES</u>!! You know me. I wouldn't disappoint you. I felt sorry for Sonia. The poor girl looked so helpless and forlorn after my brother left and then her husband Leroy. I FELT sorry for her. The poor thing was so alone, helpless and gorgeous, what else could a humanitarian like me do? I have feelings too you know. Yes indeed. But imagine if I had made her pregnant too! Just try and figure those relatives out. Daughters would be aunts and nieces and brothers and mothers. All at the same time. I'm not even going to try and figure out all these relationships. I may be crazy but I'm not that crazy. If I weren't already crazy, figuring out these tangled web of relationships would make me crazy. As I say we were a close family!! ☺

It is notable that, on page 2 of this letter, Heidnik summarizes the actual reasons that the authorities took his infant daughter away in 1978: "Maxine's welfare, and abuse, and mental illness and retardation." The four reasons, unpacked, were: (1) "Maxine's welfare" – concern for the proper care of a newborn by two inadequate parents; (2) "abuse" – concern about Gary's poor care of Anjeanette during her pregnancy as shown by her lack of weight gain and signs of abuse; (3) "mental illness" – concern about Heidnik's ability to parent because of his schizophrenia; and (4) "retardation" – concern about Anjeanette's ability to parent because of her intellectual disability.

Not surprisingly, Heidnik quickly forgets the real world reasons for losing custody of his daughter and reverts to his own paranoid explanation: "racism, revenge and money. Nothing else." He rails against the social worker, Ms. Doe, who he characterizes here, and elsewhere as a rabid feminist and Black Power racist. He laments that "nothing brings out the racist attitude in blacks and whites like mixed children and miscegenation." From this discouraging state of affairs, however, Heidnik makes an interesting reversal to his admiration for Martin Luther King as "one of the greatest men of our age." Heidnik asserts that he was "proud of America when it made his birthday into a national holiday" and sees this as hope for future race relations in America. He asserts that King's "REAL message" was not just ending discrimination, but eliminating segregation of the races entirely so that we can "live together as equals and brothers."

Heidnik then moves from his idealism about Martin Luther King to his idealism about Maxine Roberts. He praises Maxine over and over, depicting her as "very hard working, dedicated to her children, morally honest, prefers working to accepting welfare, and does work at great sacrifice to herself. In fact, "I admire the woman so much I named my daughter after her." As one of the five Board of Directors of his church, Heidnik mentions Maxine many times in this correspondence, but always in positive terms. He repeatedly affirms his trust that she would never have anything to do with trying to steal his church fortune. His idealistic view of Maxine is all the more striking because he knows that she "HATES me," "despises me," and "dislikes me so much." Heidnik says he does not know why, but guesses that it may have to do with his philandering ways. He dated Maxine briefly before she "dropped me (I don't blame her) and started dating my brother."

Heidnik goes on to describe his empathy for Maxine because of the way his brother Terry abandoned her. "My heart bled for her" and she "almost committed suicide when he left" (an act which is of supreme importance in Heidnik's estimation). He asserts that his brother deserted Maxine because "he'd had enough of crossing the color line and had indeed been discriminated by both races." Worn down by society's intolerance, his brother Terry decided to return to "the white world."

From a psychological standpoint, there is a deeper significance to Heidnik's idealism. One of the hallmark features of a severe narcissistic personality is "splitting." This means that the person splits his/her perception of the world into pure extremes of good and bad. People are either all good and admirable (like Martin Luther King, Maxine Roberts, and me, at least so far) or all evil and disreputable (like Detective Devlin, Sonia Garrett, and the two social workers, Ms. Doe and Ms. Smith). There's nothing in between, no ambivalence, no gray area. Splitting is a sign of a very primitive psychological defensive system. It harkens back to the infantile perceptual world of preschool children, who understand little of the world. They experience life and caretakers in simple terms of either love and security or fear and insecurity.

The primitive defense of splitting is reassuring to a weak personality like Heidnik. There is predictability and stability in one's belief in love, safety, and goodness. But there is also predictability and stability in one's paranoia and hatred. Paradoxically, there is an illusion of security and control in being alert and prepared for the dangers of evil-doers. Psychological splitting is also evident in Heidnik's portrayal of his parents. Heidnik would never say anything derogatory about either his father or his mother, neither in his letters nor in his interviews with me. Even when confronted with evidence to the contrary, he consistently described his childhood and home life as if he had been raised by Ward and June Cleaver.

Although Heidnik makes an occasional flight into idealism and trust, his tendency is always stronger toward paranoia and distrust. He spends the last eight pages of this letter in nonstop grievances about other people's greed and hypocrisy their intentions to steal his money and block him from contact with his daughters Angelique and Maxine.

At any rate Sonia rated a mention in my book "40th St. Soaps." I don't mention her name but she's the sweet faithful* paramour who borrows my car and --- loans it to her real boyfriend, who in spite wipes it out!! Isn't Sonia a nice girl? If you like maybe I can arrange a date? (just <u>kidding</u>!!! Don't get mad Joanne). Anyways – Sonia is the quintessential* example of venal. She'd do anything for money, and when they coined the word I think they envisioned her. (I may be philanderer* and a <u>little</u> venal, but this woman makes me look like an angel). She certainly knows all about the church and what it's worth and it's weaknesses. She learned it all from a very impeccable and unimpeachable* source – me. I told her everything. I even suspected she may have been in the plot to frame me and steal the churches money so I used her.

So I wrote my daughter a phony letter that I had changed the Board of Church Directors. I'm positive she'd have shown the letter to Sonia. I do suspect Sonia of being implicated. They wouldn't have to pay her OR my daughter Angelique much. Yes, my own daughter would join in such a scheme. She's also VENAL. Just as much as the rest of them. I'd like to think she'd never sell out her very own father for money but I KNOW better. She also knows about the church and HOW much it was worth. She also had a terrific source of information – ME!! The mother though is the key. She's the one they would need since she was on the board of directors. They need her vote, (once they eliminated me to get the money. Lynn loves her children and would sign anything they told her to sign. Also Lynn was one person in the dark about how much money was involved. Sonia could have manipulated her easily. If she had any problems manipulating her they could have used their big gun. Angelique. Lynn would jump off a cliff if Angelique asked her to. Sonia has more brains than all the rest of them put together. In 85, when Angelique stormed out of the house, she not only refused the $100 for her birthday but Sonia concealed the post office box, so I couldn't even send money to her. When people as venal as these two refuse money, there has to be a good reason. It may very well be they were part of the plot to frame me and were now worried. Of course I'm only <u>guessing</u>, but they do act suspicious.

I really* do love my daughter, and want to restart relations, but I'm not going to be a fool about it or stupid, or blind. The imperfections in her character are not, after all her fault. They're Lynn's fault, and Lynn is paying the price for this now (as well as me). If Lynn had not barred and kept me from seeing Angelique as a little girl I'd have straightened out our daughter a little and she'd be a much better woman. But Lynn was very jealous of her daughter's affection and didn't want to share it with anyone. She didn't want her daughter to love anyone but her. So when Lynn saw that Angelique was actually beginning to like me, she cut off my visits. Completely* and wouldn't even let me see her. She wouldn't even accept money or presents from me unless I left them at the door. During a very memorable Christmas of something like 71 or 72, she told me to put the Christmas presents on the doorstep and GO away. I could NOT see my daughter. And stubborn as I am I refused to give her money or presents unless I could see my daughter. You know Quid Pro Quo. I gave you money, you let me see Angelique. It did not work!! She wouldn't let me see her, even if it meant starving.

And then the state started cutting her welfare payments, as her children matured and moved away. After a couple years, I started to look good to her again and she'd also "worn" out "poor" Stevie. Fool that I am and I am a <u>FOOL</u>! I blew the opportunity also. I was able to function a little bit better (about 15 minutes) and did manage to give her some "small" measure of satisfaction. But one time, when she asked me to "entertain" her I told her no, I wanted to play with Angelique, and me and Angelique started playing with a rubber ball. FOOL!! I committed a DOUBLE whammy, not just one. First of all I had <u>scorned</u> her and second I was usurping HER daughter's affection (she doesn't give me much credence for my part in the conception). She of course threw me out very quickly and didn't ever relent. I tried to visit again in 78 and she called the cops and almost had me arrested.

Later in 83 she saw things a little different and tried to reconnect. She needed me then since she was being evicted from a boarding home AND, she felt if she went back with me we could get our daughter back. She was so determined and desperate. Phone calls, every 5 minutes, 24 hours a day. But it did no good. She was evicted and wound up abandoned by her children in Ancora. Even when I visited in 86 and would give her $5 she'd spend most of it on a call to Angelique. They wouldn't let her call them collect. They'd only let her call if she paid for the call. And as badly as Lynn needed money, she's spend it all on a phone call to Angelique. Is that LOVE?? I think so. Tremendous LOVE, but perhaps too much. Especially since Angelique has almost no love for her mother (or her father).

If you go to talk to Lynn (who is probably still at Ancora) start talking about Angelique and how pretty and nice she is. Lynn will then consent to see you and talk to you. One of these people Lynn, Sonia, or Angelique KNOWS and may be persuaded to TALK about my being framed. I'm equivocal about it though. I want them to talk and clear me but I also don't want them to get into trouble. No not even Sonia. I like all of them, especially my daughter and DON'T want them in trouble. But they KNOW something. You're an investigator, and a DAMNED GOOD ONE!! (I've seen you in action. It's only your writing* that doesn't impress me, both literary *style and penmanship* ☺*). So maybe you can pry some information from them. Sonia is your key. She'd know more than all the rest of them. I doubt if she'd even tell her mother what the purpose was for she wanted her to sign, and I doubt if she'd share the money with her mother. Sonia would though share some with Angelique. They're close. They are after all sisters and---??*

PROLIFICALLY and
relatively ??? yours,
Gary

P.S. I'm taking off a couple days of writing* my book for the holidays, so I've more time to write you. Stay tuned for my next holographic missive (formus opus). I think it will be about lawyers, solicitors*, cr_ _ _ s. The ones who Shakespeare damned and condemned and the ones whose degree gives them a license to steal. ☹ *yuk!*

P.S.S. Can I write or can I write? Isn't my literary style entertaining and holds your attention? Wait till you read my book!!

I hope my candidness doesn't upset you ☺☺☺☺☺☺☺☺. *I'm worried can't you tell.*

As noted earlier, Heidnik began this letter by referring to my wife, Joanne, which was a set up for some manipulation to come. His comment about Shakespeare in the postscript is also a personal reference, reminding me that I had given him many books. He is seeking to exaggerate the intimacy of our alliance in anticipation of springing his trap. He begins by buttering me up with exaggerated praise. He declares that, "You're an investigator, and a DAMNED GOOD ONE!!" He needs my mobility and credibility to get to Lynn, Sonia, and Angelique to "pry some information from them." More importantly, he wants to use me to trick Lynn (one of the Board of Directors) into signing away her share of the church fortune. The proposed method is to take advantage of Lynn's current mental incapacity (she is in a state psychiatric institution) and her vulnerable willingness to do anything to gain love from her two estranged daughters, Sonia, and especially Angelique.

Heidnik reveals his true goal when he expresses doubt that Sonia would "share the money with her mother" (Lynn). This reference to money appears completely out of context in the very last sentence. It has been five full pages since he made reference to the money, saying that he suspected that Angelique knew "how much the church was worth." Heidnik is so close to springing his trap on me that he can barely contain his eager greed. He adds a P.S. to the letter. He adds a P.S.S. He is too excited to stop writing. So he squeezes a final comment into the margin: "I hope my candidness doesn't upset you." He is so giddy that he draws ten smiley faces. His sarcasm about being too "candid" is his way of saying "we can talk frankly now. You know, and I know, that we want that money." As he first attempted with his "let's play a game" in letter #9, Heidnik wants to lure me into becoming his partner in crime. His restraint is short indeed. He will propose his plan in a letter written on the very next day when he instructs me to set my honesty aside and "put yourself in the criminal's mind."

LETTER #15
"Put Yourself in the Criminal's Mind"

December 25, 1988

Heidnik waits before springing his Christmas Day trap. He begins his letter by thanking me for returning the prologue and first-draft pages of his proposed novel, "40th Street Soaps." It is notable that he never asks for my opinion of his writing, not here, nor any time that he sent me chapters or sections to read. You would expect any first-time novelist, or even an experienced one, to be eager to hear some reaction to his creative work. Not Heidnik. He is so narcissistic that he gives no thought to what others might think. It's not that Heidnik doesn't care what others might think of his novel. Rather he can't imagine the possibility that others might have an opinion different from his own. He thinks he is writing a brilliant novel. Therefore it is brilliant. Period. Fact. Reality – for Heidnik.

He then tells me his "bad news." Betty, his wife, is selling his letters and book manuscript to a collaborator who is writing a tell-all book about him. Heidnik is proud of himself, however, for detecting Betty's dissimulation and brags that he can now out-smart her. The odd thing is that Heidnik already told me this information just two days before. One explanation might be his poor memory. Or maybe, after cranking out 42 pages of letters in just two days (not to mention working on his novel), Heidnik simply cannot keep track of what he has said or not said. From a clinical standpoint, the frenetic and emotional outpouring of his letters looks like the symptoms of mania. He is bursting with ideation and cannot stop himself.

Heidnik then shifts to his favorite topic – suicide. As he asserted previously in letter #11 (page 5), he is not afraid of death, he is afraid of pain. This time, however, Heidnik makes an interesting revelation of the origins of this fear. At age 27, his mother suffered an extremely painful death by suicide. He twice describes his mother as "a pretty classy lady" and confesses that even today, 18 years after her death, "I miss her terribly." The reawakening of such acute feelings of loss precipitates an emotional shift to weakness and Heidnik suddenly summarizes his lifetime of miseries: "I was framed, my 'wife' was taken from me, my kid was taken from me, and I spent 5 years in jail and people... literally tried to kill me. And the worst crime of all is NOBODY CARES!!" With this reversal of emotion, we again see Heidnik's characteristic shifting between control (strength) and loss of control (weakness). Given his intolerance for feelings of weakness or vulnerability, Heidnik nearly always ends his letters in a state of strength and control and this letter is no exception. He ends strong – by springing his trap.

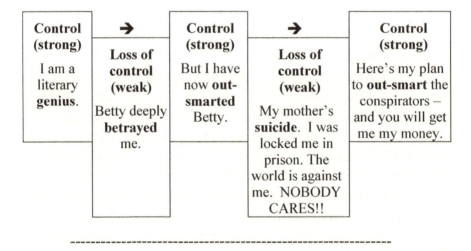

Dec. 25, 88

Dear Jack

Last night the mailman brought me the return of my prologue and the nascent inchoate copies of my "40th Street Soaps." It gives me an improved overuse of my efforts, a retrospective time-warp perspective if you will. Anyways with the advance of years I could look on it more objectively and see areas for improvement – LOTS of improvement. There were some good points too though. I especially liked my line "Cerebrally enlightened." Do you think that one may catch on, ha, ha, ha, ha!

Well thanks for sending it to me. It'll be very useful* in my next chapter. I've also got an extra two pages of my chapter on Nancy. It may give you a smile or two. Do they call groups like A.A. "self-help," or "self awareness," or "group therapy" or what?

Well so much for the good news, now for the bad news. Bad news for both of us! You may be having some competition. It seems everybody's writing* a book and my sweet lovely wife is trying to get into the act also. I'm almost 100% positive she's been selling my letters and manuscript to someone else who is writing* a book. She's either selling and/or collaborating* with this individual. It became patently obvious in her recent letters of Dec. 16, Dec 18, Dec. 20. Sorry to be the bearer of bad news (I hope you don't kill messenger☹.) Do you suppose I could have a little fun with those two and feed them some "interesting" news, for their book? As of yet they don't know I'm on to them, and they certainly haven't told me anything. My wife of course always thought me naive and she's right. But sometimes I can catch onto some things.

By the way, to repeat myself again, I'm not helping you because I'm afraid of death or even think you can help me get a McNaughton decision. "Fat Chance"! Anybody whose made as many suicide attempts as me can't be afraid of death. I've looked forward to it for too long, to be afraid of it. The only thing I fear is "Pain." I also don't want to die like my mother. She took some kind of mercury based hair dye and "suffered." I can still vividly remember my stepfather's description of her agony and nobody could help. Sad!! They put me in charge of her funeral and I "botched" it. The only thing I did right was Niagara Falls. That was a touch of class she'd have appreciated. Mom was a pretty classy lady, all right. Just look at the day she picked: Memorial Day. That was class. She didn't leave a suicide note or at least I don't think she did. I was too STUPID to ask anybody. But Mom wanted to be cremated because she just couldn't stand the thought of an abandoned gravesite* with weeds and trash, and NOBODY every coming to visit her. She *needn't have worried. I'd have visited her. That's one of the reasons I like going to Niagara Falls. But I've not gone nearly enough. Maybe she was right after all. Anyways Mom was a pretty classy lady all right. I miss her terribly.*

But the point I'm trying to make is I'm trying for justice!! I was framed, my "wife" was taken from me, my kid was taken from me, and I spent 5 years in jail and people literally tried to kill me. And the worst crime of all is NOBODY CARES!! I've been to A.C.L.U.; attorney Jack Bulkin; Senator Arlen Spector; Prison* Society; F.B.I.; Justice Department; Phila Daily News; *hired an attorney to try and start a grand jury investigation, told hundreds of people, even went to B'nai Brith (they turned me down because I'm not Jewish). Well I'm persistent if nothing else.*

You're next on my list. Your specialty is investigating, and I've seen some samples of your work. I'm VERY IMPRESSED!! Your* strong point is you know how to ask QUESTIONS, the right kind of questions that get to the nexus of a problem. The problem is though getting you started asking these questions. If I can just get you to ask yourself <u>first</u>, some of the <u>right</u> questions, then asking others the right questions it would be akin to setting a burning ember alight, that would grow into a raging bonfire. We may even set fire to the corrupt houses of some people that need their corrupt and fallacious mansions burned.

The problem is how do I light that first <u>spark</u>?? For one thing I've got to convince you of my credibility. That was my reason for asking the question didn't five years in jail seem a little suspect for a first conviction of three MISDEMEANORS*, especially with so many mitigating circumstances*, and a judge renowned for his "light" sentences. That question, I think warmed things up, but no spark. Then I mentioned the money in 78 was about $125,000. In terms of today's dollars with respect to inflation that comes to about $250,000. A quarter of a million. And it WAS VULNERABLE!! No attorney is overviewing* it. No auditors, no government agency, no family relatives, no church members, only ME!! The mention of the money seemed to warm up the spark a little more, but you seem to be missing part of the question. That it was ONLY ME standing between these crooks and all that money. I tried to bring this fact out with questions and it didn't work.

So I'll try the more direct approach. Can you see that the only obstacle to them was ME!! I was their only roadblock, their only impasse. They sure as HELL weren't going to let things like morality or honesty stand in their way. You may be having problem with this since you're an HONEST MAN!! You'd have to be a crook or think like a crook to see the points I'm trying to make. I'm not trying to **suborn** [WORD IS HEAVILY BOLDED BY HEIDNIK] you or get you to do anything unlawful or immoral, but trying to get you to see reality. So put yourself in a criminal's* mind frame and think like a crook!! Here is all this nice juicy* money and you want it. You want it very very badly, but the only thing stopping you is – ME!! What should you do, preferably LEGALLY!! So you won't have to go or take a chance of going to JAIL. There are several possibilities I can think of. One is open to a crooked and immoral cop. Another is contained in my medical files. You may think of some more that I haven't. TRY: If I told you what my suspicions were or what actually was tried you'd think I was crazy!!

So I'm putting it into a question. When you answer I'll give you some information that will "blow" your mind. It's possible I may have lit the spark in an unexpected area; my broker (Mr. Robert Kirkpatrick III) you may have hit on something there. He could very well be involved. He could have been a main player, along with Devlin. He certainly would have NO moral compunctions against being involved. I've known that man 15 years and the only thing he seems interested in is money! As for Maxine Roberts, most certainly look, but I don't think you'll find anything there. Try Sonia Garrett. That's a good possibility. Susan Carson may have some potential too but I think she may have tried a "grab" on her own, (the $30,000 in Provident Bank). I don't think she was part of the other main conspiracy.

A little tip I can give you in your investigation. If people know you're friendly to me or trying to help me they WON'T help you! I know it goes against your nature but if you want people to help you, don't let them know your true motives. That you're looking for justice and honesty. You won't get much from them if you do. There really is some positive information about me, but *people don't think of me in positive terms only negative. And this has been true ALL my life. As you investigate you'll soon find it out. People do NOT like me, and never have. Even though I've never done anything to them and pose* no threat. They like to hurt me. Check. You'll see I'm right?*

<u>Electrically</u> yours
Reddy Kilowatt

P.S. Any toys you can send to Jimmy would be appreciated. Just have them sent in my name. It'll be ok! But no live "Birdies" what junior would inadvertently do to them is too cruel to contemplate! Thank you, and Merry Xmas.

Heidnik waited until page 3 to present his con to get me to steal the Church fortune for him. He starts the con by trying to butter me up with the same compliment he used in the previous letter #14: "Your specialty is investigating. I'm VERY IMPRESSED!!" He recognizes my skepticism because he states, "I've got to convince you of my credibility." Since he failed to seduce me in letter #9, he devises a new three-step con. He first tries to wet my appetite by highlighting the size of the prize – $250,000 (close to $750,000 in today's dollars). Heidnik is as blunt as he can be: "Here is all this nice juicy* money and you want it. You want it very very badly." But then he has to overcome the barrier that, "You may be having a problem with this since you're an HONEST MAN!!" So the second step is to invite me to "think like a crook." "I'm not trying to **suborn** you or get you to do anything unlawful or immoral, but trying to get you to see reality. So put yourself in a criminal's mind frame and think like a crook!!" Contrary to his pretext, Heidnik is <u>absolutely</u> trying to suborn me. In fact, he actually traces the letters of "suborn" over and over so that the word appears in heavy bold. This is significant as one of only two instances in the 150+ pages of his letters. His usual convention to show emphasis is to use capital letters, underlining, or exclamation marks.

The third step of Heidnik's con is the most ingenious. He emphasizes in capital letters that the scam can be done, "LEGALLY!! So you won't have to... take a chance of going to JAIL." He tries to convince me that I can make an easy fortune and it will be perfectly legal. Suspecting, however, that I'm lacking in the necessary skills of criminal manipulation, he gives me instructions: "I know it goes against your nature but if you want people to help you, don't let them know your true motives... You won't get much from them if you do."

Finally, Heidnik employs one last manipulation to seal the deal. In his postscript, he asks me to do him the personal favor of buying Christmas presents for his son. As we now know, this is a textbook trick of inmates and con men, who will request "small" favors" while incrementally increasing the size of the favors until the guard or staff person has violated a major rule and can be blackmailed. Heidnik has been carefully luring me into his grand trap with increasing personal familiarity and favors: He addresses me as Jack rather than Dr. Apsche, he uses my wife's name, and my favors to him have included hand-me-down books and magazines, and a previous offer to buy Christmas presents. To further ingratiate himself, Gary even enclosed a Christmas card to Joanne and me. Everything appears ready for me to fall.

LETTER #16
"Let Her Know I Am Remorseful"

December 30, 1988 (estimated)

Unfortunately, I've lost the first two pages of Letter #16 so the date is uncertain. But it must have been written after December 25 and just before New Years Eve because – drum roll – that will be the night that he chose to kill himself.

It is interesting to read this letter with the awareness that these are meant to be Gary's parting words to the cold cruel world. He focuses on three topics as he prepares to die. First, he reiterates the plot to steal his church fortune and chooses this final opportunity to add Dr. Bora, his prison psychiatrist, to the imagined ring of conspirators. Second, he addresses his relationship with me – by consoling me for not getting paid by Peruto for my services at his trial. And, lastly, Heidnik expresses remorse for harming Lisa Thomas, his third and youngest victim. Absent the content of the missing two pages, these are Heidnik's three greatest concerns before he dies. The conspiracy, remorse, and – me?! The reasons for my surprising importance will be revealed in dramatic fashion in letter #19.

In the meantime, this fragment begins with Heidnik's criticism of Dr. Bora, the prison psychiatrist at Graterford prison. He mentioned her only once before, very briefly, in Letter #2: "I never trusted Dr. Bora. What makes you say that I did?" Heidnik reiterates the same sentiment here. He contends that Dr. Bora conspired with the Parole Board to repeatedly withhold parole and keep him in the state prison rather than transfer him to the psychiatric hospital in Coatesville. According to Heidnik, the circle of conspirators is led by its two "ringleaders," Detective Devlin (his arch villain) and Ms. Smith (the social worker at Selinsgrove) and is imagined to include Dr. Bora (the prison psychiatrist), Dr.

Liebold (who administered the blood test to Alberta at Selinsgrove), Audrey (his upstairs neighbor), the Parole Board, and possibly the Superintendent at Coatesville. He also includes "Dr. Williams," who is the doctor who once put him on suicide watch (he misnamed her as Dr. Wingate in Letter #8 and Dr. Wainright in Letter #10.) Heidnik reaffirms that the conspiracy was driven not by racism, as he had originally believed, but by greed to steal his church fortune. Remember, of course, there are many more suspects in Heidnik's imagined conspiracy, who are named at other times, such as Anjeanette's family, his stockbroker Kirkpatrick, and his attorneys Levine, Pressman, and Bulkin.

As for Dr. Bora, you are under a misconception of her. I do not regard her in a kindly light and am convinced that she was one of the leaders of the conspiracy against me. I got the distinct impression she was playing "mind games" with me. About the first week of every month, she called me into her office to cheer me up with the news, "I think we're going to parole you this month!" This was the upper. Then towards the end of the month she or the P.R.C. would inform me, "Nope. No parole this month." This was the downer. Up and down, up and down, every month. It was a veritable* roller coaster. It was obvious they were trying to exert psychological pressure on me, but for what end? I thought that part of it was due to having been contacted by a Phila. Detective Devlin. He was the one who organized and led the frame up and put me in jail in the first place. I was thoroughly convinced that their purposes for lying to me was racially motivated and because I violated the "blue code." I also knew that they were all lying to me. When they said I wasn't being paroled* to Coatesville because Coatesville had so far refused to accept me, I knew this was pure chimera. I had written not once, but several times to the Superintendent of Coatesville he assured me that I'd be accepted as soon as the parole board contacted him. So Dr. Bora and the Parole Board were obviously lying. But why? Just how much vengeance did they require of a white man who committed the sin of miscegenation*? Wasn't 5 years of incarceration enough blood for them?

It then occurred to me that maybe there was another motive for their lies. Perhaps they had designs on the church's assets*. So I designed a little experiment. I am fairly certain that the prison authorities read all my mail avidly, so I wrote a spurious letter to my daughter, that I had changed the membership of the Board and that many like her mother were no longer on the Board. I'm not bragging, but this is actually a very ingenious move on my part. Since the only way they could pilfer the churches resources was to control the church board or by circumventing it entirely, the selection of a new and COMPETENT* board would block this. Do you know what their response was? When they realized that they could no longer steal that money, they paroled me. Two weeks after the letter, NOT also incoincidentally*, everyone seemed to lose interest in me and they ceased to persecute me. For more than 5 years I thought all the punishment and harassment was racially motivated but now, in hindsight I believe it was mostly money, at least by the leaders. Two of these leaders seeking these illicit profits were Detective Devlin and Dr. Bora. Mrs. Smith was also a ring leader, but her motivations were different. I believe she was motivated not by money, but by the lies of Devlin and Anjeanette's family, and was suborned, just like so many others in this frame up, like Dr. Liebold, Dr. Williams, etc. They could have recruited Dr. Bora with offers of money.

As to the charges of malingering, I say "Rubbish." To be a malingerer I would have had to have had a purpose. What would have been my purpose; to stay in jail? My minimum sentence was up and I was unequivocally* qualified for parole. I had income, a place to go, no misconducts* or disciplinary problems etc. If to be paroled all I had to do was talk, why wouldn't I talk?" [Author's note: Heidnik was mute for nearly 3 years.] Since I was a 100% disabled service connected veteran, applying to a veteran's hospital for a service connected illness they had to accept me, whether I was talking or not. Their only reason for denying me parole was entirely mercenary. Once that money was removed from their grasp, there was no longer any reason for their charade and so they not only

SOCIAL NETWORKING

TIPS FOR PARENTS

For additional information on this topic:

◀ Visit **www.ConnectSafely.org**

◀ Visit your local library
   dude mencial ledeo
   Teleserve

Dave Dudley
Tosca

Levers in the Bible
g.g. worms

This series of Internet Safety Bookmarks are available to download and print locally at the Web site of the Illinois Library Association:

◀ **www.ila.org/netsafe**

SPONSORED BY
© 2006 ConnectSafely.org
Illinois Library Association

SOCIAL NETWORKING
TIPS FOR PARENTS

Be reasonable and try to set reasonable expectations. Pulling the plug on your child's Internet activities is rarely a good first response to a problem—it's too easy for them to "go underground" and establish accounts at a friend's house or many other places.

Be open with your children. Encourage them to come to you if they encounter a problem online—cultivate trust and communication because no rules, laws or filtering software can replace you as their first line of defense.

Talk with your children. Find out how they use the services. Make sure they understand basic Internet safety guidelines, including privacy protection and passwords, the risks involved in posting personal information, avoiding in-person meetings, and not posting inappropriate photos.

Consider requiring that all online activity take place in a central area of the home, not in a child's bedroom. Be aware that there are also ways children can access the Internet away from home.

Try to get your children to share their blogs or online profiles with you. Be aware that they can have multiple accounts on multiple services. Use search engines and the search tools on social-networking sites to search for your child's identifying information.

© 2006 ConnectSafely.org

SPONSORED BY

paroled me, but finally* everyone lost interest in me.

So as you can see, I've no respect for Dr. Bora. She not only sold her integrity but the honor of her profession* for profit.

Peruto, Jr. informed me he had paid you something like $5,000 or $10,000 for your services. I was chagrined to learn he paid you nothing. It impugns his integrity.

About your interview with Lisa. did she have any comments on the case? Does she hate me still? If you see her again please extend my sorrow to her of what happened and let her know I am remorseful.

Very truly* yours,
Gary

Heidnik makes two very interesting comments at the end of this letter. First, he repeats, almost verbatim, the same ploy that he tried at the beginning in Letter #2, when he claimed that, "Mr. Peruto told me he paid you something like 5 or 10 thousand. You say you were unpaid. Is that true?" At that time, Heidnik's motive was clear: He suspected that his lawyer and I were in cahoots to write a Heidnik book together. He intended to plant the seed of distrust in my mind and play me against Peruto. Heidnik's comment was a transparent ruse the first time, so why does he do it again, almost three months later, and after I have presumably earned his trust? This issue must be of great importance to Heidnik because he either remembered his exact words and/or kept a record of what he wrote in Letter #2.

There is a slight difference in phrasing between the two letters that may suggest a reason for repeating his ploy. In this letter, Heidnik adds his "sympathies" to me for having been ripped off by Peruto. Of course, the supposed insult never really happened. I took the defense team job without any promise of pay, but eventually I was paid for my efforts. By saying that Peruto has impugned his integrity, Heidnik may be trying to compliment me for maintaining my own. After all, I have passed his two honesty tests in Letters #9 and #15 by not succumbing to the lure of his fortune. In his previous letter #16, Heidnik remarked that, "It seems everybody's writing a book." My guess is that Heidnik is getting paranoid that Peruto is writing a book or, worse yet, Peruto might try to re-team with me to write <u>this</u> book. Or maybe Heidnik fears that a shrewd and unscrupulous lawyer like Peruto (in his view, not mine) will take advantage of my naive honesty. He wants to protect his book, which he thinks will be his legacy, by turning me against Peruto and keeping the book in my hands so that he can control its content.

    Heidnik follows this manipulation with an extraordinary statement of remorse. It stands as a rare moment of sincere and appropriate concern for one of his victims, Lisa Thomas, who endured three months of abuse in his cellar. His last sentence is, "Please extend my sorrow to her of what happened and let her know I am remorseful." He is careful not to confess any specific crime (it is vaguely termed "what happened") and he does not admit any fault or responsibility, but Heidnik clearly feels bad for abusing her. He wants Lisa to know that he feels sorry. But what makes his expression of remorse so believable is that this apology was intended to be his last words on earth.

    Clearly Gary is trying to make amends in some way at the end of his life. He wants to know if Lisa Thomas still hates him and if she forgives him. I did interview Lisa, but I would never ask her that question for Heidnik. I found Lisa to be sweet. She was trying to make sense of her trauma and, surprisingly, she didn't seem to harbor any hate in her soul. I never told Heidnik that or anything else about Lisa. I felt and still feel that he did not deserve to know anything about any of his surviving victims.

    It is also notable that Heidnik expresses his final farewell in a straightforward fashion that is entirely unique. With the exception of two letters in which he used "respectfully," Heidnik typically ended his letters with attempted humor or irony as below:

- Cogitatively yours, (Letters #7 & 8)
- Your favorite lab specimen, (#11)
- Philologically yours, (#12)
- EGREGIOUSLY GRIEVED, (#13)
- PROLIFICALLY and relatively ??? yours, (#14)
- Electrically yours, Reddy Kilowatt (#15)
- Resurrectically yours, Lazarus (#17)
- Missively yours, (#19)
- Veraciously Yours, (#20)
- Assiduously Yours, (#21)
- Pissed off, (#22)
- Still suspiciously yours, (#24)
- Hopefully yours, (#25)

Unlike his other letters, Heidnik simply says, "Very truly* yours, Gary." He adds the emphasis of "very" to a sincere and direct farewell. When he wrote these words, Heidnik clearly intended to be dead in a matter of hours.

I vividly remember the events of that New Years Eve. I was home with my wife, my daughter, and two step kids. There was a knock on the door and there was my nephew Robert in his park ranger uniform. He heard on KYW that Heidnik was found unconscious after attempting suicide and was in a coma. My immediate reaction was sadness, which shows that, in some weird way, I was attached to the crazy SOB with all his ramblings and rhetoric. I thought, wow, what a way to end my time with Heidnik.

Following his news announcement, Robert brought a case of Heineken into the house that he had confiscated from a group of teenagers in the park. He promptly declared, "Lace 'em up," which meant that it was time for table hockey. He and I were fierce competitors and it broke down this way. If I drank coffee, I was unbeatable. If I drank beer, I was a sitting duck! Well, we had beer and we listened to tunes on KYW and played hockey. Looking back, hanging with my nephew was some of the best times of my life. He was an Airborne Ranger and made 86 parachute jumps, including one out of a hot air balloon. I was some sort of a hero in his eyes because I survived Vietnam. On the day Robert enlisted, he and I took a walk and discussed the reality of being owned by the US government and being willing to do whatever it takes for your platoon. Robert understood that and did extremely well in the military, frankly better than I did because I have issues with authority. So I remember this night had mixed feelings of sadness about Gary's suicide and the joy of a great night with Robert and my new family.

LETTER #17
"Greetings From the Crypt"

February 4, 1989

Letter #17 was a surprise to me. I presumed that Heidnik was either going to die or would be too brain damaged to continue our project. So this letter actually felt like it was "greetings from the crypt," both eerie and surreal. Even before his suicide attempt, I had no clear idea where the Heidnik book was going. Now I was even more confused about my purpose and my relationship with him. I was glad he was alive, even though I knew he was destined to be executed by the Commonwealth of PA. In my strange way, I found some humanity in this wretched and violent man. He was a victim of social ridicule and a system that didn't give a shit about the mentally ill, and he was unable to escape the obsessive deviant fantasies that were dominating his mind. I never forgot his crimes, but I did look for the person beneath the monster hype. Was I manipulated by Gary? Probably so. He was a vile sexual predator who got off on torturing women. Yet there were times that I could find some good parts in this man.

I don't know why Gary did not die in this or any of his suicide attempts. This time he ingested a lethal dose of his antipsychotic medication, Thorazine, which he had stockpiled in his prison cell. A guard noticed his unconscious body was half-fallen from his bunk at 3AM on New Years Eve and summoned emergency medical assistance. The lethality of this suicide attempt again shows that the malingering tag that the prosecution tried to pin on Heidnik at the trial was pure bullshit. Heidnik was unconscious for five days in a coma and came as close to death as someone can without dying.

Malinger to what end?

Now, in the aftermath of his self-poisoning, Heidnik complains of bed sores, huge gaps in his memory, numbness on his right side, and trouble with his handwriting. It is likely that he suffered both temporary and permanent brain damage from the overdose and he seems aware of his diminished capacity. It took him a month to recover enough mental and physical functioning to compose this letter to me. He may be weaker, but his braggadocio remains in tact. As a self-proclaimed master of suicide, Heidnik boasts of the multiple times that he has narrowly escaped death. His spirits are high and he is playful. Most of all, he is curious what the newspapers have had to say about his near suicide.

Feb 4, 89

Dear Jack,

Greetings from the crypt! I'm back again after having been dead or awfully close to it. I wasn't so lucky this time though. I've got nerve damage on my right side: some numbness in my right hand and back. It seems to have some effect on my writing* too, which looks even worse than normal. Also I got a bedsore on my left back. The dead skin is about to fall off though, and I'm wondering just how bad the damage is. Perhaps even worse as I seem to have a lot of "holes" in my memory. I lost a couple of weeks in December and January. I can't remember anything that happened like going or being in the hospital or talking to the doctors. Nothing. My memories start again when they locked me in the "bug" cell in the prison hospital. Apparently I was unconscious for 5 or 6 days, and came very close to not making it... again.

This is my third time at knocking on those pearly gates and not being allowed in. THREE times. Can you believe it? Most people never get past the first time. I must have more lives than a cat. You already know about the time in 86 in the garage. I <u>think</u> I've told you about trying to hang myself in D.C. and now. There were also a lot *of narrow escapes, like in 84 I was living in my van for a couple of months and I'd try to heat it up inside with a kerosene heater. The flame in the heater would get real low and smoke but wouldn't go out – quite. The doctor explained to me that the problem was no air in the van. Also the heaters lots of times put out carbon monoxide, when they don't burn right. Another time my polyester* blankets fell up against the heat, instead of burning, they just melted. If I'm not mistaken polyester* burns, and or makes toxic gas when it melts or burns. That would have been a very painful way to go – live cremation.*

Some people would interpret all these narrow escapes as meaning I've got more lives than a cat or maybe I'm immortal. I have a different interpretation. I think it's my destiny*, that it's pre-ordained by God, that I'm to die in the electric chair and nothing is going to change that – NOTHING. I don't know why God would want me to die that way but apparently He does. Consider also, that I never killed anyone, but these two death were accidental, but that doesn't matter. Also I got sold out by Peruto on the death penalty* phase of my trial. He didn't defend me on that issue, only on the insanity part. (He figured he'd get more money for his book if I got a death sentence.) Anyways the electric chair seems to be determined for me by God. There just doesn't seem to be any other explanation. I'm sending you the report, I was given. You can see from it that the guard found me at three A.M. If he'd only have been a ½ hour or hour later, I'd be gone now. Also if I hadn't had some kind of seizure and was lying ½ off the bed, he wouldn't have never known, since as you already know, I always sleep with my head under the blankets. The guard wouldn't have noticed anything in that position. Also, in 86, Tony came home unexpectedly, he wasn't due for hours, and why the hell he got so nosy as to look into the garage, I'll never know. Then in 87, when I hung myself in the shower, why in HELL did the guard decide to check on me. In seven years of jail I've only been checked several times. And he checks just in time too. ½ a minute later and it would have been too late. One near miss I could say it was coincidence, but THREE times is just too often to be a coincidence. There has to be a reason, and it can only be God!

By the way, as you can see, I'm no longer at Fairview, but back in R.H.U. at Western. Imagine that. Being sent back after only 2½ weeks. Yippee – I'm cured! ☺ Fairview was AWFUL. They kept me in a room all by myself, and I had an attendant watching me constantly 24 hours a day. I couldn't even pee, without someone watching me. The food was lousy and the place was cold. I probably lost 5 pounds while I was there. So I'm glad to be back. Again though I've been in a news blackout and I'm curious* what the papers said. Could you send me some Xerox* copies of the latest news stories. I also understand Peruto said I'm brain damaged or something. Could you send me copy of that article too? Unfortunately* he's half right, but the damage seems to be mostly to my memory. It's hard to know what you've forgotten when you don't remember what it is you've forgotten.

 You might like a laugh, so I'm enclosing a letter I got from someone. If you think I'm a fruitcake wait'll you read this guy's letter. You'll fall off your chair laughing. ☺

 By the way, there's a psychologist at Fairview, named Dr. Camile (a man). I didn't talk to him, since I'm sure he was writing* a book also, but he actually quoted me the figures of what the church was worth in 81. He tried to get me to talk by shocking me with that information. If he knows the actual figures for 81, then EVERYONE must have known. This could be a big break for us if he'll talk. Let me know how you do with him.

 Also, how are you doing with Bulkin. Did you get the 78 transcripts yet. You haven't mentioned anything about that.

     Resurrectically* yours,
     Lazarus Lazarus

 It is interesting to observe what topics are of most concern to Heidnik in his fuzzy post-suicidal condition. Despite his apparent memory damage, he picks up with one of his main concerns from the previous letter. He is convinced that Charles Peruto is writing a book about him. He declares that, "I got sold out by Peruto on the death penalty* phase of my trial. He didn't defend me on that issue, only on the insanity part. He figured he'd get more money for his book if I got a death sentence." Heidnik also asks for more information about an article in which Peruto stated that he was "brain damaged."

Given his loss of memory, it is surprising that Heidnik reports a <u>new</u> memory that excites his hopes for vindication for the "injustices of 78." He remembers a psychologist (actually a psychiatrist) named Dr. Camile, who treated him at Fairview State Hospital for the Criminally Insane, where he was hospitalized from 1978 to 1981. Dr. Camile supposedly "quoted me the figures of what the church was worth in 1981." Convinced that, "This is PROOF," he is buoyant with renewed hope of validating his conspiracy theory. He is also eager to know if his former attorney Bulkin has sent me the transcripts from the trial of 1978. All in all, Heidnik's tone is upbeat in this letter and even jocular as he jests about some "fruitcake" who wrote to him in prison.

Ultimately, Heidnik attributes his survival from suicide to Divine intervention: "One near miss I could say was coincidence, but THREE times is just too often to be a coincidence. There has to be a reason, and it can only be God!" He wants to sound philosophical, even pious, but his declarations are pure egotism. "I think it's my destiny*, that it's pre-ordained by God, that I'm to die in the electric chair and nothing is going to change that – NOTHING. I don't know why God would want me to die that way but apparently He does." Heidnik closes his letter by signing his name as "Lazarus," the man who was raised from the dead by Jesus. Behind Heidnik's attempted humor is the ultimate egotistic belief that Jesus personally saved him from death.

III. THE SCHISM

LETTER #18
"The Local Drug Lord"

February 10, 1989

So everything appears hunky dory in Heidnik-land. He has survived a deadly suicide attempt and, after a little rehab time to recover his ability to think and hold a pen, he is back to his usual games. His "greetings from the crypt" was written as if nothing is different in our relationship. But, one week later, our correspondence is about to be shattered. I'll call this period, "The Schism," because a rift is about to form between us. Neither of us is expecting trouble, but Heidnik's neediness and my impatience are about to collide, or in psychotherapy parlance, his transference and my countertransference have created a powder-keg that is ready to explode.

I'll take responsibility for lighting the final fuse. I don't know about you, but I had reached the limit of my patience with Heidnik and his self-serving letters. Yes, I genuinely felt bad for him when I heard about his suicide and I was relieved to hear of his recovery, but then I started to feel extremely annoyed with him. Heidnik's brush with death did not change him in any way. He had no insights about the value of life, no resolutions to be a better Gary, no remorse over his crimes, nothing. It really pissed me off to see him go right back to his conspiracy bullshit and gloat about his rescue by Divine Providence. If Heidnik was prepared to kill himself, then isn't it time to get real? After 17 letters and 125 pages, I felt that Gary should have reached inside himself and pulled out some honest revelations about his real thinking and feelings. I wanted the truth of his crimes, not more bullshit.

My growing impatience was also being fueled during this time by sleep deprivation caused by combat nightmares. Every night I was back in the Nam. Sometimes I dreamt of the little old man in the straw hat who I killed at the burning village. Sometimes I dreamt of being on ambush patrol in the jungle. In that nightmare, I see an NVA soldier advancing on my position. I aim my M-16 and squeeze the trigger. Click. My gun jams. The NVA looks straight at me, aims, and fires his AK. I see the muzzle flash and feel my chest burning with pain. I would wake in a pool of sweat and feel the actual pain from the phantom AK round. Each time I experienced the shooting as absolutely real. It was terrifying and I would be afraid to go back to sleep, even I was able to calm myself enough to do so.

With that reality robbing me of sleep, I was one moody SOB most of the time. I was fed up with Gary's bullshit and was ready to call him out. Something else had changed that made it possible to confront Heidnik. I finally had the offer of a real job and writing a best seller no longer mattered much to me. I hadn't made much progress on the book anyway and the thought of starting a new life and career made the Heidnik project feel like a ball and chain. So I sent Heidnik a very frank letter asking him about his deviant fantasies and suggested that he stop bullshitting himself and me.

In the meantime, I was confronting myself. On the positive side, I had a new wife whom I loved, two nice step kids, full custody of my daughter, two collies, and a house. I was still staying clean of sex and cocaine and made a new decision to quit my unlawful ways of earning money. In those years, I had many friends who were involved in a variety of illicit money-making enterprises, including drug manufacturing and distribution, money lending, and money laundering. Many were Vietnam homies and, to be honest, none of us gave a fuck at the time. Before you judge me, remember that most of the American public had turned their backs on the boys returning from Vietnam and most of us were subject to at least one instance of being spit on or called "baby killers." Vietnam veterans were treated like pariahs not heroes. I'm not justifying anything that I did. It was wrong and I know better, but don't judge my friends unless you have ever walked in their shoes.

Professionally, I could no longer do counseling with Vietnam Vets, which had been my livelihood before the Heidnik case. It exacerbated my own post-traumatic symptoms and I couldn't sleep because of my flashback nightmares. I was emotionally exhausted. My head was buzzing inside with a sort of a constant "white noise." I needed sleep and rest and there was no way I was going to the VA for help.

So this was my dismal state in February 1989. It is less than a week after Gary's "greetings from the crypt" and my confrontation letter to him. He wrote me two letters on the same day. The first letter, #18, is friendly and personable. The second, #19, is angry and attacking. Letter #18 must have been written first because Heidnik becomes so furious in letter #19 that he entirely stops our correspondence for the next eight months.

Letter #18 begins quietly enough with Heidnik's literary insights about a used copy of *Romeo and Juliet* that I had given him. He is proud of his realization that Tony and Maria in *West Side Story* are modernized versions of Romeo and Juliet. He takes delight in the coincidence that the character names of Romeo and Tony are combined in his own character "Tony, the Romeo of 40th Street" in his self-penned novel, "40th Street Soaps." Heidnik uses the word "auspicious" twice, first regarding this insight, and then to describe the congruence between his daughter's intended name and that of my wife, Joanne. As discussed previously in letters #8, #12, #14, and #15, Heidnik nearly always had a manipulative purpose or ulterior motive for emphasizing our "bond," particularly the coincidence of my wife's name. In this instance, however, I don't see any immediate purpose other than asking me to get information about the Roderick Frey case.

Frey had been convicted of first degree murder for hiring two men to kill his wife in 1979 and, like Heidnik, was sentenced to death by electrocution. Ten years later, Frey was challenging the constitutionality of a mandatory sentencing provision as a way to escape execution, which obviously had major implications for Heidnik and 98 other inmates on Pennsylvania's Death Row. On February 7, just a few days before Heidnik's letter, the State Supreme Court upheld the death sentence for Frey. It would be upsetting news for Heidnik, who was fearful of the pain of electrocution, but for now he does not know and his mood is breezy and light. He feels confident and comfortable in his position with me because he openly teases me (again) about my "dried prunes" writing style and is proud to show off another sample from his now 300+ page novel, "Life in the Slow Lane."

Feb 10, 89

Dear Jack,

I've recently been perusing your copy of Shakespeare: to wit, Romeo and Juliet. Upon reaching the balcony scene*, I was suddenly overcome by the revelation that West Side Story is a contemporary musical version of Romeo and Juliet. That was a very pleasant surprise since I'm very fond of West Side Story, and know it well.

Then while divining who was which counterpart in each story, for example Juliet was Maria, and the Prince was Officer Krumpkee, I was struck with a second revelation*. I'm sure you're familiar* with Mr. Cyrus Green as well in my book, "40th Street Soaps." Back in 84, I nicknamed Cyrus "the Romeo of 40th Street. The Great Lover." (He really lives up to that nom de guerre also). While trying to recall the name of the male star of West Side Story, who is of course Romeo's counterpart, I remembered it is Tony. WHAT A SHOCK! Very few people actually know Mr. Green as

Cyrus since he goes by the name of --- Tony!

Isn't that fascinating and perhaps – hopefully, in some way auspicious. Of course it's not quite as fascinating or hopefully auspicious as your wife's name being Joanne: The same name Anjeanette and I chose for our daughter denied.

I'm not really superstitious and should be careful* assigning too much value to these very intriguing coincidences. Perhaps my attitude should be what was best expressed by a certain ancient bard when he uttered, "What's in a name? That which we call a rose by any other name would smell as sweet." ☺ (How'm I doin'? Is this effective writing* or just dried prunes"? ☺)

As the cerebral edema recedes*, my cogitative acuity is rebounding with a vengeance*, but I'm still having mnemonic difficulties. My penmanship seems vastly improved also.

By the way I'm enclosing several pages from my book "40th St. Soaps" about Tony. It's not one of my better writings*, but you may get a smile and a little insight from it. Don't pay any attention to the page numbers though. I've written almost 300 pages.

Another favor I'd like to ask. I'm still in a kind of news blackout. I only know vaguely what's going on in the world. I just overheard the guards talking about somebody's case having been lost and now he's going to appeal to the Supreme Court. I don't want to ask anybody here, but I suspect this is the Roderick Frey case, they were talking about. It concerns the death penalty. It went before the State Supreme Court in September, and now it "sounds" like they reached a decision. If so, could you send me some information or preferably some newspaper articles on it? Thank you.

While at Fairview an interesting thing happened. Late at night I overheard a couple of guards talking. The one was talking about how the Puerto Ricans knocked down a fence with their cars, threw rocks and bottles at a house, filled the yard with trash, vandalized a car, and made many threats so the person was afraid to go out at night. When I heard this I thought they were talking about me, but the guard was talking about his father-in-law. He said he was forced to sell his house at one third of its value and "do you know who bought it," he asked?

"No," said the second guard.

"A, Puerto Rican," says the first. "They're the only ones who'd buy it."

"Of course," concurred* the second.

I know you know about the nine bullet holes in my garage, and you've seen all the trash in my yard and the broken fence. Well I didn't do that, my Puerto Rican neighbors did. I've actually seen them do much of the damage, personally, but have been afraid to swear out a private warrant against just one or two of them. To do that would have been equivalent to suicide. They've broken windows in my house, thrown rocks and bottles at my house and cars. They put several large dents in and damaged the front door of the house. They've filled my front yard with tons of trash, not one but several times. They also knocked over the main post to my fence, then destroyed the gate it was attached to. They also broke the windows in my garage as well as two in the house. I replaced the windows with plexiglas*. The door with the broken glass was replaced by a solid metal garage door.

This all happened at 3520 N. Marshall of course. They repeatedly vandalized my mailbox and would tear up my mail. Then they would put large rat traps in it, concealed in brown paper bags, hoping somebody like Betty would reach in, and "pow." But Betty recognized it as a trap and I "defused" it. Finally they blew up the mail box, and ripped it OFF its post. I installed a new one on front of the house then, which they left alone. Ironically, they used to hide their drugs, temporarily, in my mail box, before they destroyed it. They'd also hid their drugs in the trash in my front yard. One of their first forms of harassment* was parking different cars in my driveway, so I couldn't get my car into the yard. I tried to counter this by always parking either my 72 Dodge or Tony's car in the driveway, so we'd always be able to get in and out. Also I'd call 911, and have their car, when it blocked my driveway, ticketed. That sometimes worked and sometimes didn't. When I first bought my house, the Puerto Ricans weren't even on my side of the street. My property actually covered three addresses, 3516, 3518, and 3520. The house on my right; 3514, wasn't even occupied at the time. It had been damaged in a fire, and the roof was half burned off, and the inside damaged. It was really only an abandoned shell.

Then this Puerto Rican bought it and began to literally pour thousands and thousands of dollars into it's repair. The guy was only about thirty and had a gold tooth in the front of his mouth. I never could learn what his name was. Who he was, actually, was the local drug lord. He completely* controlled the drug trade in our neighborhood and was the "boss" over all the other local Puerto Ricans. When he'd give orders, they'd jump. One of several were always in close proximity to him whenever he'd venture outside. A large, aggressive, and very loud Puerto Rican served as his chief Lieutenant. The guys nickname was "Angel" and he personally performed and led most of the vandalism directed against me. I didn't discover until later though, the reason the drug lord bought 3514, and was willing to pour such quantities* of money into a worthless, burned out shell of a house. The reason was that house commanded a tremendous view of that part of N. Marshall St. He could see not only everything in front of his house, but almost all the way up and down N. Marshall.

The drug lord though had a problem. He decided he wanted another driveway and garage – <u>mine</u>. I was slow to catch on at first, but I soon realized what he was up to. He not only wanted my driveway badly, he wanted it CHEAP!! Dirt cheap, and was pretty positive he could get it by intensifying the harassment* I was undergoing. He made several proposals to me to at first buy my house and then to simply buy my driveway. I figured that if he wanted my property* so bad, then pay me big bucks for it, although really and truly* I didn't want to sell.

(to be continued next week)

Of all Heidnik's stories, I believe that his "local drug lord" story may be his most credible for two reasons. First, Heidnik has no axe to grind this time. He is not trying to marshal evidence to disprove charges against himself nor is he trying to show that he was framed by people seeking to steal his money. Heidnik is simply telling the story of how he was bullied, harassed, and vandalized by a drug pusher in his neighborhood. He admits that he was afraid to file charges with the police for fear of more dire retribution by the drug lord, but Heidnik remained stubbornly determined to hold onto his property.

The second reason I believe this story is that there is external validation. A Puerto Rican cocaine dealer by the name of Luis Antonio "Sexo" Ortiz was gunned down in September 1988. Such a case might have escaped media notice except for the fact that the murder occurred on the 3600 block of North Marshall Street. Ironically, the story was reported in the newspapers because this was now famous as the site of Heidnik's house of horror. Gary would have been happy to know that the parade of curiosity seekers who came to see his house probably put a major damper on his neighbor's drug business.

The resolution of Heidnik's story, if there was one, is missing. His letter ends abruptly at the bottom of page 6. Heidnik wrote "to be continued next week," which showed his intention to complete his story later. In any case, there is not a hint of ill feeling or anger anywhere in letter #18. Within hours, however, he will explode in rage.

LETTER #19
"Don't Open That Can of Worms"

February 10, 1989

Letter #19 begins pleasantly enough. Heidnik thanks me for sending "nice pictures" of Niagara Falls and some newspapers for him to read. To emphasize his appreciation, he adds the comment, "You really came through for me this time." Heidnik then goes on to say, "You're a nice person" and apologizes for possibly "offending" me by refusing my request to visit him in prison or talk over the telephone. He declines to reveal the reasons for his refusal, but assures me that they are "very good ones." The last time I requested a visit (and I was similarly rebuffed) was at the end of letter #7 seven weeks before. At that time, Heidnik refused my visit because he was under the short-lived, but ecstatic illusion that his estranged wife Betty loved him after all and he wanted to reserve his limited visitation privileges for her.

Then Heidnik suddenly turns hostile in mid-sentence. He assures me of his desire to continue our correspondence, but complains that our relationship is "decidedly unilateral." This precipitates a flurry of angry complaints and a sharp warning: "Don't open that can of worms."

Feb 10, 89

Dear Jack,

Your nice pictures of Niagara Falls arrived, and also your Express delivery with the newspapers. Thank you. You really came through for me this time, and I will reply to the newspapers in a separate letter.

As to your requests for a personal visit and/or a phone call – NYET!! You're a nice person, and I hope you aren't offended by my *seeming maliciousness, but I have my reasons. However I'm still willing to continue our relationship through correspondence, which seems to be decidedly* unilateral. I'm beginning to think you've injured your hand or something and are unable to write. You've sent me good news but are very equivocal about exactly what most of it is. How about elaborating on it a little – PLEASE! I can appreciate you're* busy, but surely it won't take very long to write several pages, rather than just one. Also you seem to suffer from mnemonic problems also. I sent you several pages from my putative manuscript and other things, asking you to return them. I even gave you permission to photocopy them. I have no doubt you'll return those items as you promised me, but it annoys me having to keep asking. Getting you to answer my many questions is also a frequently protracted affair. Please don't be offended, but if I don't complain, the situation will only get worse. Also I'd prefer to think that your recent reluctance to write, and tantalizing but inchoate announcement of "good news," are not simply attempts to <u>manipulate</u> me into granting you a visit. This reluctance to write of several months is casting shadows on your credibility. And as you know I'm very paranoid. I've been extremely* candid and prolific with you, like for instance my 28 page letter of December. So how about relieving some of my creeping suspicions by writing* more, and accepting my moratorium on visits.*

    Another suggestion is that you apply for my records at D.C. Especially my medical records and Doctor <u>Wainright's</u> reports (I think I've finally got the name right). I'll sign any release forms you need to get that information. Dr. Wainwright's report will go a long way to cement my credibility, if it was ever in doubt.

    Also let me repeat my two other questions in this letter.

    A. What and is there some news on the Roderick Frey case (death penalty)?

    B. Was 3520 Marshall Street structurally damaged?

    Thank you.

Missively yours,
Lazarus

> *P.S. I hope you **don't** [WORD DOUBLE INKED BY HEIDNIK] find me difficult, but you know my medical history, perhaps even better than I.*
> *(Don't open that "can of worms" we may never get it closed again.)*

Why is Heidnik suddenly so angry with me? What is the "can of worms" that should not be opened? This letter is the emotional climax of my correspondence with Heidnik. After this letter, he will end all communication for the next eight months and our relationship will never recover from the schism.

As noted above, Heidnik's violent change of attitude occurs literally in mid-sentence when he observes that our relationship is "decidedly* unilateral." His realization that our so-called "relationship" is very one-sided is entirely accurate. We are not equals. We are not friends. There is no reciprocity. In essence, he does all the giving and I just take. Is it possible that Heidnik has poured his heart into writing 135 pages and 19 letters before he finally realizes this truth?! Although he has complained previously about the delays and brevity of my letters to him, this time his irritation flames into rage. He is outraged by the gross inequity between us. But why now? What has changed in the six months since the correspondence began?

The answer is a common phenomenon that occurs in psychotherapy called "transference." Although I am not Heidnik's therapist, and he is not my therapy patient, the correspondence has evolved into something very much like psychotherapy – for Heidnik. Essentially, in transference, the patient forms intense emotions toward the therapist, which often include feelings of love and idealization. Such feelings may arise over the natural course of therapy as the patient reveals more and more intense personal information to the therapist. The patient experiences a special kind of acceptance from the therapist, which makes it possible to safely explore even deeper emotional material. Further, as the patient comes to trust the therapist with more and more of his deepest secrets and feelings, the more important and special the therapist becomes in the patient's life.

Since the patient has such strong positive feelings toward the therapist, he naturally wants to believe that he, in turn, is special and liked by the therapist. But the cold fact is that the patient hardly knows a thing about the therapist! It is the duty of the therapist to maintain a professional boundary and this is done to a large extent by carefully withholding nearly all personal information. Therapy is a very one-sided relationship. The patient reveals everything personal; the therapist reveals nothing personal. For this reason, the patient is induced to speculate and fantasize about the therapist's private life. Transference is the term for the feelings and beliefs that the patient "transfers" onto the "blank slate" of ignorance about the therapist's personal life. In psychoanalytic theory, it is believed that the patient is also transferring deep "unconscious" feelings and dynamics (which originated in early childhood) onto the therapist. Transference feelings can be extremely intense and feel absolutely true to the patient, especially for someone like Heidnik, who has major personality problems and a lousy sense of social reality. Therefore it is the ethical duty of the therapist to be alert to and appropriately manage "transference" when it emerges, so that the patient does not feel rejected or get carried away with unreciprocated feelings and fantasies about the therapist.

In this case, even though our correspondence is not face-to-face psychotherapy, Heidnik had been revealing intimate personal information and formed an intense transference towards me. In the acute isolation of Death Row, Heidnik became more and more dependent on me as a trusted outlet for his feelings – as if I was his therapist. I had become the <u>only</u> meaningful personal bond in his life. With the possible exception of his brother Terry, Gary had been totally shunned by everyone he had ever known – his wives, girlfriends, children, disabled friends, and parishioners. Heidnik can talk to no one but me. He can trust no one but me. By necessity, I was filling the void of his loneliness by becoming his entire social world. He needed me to fulfill all of his social and emotional needs by being his friend, confidante, family, and parent – all rolled into one. He invested everything in me through this intense letter writing. The more that he poured himself into his letters, the more he needed me. His depth of dependency has grown so gradually that neither of us was aware of it. He had forgotten the true character of our relationship – which was "business," not friendship, and not therapy – and he lost sight of the cold fact that our relationship was, indeed, "decidedly unilateral."

For my part, I was simply asking Heidnik for information for my book and he was willing to provide it without compensation. I was not acting in the professional capacity of a therapist so I was not paying attention to the signs of Heidnik's growing dependency and transference. Basically, it was not my job. I was polite and professional, and rewarded his cooperation with small favors, such as sending him used books and newspapers, but there was no personal bond of any kind, and certainly no fond regards from my end.

But, for Heidnik, I had unknowingly become his most important bond. As he poured his feelings into page after page, his transference grew and he developed strong feelings toward me. Until this moment in Letter #19, I do not believe that Heidnik realized the depth of his emotions or dependency on me – and he is devastated. He realizes that, "Jack is everything for me, but I am nothing to him. I have been giving everything to someone who probably does not even care about me!" For Heidnik, the realization feels like the ultimate betrayal and humiliation. This insight is unbearably painful for him and he lashes out at me in the letter. He reacts at the primal level of a small child abandoned by his caretaker.

He flails and screams, demanding love and attention, desperate to restore a position of security in his bond with me.

Neither of us was prepared for this violent explosion of emotion. The catalyst, innocently enough, was my gift of the pictures of Niagara Falls. Niagara Falls held huge psychological meaning for Heidnik. It symbolized his beloved mother and was his favorite place in the world. It was the sacred place where he spilled his mother's ashes after she committed suicide in 1970. It served as the grave where he came to visit her memory as often as he could. It was the place where he brought his new love, Anjeanette, in August 1977. It was the place he wanted to bring his new bride, Betty, in October 1985, but he was not allowed to leave the state because of his parole restrictions. It was the place he planned to take Betty for a second honeymoon when he was free to travel again. I knew how much Heidnik loved Niagara Falls from our conversations and his letters (it is mentioned in Letters #7, #8, #15, and #19). That is why I sent him the pictures. Clearly, he was touched by my gesture ("You really came through for me") because it is the very first thing he addresses in his letter.

Paradoxically, however, by touching Heidnik's heart with memories of Niagara Falls, I also touched a landmine of primal hurt and rage. The emotional logic is thus: "Jack, you must really care for me because you know how important Niagara Falls is to me. You know me better than anyone in the world. I have trusted you with my deepest secrets. You really came through for me…" He feels the rush of warm feelings that come with his thoughts of Niagara Falls, the mother he loved so much, his devoted and innocent Anjeanette, and… Betty. "Wait a minute," he thinks to himself. "Jack is not like my loving mother. He is not pure and giving like Anjeanette. He acts more like Betty, who betrayed me. Like Betty, he only pretends to like me so that he can exploit me for his book." And Heidnik is doubly hurt and outraged that I dared to demand <u>more</u> honesty from him in my confrontation letter.

Thus, my personal gift of the Niagara Falls pictures triggered Heidnik's realization of the very opposite – that I <u>never</u> gave him anything personal. Like a thunderbolt, he realizes that our relationship is, in truth, "decidedly unilateral." He does all the giving and sharing of his soul, but I give him very little and share next to nothing. It is too painful for him to believe. If it is true, then he has been a ridiculous fool and is utterly unlovable and alone. So Heidnik tries to hold onto the possibility that I <u>do</u> care about him. He hopes that his own paranoia has created this painful doubt that I don't care about him. He launches into a series of childish demands for me to <u>prove</u> that I care about him. But then each demand is quickly followed by an apology or retraction because he is terrified of losing me. So he flips back and forth between raging demands to prove that I care and apologetic excuses that will preserve his bond with me. The reversals of emotion are quintessential Heidnik, shifting between control and loss of control, between strength and helplessness. The following chart shows the chronology of more than a dozen of these angry controlling demands within this two-page letter, each followed by retractions and apologies.

The upshot of Heidnik's letter #19 is a demand that I show that I care about him. His weak side is saying, "I've been pouring my guts out to you. I'm dependent on you. I'm hurt. I need reassurance that you care about me." His strong side is saying, "If you dare to reject me, I will reject you first. I will punish you. I will not meet with you. I will not write to you. Now you can wait for me. You can feel what it's like to have your important questions go unanswered. Let's see you write a 28 page letter to me!"

CONTROL / STRENGTH **Complaints and demands to prove that I care about him**	LACK OF CONTROL / WEAKNESS **Retractions and apologies so that I won't abandon him**
"NYET!!" No visits or phone calls – until you prove yourself	but… "you're a nice person." Don't be "offended by my seeming malicious" refusal.
This relationship is "decidedly unilateral"	but… I'm "still willing to continue" it.
You hardly ever write me	but… maybe "you've injured your hand… and are unable to write."
"PLEASE!" elaborate on your "very equivocal" good news	but… I can appreciate that "you're busy."
"Surely it won't take very long to write several pages, rather than just one"	
I sent you my manuscript and want you to return it "as you promised me"	but… maybe you "suffer from memory problems" like me."
"It annoys me having to keep asking" you.	
"Getting you to answer my many questions is also a frequently protracted affair"	but… "please don't be offended… If I don't complain, the situation will only get worse."
Your "reluctance to write, and tantalizing… good news" is a way "to manipulate me into granting you a visit…" and "Your reluctance to write of several months casts shadows on your credibility"	but… "as you know I'm very paranoid."
"I've been extremely candid and prolific with you." I've even written "28 page letters"	but… these doubts could just be "my creeping suspicions" (my clinical paranoia).
"Relieve" my doubts "by writing more and accepting my moratorium on visits."	
Prove yourself by getting my medical records and Dr. Wainright's reports	but… maybe you need to see these documents to "cement my credibility" and relieve your "doubt" about me.

Prove yourself by answering my two important questions – promptly and directly. Am I going to be electrocuted (the Frey decision)? Was my precious house at 3520 N. Marshall damaged?	
I am "missively yours" = <u>I'm</u> the boss this time! (a missive is a message from a superior)	but… I'll make a joke by signing my name as "Lazarus" so that I don't offend you.
	P.S. "**Don't**" abandon me if I act "difficult." As a clinician, "you know my medical history." I'm a paranoid schizophrenic and can't help myself.
So "don't open that can of worms" and insist on visiting.	because… I'm afraid our relationship will never survive this conflict.

In essence, Heidnik wants me to break my professional boundary and become vulnerable too. Although this is not therapy and I am not Heidnik's therapist, I decided to respond as a professional therapist is trained to do. When faced with transference, the therapist must be careful not to respond emotionally (what is termed "counter-transference") and/or become overly personal with the patient. Instead, it is important to maintain one's professional stance with the expectation that the most immediate and violent emotions of the transference will subside and then it will be possible to discuss and analyze the feelings in a therapeutic fashion. In Heidnik's transference fantasy, he would love for me to write a deeply personal 28 page letter in which I disclose all sorts of details about my private life. Obviously, that is the last thing I would or should do. I opted to do nothing and wrote no reply. Besides I was about to move lock, stock, and collies to Illinois and I was glad to leave Heidnik behind.

In February, after eight months of unemployment, I received an unexpected job offer. My close friend Ron was an administrator at the University of Illinois at Urbana-Champaign and my other friend Jimmy was a Vice President of something. They offered to hire me as a psychologist to do something in their department. It looked like a great opportunity and I'd be working with my friends. That was all I needed. We started packing up for the grand move to Ivesdale, Illinois, population 267!

Joanne was first to go. My friend Ron loaned her his new Volvo station wagon to make the trip with the three kids and two cockatiels. Joanne was never, shall I say, a great driver. She appointed our oldest daughter Amy as the navigator, while Melissa was relegated to the backseat with Joey and the screeching birds. Joey was always thirsty, or hungry, or had to pee. The last straw was when Joey brought the bird cage into a McDonald's. The birds freaked out and started squawking, then Joey started squawking, and then the store manager started squawking, and asked them to leave. They were stopped for speeding, got lost a hundred times and, by sheer dumb luck, found Ron's farm in rural Illinois.

I stayed behind to load the rented truck, take care of the collies, and sell whatever I could. I disposed of the trappings of my gangster life – my Rolex watch, Smith & Wesson 669, Mossberg semi-automatic pump shotgun, Colt 25 automatic, Carter Arms Bulldog 44, and 357 magnum – as well as my stereo, fish tanks, and anything left over. The packing was going well until I went to clear out the shed. It seems that Joey had been depositing our garbage in the shed all winter instead of taking it down to the street for pickup!

After several days, the truck was packed, the house was cleaned, and the collies and I mounted up. Nikki was an elegant, chestnut sable, while Shanus was tri-colored and had a Pepi Le Pew-ish face. Nikki sat looking out the windshield and chatted with me for the entire ride. Shanus was sick and looked green all the way (yes, a green dog). I stopped frequently to give my collies some water and peanut butter crackers for nourishment. I arrived at dusk with no idea where Ron's farm was hiding. All I could see was endless frozen cornfields and an occasional skeleton tree. Then I stumbled on a hand-written sign in the middle of nowhere pointing the way to "Jimmy's birthday party."

Ron welcomed me with a big oil can of Foster's beer. I first met him while selling cars at Keats Ford in Trenton, New Jersey. Ron was a big, strong, crazy guy, who played semi-pro football and was the only white player in an all black league. He was feared, loved, and respected. One night in a bar, some big guy started a fight with a friend of ours. Ron lifted the dude over his head and bounced him off the bar. Then he casually finished his beer. Ron was a wild, goodhearted man, who I loved like a brother and I miss terribly.

Ron then told me the bad news. My job was frozen (no job!) and the house that we were going to rent was sold (no home!). The good news, at least, was that Ron's wife Suzie found us another house to rent. So we had a house, but I still had no job. Thus my life in Illinois began as badly as it had ended in PA, confusing, difficult, and scary. Do I have what it takes to get my shit together to be a good husband and father to this family? Can I climb back up the mountain of respectability? I was determined to give it my best shot, which all too often seemed to fall short.

Rural Illinois was a wasteland of flatness, farms, and strange people. Joanne got a low paying job at an elder care facility. The kids were enrolled in school. Melissa was bored and began to play chicken with freight trains, smack her brother with her book bag, and plotted her escape from hell. Joey took up fist fighting with the bullies at school and held his own. Amy adjusted well and found other intellectuals with whom she could share her disdain for parents and other proliferate. I involved myself in body building, running, drinking beer, meeting Joanne for lunch, and threatening the Sheriff of Tolono, Illinois. I was waiting in line one day at thelocal post office and the Sheriff addressed me once too often as "boy." Maybe he didn't like my newly shaved head, but I lost my temper and jumped up in his face, daring him to, "Call me boy again, mother fucker, go on…" I was restrained and separated by his Deputy and another customer and the Sheriff promised to get me back. I lunged at him once more, but he wisely retreated and took his fat ass outside. Granted I've got problems with authority, but the Sheriff was directly provoking me.

When I picked up Joanne at work that afternoon, I greeted her with a can of Fosters beer and my freshly shaved skull. "Rough day, hon?" she asked. After telling her the story, she suggested two things: One, I should stop running long distances alone on remote country roads and, two, we should get the hell out of Dodge and fast.

LETTER #20
"Your Hostile Perspective"

October 17, 1989

Getting out of Illinois was no easy trick. We had three kids, two birds, two collies, an old Jeep Wrangler, and a partridge in a pear tree. To pay for the move, I asked for and received an advance on the money from the Heidnik trial from Chuck Peruto. I called a realtor, who assured me he had a great rental house ready for us back in Pennsylvania. I sent him a deposit from my advance. My mother even paid for all of the kids to fly home. So we took the kids to the airport and everyone got a farewell hug and kiss before boarding, except Amy. As the stepdad, I got a pat and head turn. Joey was terrified of flying, but he chose that over being strapped to the hood of the jeep like a deer.

We went back home to finish packing for the move. I bought a car tire with the last dollars in the checking account and then decided to treat ourselves to a farewell-to-Illinois dinner. I suppose that I am admitting to check fraud, but I told myself I would send them the money when we got back home and I landed a real job.

We gave the birds to one of the movers because it was zero degrees outside and the heat wasn't working in the jeep. We loaded the clothes and collies and off we drove. I admitted to myself that I had failed up again. This was a tail-between-my-legs return to PA. I was silent during the long the ride home. I told Joanne that it was just too cold to talk, but I was feeling utterly defeated. I had no faith in myself. I was just a broken-down Vietnam vet with no prospects and a family to try to care for.

What else could go wrong? We arrived and walked into our new house to find a massive 4 by 4 foot hole in the kitchen ceiling where the previous tenant had fallen through while trying to hide from the police. The entire place reeked of cat piss and the master bath had pubic hair on the sink and commode. One bedroom smelled so bad that even the cat wouldn't go in there to piss. The backyard was a trash dump with old rusting appliances and collie-sized weeds. Welcome home. I called the realtor to come see our lovely home for himself. His smile disappeared as I grabbed him, dragged him into the cat piss bedroom, slammed him against the wall, and suggested that the carpets be removed, floors cleaned, walls painted, and ceiling fixed – or else.

Days and weeks passed and our furniture had still not arrived. We wondered what was wrong. We had no phone either and finally got in touch with the movers. They had been trying to contact us for a month at the phone number that we gave them, which was my loving crazy mother. They told us that she said, "I never hear from the son-of-a-bitch and I don't know where he is!" When I asked why she said that, she complained that they were bothering her. We were just a mile down the road! So now the moving bill included a month of storage as well.

Meanwhile, Joanne found another house that was clean and well maintained. We rented it on the spot. Since we had nothing but our clothes and an air mattress, we were ready to move right in. But the realtor and his asshole attorney partner had the nerve to threaten a law suit for breaking our lease. I promised them that they would have a series of accidental mishaps and perhaps worse. You may not like me for this, but I wasn't bluffing one bit. They backed down.

In the middle of this drama, I was surprised to receive a new letter from Heidnik. With all the confusion of three address changes, it wasn't until November that letter #20 actually reached me. After eight months of silence, Heidnik decided to break the ice with his analysis of our break up. I was annoyed to read his insane theory that I had fallen under the spell of the diabolical Detective Devlin. I only wish that Devlin was as powerful as Heidnik imagined because he could have helped me out of my problems with law enforcement in Illinois. I had not thought about Heidnik at all during my sojourn in Illinois. I didn't give a shit about the book, Detective Devlin, or Gary's paranoid delusions. It had been a relief to be free from his narcissistic letters and endless directives to research this or that file, interview this or that person, or get this or that article. So, for me, letter #20 was an unwelcome intrusion from the past.

For Heidnik though, letter #20 was an all-important attempt to win me back. The tone of his letter has changed dramatically. He is formal, guarded, and curt. He addresses me as "Dr. Apsche" rather than "Jack." He states that, "I no longer feel you trustworthy" and he believes I have a "hostile perspective" towards him. He tries to hide any personal feelings by claiming, twice, that the purpose of his letter is "purely scientific." Yet, for all his face-saving formality, Heidnik is clearly testing the possibility of restoring our relationship. This will be the first of a half-dozen letters that seek reconciliation.

Oct 17, 1989

Dear Dr. Apsche,
For reasons of purely scientific veracity, I suggest you explore possibilities of a <u>mild</u> case of Fetal Alcohol Syndrome. My mother was a documented alcoholic and also complicated by smoking. Suggest you check my elementary school records at Henry W. Longfellow in East Lake, Ohio. Do you recall that I flunked second grade almost twice! The more you check into the symptoms the quicker you'll become a believer. Things like my "tic" for instance may have been a manifestation. Also peer problems, perception problems, etc. Hasn't my writings* and speech been characterized as "rambling"? Keep looking. It may be the pot at the end of the Rainbow. What everyone wants to know is WHY??
Veraciously Yours
Gary

> *P.S. This missive inspired by a purely scientific predisposition. I no longer feel you trustworthy, but blameless. The onus belongs to Det. Devlin, who I believe has contacted you and coerced you into your hostile perspective.*

After ruminating about our "break-up" for eight months, Heidnik has developed an explanation for why things turned bad between us. He imagines that the arch-villain of his persecutions, Detective Devlin, must have "coerced" me into taking sides against him. Yet it is fascinating that Heidnik considers me "blameless." In his mind, I am still an honest innocent, but I have been seduced by a venal and diabolical fiend.

The basis for Heidnik's conviction that I am "blameless" takes us back to the psychological process of splitting as discussed in Letter #14. Splitting is a primitive defense mechanism in which a fragile personality like Heidnik perceives the world in extremes of good and bad. People are either idealized as all good and admirable (like his mother, Martin Luther King, Maxine Roberts, Anjeanette, and me) or condemned as all evil (like Detective Devlin, Sonia Garrett, and social workers Ms. Doe and Ms. Smith). There's no ambiguity, no gray area. In this instance, Heidnik was rocked by the horrible suspicion that his trusted Dr. Apsche might <u>not</u> be "all-good." Ever since the traumatic break-up, he has been struggling to hold onto his child-like need to believe that I am all good. It has taken eight months, but he has invented the perfect explanation for this unbearable insight: The all-bad Devlin has poisoned the mind of the all-good Dr. Apsche with his evil lies. By this emotional logic, Heidnik has found a way to redeem his faith that I am still all-good and therefore, most importantly, there is hope of restoring his bond with me. That is why Heidnik focuses exclusively on an attack on Detective Devlin in his next letter #21. He must destroy the evil villain to reclaim me as his good prince.

For now, however, Heidnik needs a face-saving reason to write to me and begin my redemptive rescue from Devlin's dark power. Knowing that I'm a clinician, he comes up with the ploy of presenting new "scientific" information that he suffers from Fetal Alcohol Syndrome on top of all his other disabilities. He hopes to elicit my sympathies by emphasizing his many weaknesses – including his "tic," "peer problems," "perception problems," "rambling" speech, and nearly flunking second grade "twice." This is also Heidnik's way of asking forgiveness by attributing his prior rude behavior to his weakness as a paranoid schizophrenic. In effect, he is saying, "please don't take my prior misconduct too seriously because you know my psychiatric history and know that I cannot help myself."

LETTER #21
"Expose Him From the Grave"

November 1, 1989

Heidnik waited two weeks for my response to his eight month ice breaker. There was no reply. Given the mail delay because of my address changes, I probably had not even received his letter yet, and if I had, I was too irritated to resume the correspondence. But Heidnik will not go gently into the night. As he indicates by his closing, "assiduously yours," he intends to be persistent. He still clings to his faith in my basic goodness and he desperately hopes to win me back from his imagined arch-enemy, Detective Devlin. By attacking Devlin as a criminal, Heidnik hopes to regain my allegiance.

Nov 1, 1989

Dear Dr. Apsche,

I don't know if you got my last letter but I do have an addendum to make. You know Det. Devlin hasn't gotten off scot-free. In at least two ways he is having to pay for his culpability. Consider this,

(1) Despite all his best efforts to steal the churches money, his efforts netted him not one single nickel of profit.

(2) He has that problem peculiar* to all criminals. He has to stay alert, always be looking over his shoulder. He can never go to sleep or rest even. If he does, I just might pull off some stunt and expose him as the gangster he is. No matter how hard he tries to keep his dirty deeds buried, I may succeed in uncovering them.

With you he got careless and almost got caught. You started probing and uncovering some dirt. Unfortunately* he responded in time and stopped you --- this time.

So he's keenly aware of his danger. So next time you see him tell him I'm laughing at him and he better not go to "sleep" and he better not "relax." Never! Not as long as I'm alive. Not even after I'm dead. I just may find a way to expose him from the grave.
Assiduously Yours,
Gary

Heidnik's entire letter is nothing but a string of empty threats against an imaginary foe. He barks and growls to appear strong and in control, but he has no bite and is utterly helpless and pitiable. His shrill, impotent threats sound like a petulant child on a playground and are so exaggerated as to be laughable. He rails about his power to "expose" and destroy Devlin. He fantasizes that his enemy is afraid of him, always "looking over his shoulder," unable to "sleep or rest even." Heidnik sees himself as relentless and indefatigable. He will haunt his enemy in his every waking hour. He puffs and pounds his chest with fantasized power. It is he who stands "laughing." He brags that he will pursue his vengeance until the day he dies – and more. Yes, he is so powerful that he will even strike his enemy "from the grave."

It is pure paranoid delusion. There is no Devlin plotting to steal his money. There never was. There is no alliance between his arch enemy and me. In the profound isolation of his prison cell, Heidnik has nothing but his own distorted thoughts, twisting in and out of themselves, churning like a ball of snakes in a black cave.

I have no patience for Heidnik's delusions. The weight of his dependence feels like a burden to me now. My feeling is that I want to keep him as far away as I can. I won't write back.

LETTER #22
"YOU That's Right You!"

November 14, 1989

Heidnik waited another two weeks before unleashing his next "missive." My failure to respond to his two prior entreaties has hurt him deeply and he is volcanic with rage. For a third time, he addresses me as "Dr. Apsche," but immediately negates this courtesy by calling me a "wise guy" and "Mr. Dried Prunes" with "the intelligence of a 5 year old." He begins his four page assault by refuting my confrontation letter from ten months before in which I accused him of being manipulative. On the contrary, Heidnik wants to make me feel guilty that he has given his full cooperation for my book without asking for a penny in return. He insists that he was never manipulating and proclaims that his only reason for helping me with my book was a noble desire to achieve "equal treatment." He denies any monetary motives of any kind ever – forgetting, of course, his attempts to manipulate me into stealing his church fortune.

For all its vitriol, the letter is essentially an expression of Heidnik's primal, infantile fear and fury over being abandoned by me. He attacks me as strongly as possible. "YOU that's right YOU!" He pulls no punches for the sake of politeness or for fear of burning his last bridge of hope for reconciliation. His self-righteous shrieking for "equal treatment" is the shrieking of a helpless child who is terrified of abandonment.

As for me, I was still getting resettled. I had now received three of these Heidnik letters and I wasn't sure how, or if, I wanted to respond. What do I say in response to his ranting, off-the-wall accusations? Besides, he had never responded to my confrontation letter or my questions about his sexual fantasies. Instead Heidnik was trying to get me to join in his delusions. I declined. I was too busy trying to get my own life in order and didn't want a renewed headache.

Nov 14, 1989

Dear Dr. Apsche (wise guy)
So! You go to college and get all those fancy degrees, but you've got about the intelligence of a 5 year old, Mr. Dried Prunes.
You don't get it do you? You just don't see it? It's right in front of your nose and you can't see it. Okay, lets do some straight talking and I'll keep it nice and simple so you won't get lost.
You accuse me of manipulating. Really! And if I'm manipulating what am I striving for? YOU that's right YOU! said you were writing* a book. Isn't that right? Didn't you say you were writing* a book about me, and you wanted my help? Okay so far? You still with me? And why did you want to write it? For exercise? Hell no! You wanted to make some money. That's why! Nothing wrong with that. If you write a good book you should get paid.
But did I ever ask for a percentage, or royalties* or anything for myself? Hell no! When you say I was trying to manipulate you, you're right. But I wasn't looking to make money off you. I wanted something else. That's the sad part. Really sad. But not for the reasons you think.
Do you know what I wanted? Let me spell it out for you. I wanted equal treatment, that's what. Equal treatment. No special favors! No money! Not even to save my life. I wanted EQUAL treatment. All I ask is to be treated like everybody else. If I do wrong, I should be <u>punished</u>. But I want to be protected from people abusing and victimizing me. When I find a woman who wants to live with me and have my children, I don't want people breaking us up and taking our children away because they're a different color. If someone breaks into my house and assaults me, he should be arrested, not me. When I start a church and save, save, save, trying to do something right, I shouldn't be framed and put in jail for 5 years because some crooked cop and crooked administrators want to steal the church's money. And my wife, no matter how pissed or threatened should not

be framing me for a rape I never committed. And when I lived at N. Marshall I suppose you think I busted down the fence, vandalized my own car, piled all that trash in my yard and shot all those bullet holes in my own garage.

Don't you see? Nobody could do any of that shit to you or anyone else and get away with it. You've got rights! If you go to the law, the law will protect you! If some bastard breaks into your house and assaults you, the police would DAMN well arrest him. Well I don't want any special treatment. I just want equal treatment, like you and everyone else gets. Is that asking too much?

Read the enclosed pages from "Cellar of Horrors." You'll see that Mr. Harper not only admits to breaking into my house, but brags about it. Like he's got a right to do that AND assault me, in front of witnesses no less. Now I'm going to ask you to do something that may come pretty hard. I'm going to ask you to THINK!! Do you see where <u>he</u> says I had a loaded rifle and a pistol. That's plenty of firepower isn't it? Now see where he says I wanted to kill him? If that's true, why is he still walking around, bragging about breaking into my cellar. I had the firepower didn't I? Do you really think I'm such a bad shot at three feet I couldn't hit him? Even so why didn't I keep shooting. If I'm the bloodthirsty killer I'm supposed to be, WHY DIDN'T I KILL HIM?

If you can't see the truth here, you need glasses. The judge saw it. As a matter of fact I'm sure the judge was surprised I didn't shoot him. They even admitted to breaking in my house. So you see you have positive PROOF! That I've at least told you the <u>truth</u>. So why wasn't Mr. Harper arrested? If he broke into your house you'd have arrested him, probably right after you shot him. So don't you see? That's all I ask for. Equal treatment. The law says it's my right. We live in America, not some third world country run by dictators. Why can't I have the same equal treatment as everyone else?

That's the sad part. The real sad part. That I have to try to manipulate someone like you to get what should be already* mine – EQUAL treatment. I shouldn't have to scheme and maneuver* for this. It's supposed* to be mine as a law abiding American citizen. (In 76 I was a law abiding citizen, right up till Nov 86).

So if you think me trying to manipulate you into me getting

equal-treatment is something evil, or self-serving, then you're really in bad shape and you deserve to be punished. Do you know what that punishment should be? Well it should be crooked cops, crooked judges, crooked* politicians, and bastards selling drugs on your front doorstep, breaking into your house, stealing your wife and kids.

Maybe you think that now you're living out west, you're safe. That these problems are mine and belong in the inner cities. Well buddy I've got news for you. You can run, but you can't hide! All these problems will catch up to you sooner or later, no matter where you go.

So if you don't care about what's being done to me, then do it for yourself. If the concept of equal-treatment is too complex for you, then you deserve everything you get, and you've got a worse mental problem than me. You're the one who's* sick, not me. You need help, not me!

Pissed off
Gary

Letter #22 is a laundry list of the injustices Heidnik believes that he has suffered in his lifetime of perceived rejection and persecution. Notably, the list begins – and ends – with yours truly:

- Your book about me (= <u>my</u> book) has been taken from my control.
- People have been "abusing and victimizing me" my whole life.
- The crooked authorities took away my love, Anjeanette, and my child because of racism – March 1978.
- My tenant, Mr. Harper, was a crooked former cop, who broke into my house and assaulted me – 1976.
- Another crooked cop, Devlin, and the crooked authorities framed me and put me in jail for five years to steal my money – May 1978.

- My wife Betty falsely accused me of rape – December 1985.
- The neighborhood drug pusher bullied me and vandalized my property – 1985-1986.
- An author has written a condemning book about me [Ken Englade's *Cellar of Horror*].
- The authorities lied that I tried to kill my tenant – 1976.
- And now you accuse me of manipulating you – today.

Although Letter #22 is intended as a lament of his many persecutions, Heidnik has only one injustice that consumes him now – me. I have forsaken, betrayed, and abandoned him. He is in the throes of primal hurt, rage, and helplessness. Even the choice of words for his motto – "equal treatment" – is clinically revealing. He uses the phrase <u>nine</u> times in this letter, twice with capital letters. He does not ask for "justice" or "fairness," terms that might be more accurate. His choice of the words "equal treatment" is psychologically precise. "Equal" embodies his desire for an equal relationship with me. To be equal would make us into trusted, bonded friends and could restore his only caretaker and confidant. Likewise, the word "treatment" can only be me. I am a mental health professional, a therapist, someone providing treatment. Treatment is caring, reassurance, and hope.

At this juncture, Heidnik is utterly desperate. If he loses me, he loses his last finger-hold of human connection and drops into a bottomless void of aloneness. His final paragraphs are the cries of a little child clinging to my leg, "Don't leave me! Come back!" Even as I tear free from his hands, Heidnik cries, "I'll follow you. I will never let go." In his own words, "Maybe you think that now you're... safe [from me]. That [my] problems are mine... Well buddy... You can run, but you can't hide! All [my] problems will catch up to you sooner or later, no matter where you go." Heidnik knows that he is weak and dependent and believes he is being punished. So he reverses his pain onto me: "<u>You're</u> really in bad shape and <u>you</u> deserve to be punished." It is the pitiful, primitive reversal defense of a small child. His final paragraph is pure, desperate reversal: "You're the one who's sick, not me. You need help, not me!"

Now that I am receiving the full torrent of Heidnik's neediness and rage, I am all the more repulsed and determined NOT to resume the correspondence. For a third time, I did not reply to him.

LETTER #23
"A Failure to Communicate"

November 24, 1989

During the period that Heidnik was sending his angry reconciliation letters, I was going through an important transformation. In the wake of the Illinois disaster, I knew I had to make some decisive changes in myself. Melissa's birthday and Christmas were coming and I still had no job and no income. I still had a hair trigger temper. I still had nightmares and intrusive thoughts from Vietnam, but these, and my cravings for drugs and wild sex, had lessened greatly. Despite all my mistakes and failures, I had a family that loved me. I could take solace in the fact that, even in my own self-critical eyes, I was a pretty good dad and husband.

There was only one area of my life in which I had made no progress – my career. I hadn't had a steady job in almost three years. Getting hired for the Heidnik trial was a fluke that filled nine months, but it had been preceded by several months of unemployment and then followed by unemployment for eight months in Pennsylvania and eight more in Illinois. I had to get a job. Otherwise I knew I could slide back into the chaotic underworld of my former illegal and often dangerous means of making money.

I had a doctorate in psychology and what did I have to show for it? Why couldn't I make a respectable honest living in my profession? What was stopping me from getting a job? The answer sounds stupid. I suppose it is stupid. It was pride. To get a job meant that I would have to humble myself and start at the bottom. I would have to accept the authority of whoever was in charge. Ever since my father died, I had built myself into a tough guy, a self-reliant rebel, ready to fight, bowing to no one. I was all pride.

So I made a firm decision. I went back to Temple

University where I had done some important research during my doctoral training and beyond. At the time, I was considered a rising star. Now I was humbled and humiliated. I had to convince the director, a former colleague, that I would follow orders and behave myself. He knew my reputation for irreverence and clashing with authority. It took a lot of begging and cajoling, but he gave me a chance. I was given a junior level position reporting to a Masters level person, who was at least ten years younger than me. I was restricted to the adolescent behavioral unit where I worked and prohibited from walking around the facility without an escort. It was embarrassing.

As ordered, I stayed on my assigned unit and focused on my new job. I can't tell you how hard it was for me to swallow my rebel pride and toe the line. I could have lost my temper, or blown off my responsibilities, or challenged the bosses, or broken the rules because I had a better idea. I could have taken my frustrations home and gotten drunk or high. My strength came from my family. I was determined to behave properly for their sake. My temper and impulsive desires could no longer come first. I wasn't comfortable in a suit jacket, but I kept wearing it, and I turned the restrictions of my scheduled routine into a boot camp for developing self-discipline.

Well, lo and behold, I started succeeding. It was a residential treatment unit for mentally ill adolescents with aggression and severe behavior problems. Most were inner city kids from broken families and broken neighborhoods. Nearly all grew up in the chaos of poverty, drugs, crime, and violence, and most were the victims of abuse. They were tough kids, wounded and fierce, always ready to strike out. (Sound like a Vietnam vet we know?) These kids were the clinical population that most mental health professionals run away from. I obeyed my young boss, and did whatever he asked me to do. The kids were tearing up classrooms, breaking furniture, smashing their bedrooms, and beating the shit out of the staff, who were too scared to stay employed there for very long. My boss asked me to develop some behavior modification programs to restore order. I plunged in. I spent time with the kids to really understand them and started developing individualized behavior plans for each. Then I would train the staff and role-model how to implement the reinforcements. In six months we had eliminated the use of all physical restraints and the adolescent unit became a model program.

Later, Joanne also took a job on the unit as a psychiatric nurse. It was great to share the hard work and satisfaction of helping kids and families that often seemed hopeless. I could see that good treatment could save even the most troubled and anti-social kid from devolving into a Heidnik. I had a gift for working with the toughest, most aggressive kids. I understood them and could connect in a natural and authentic way. The eminent psychologist Marsha Linehan once said, "you are who you treat." I totally agree with her. As a fatherless and wounded kid who turned into a tough guy, I understood what these kids needed to safely drop their tough exteriors and take a chance at trust and change. I loved the work. I gained more and more confidence in my abilities. My self-esteem soared and my bad behavior faded into the past.

I also came to like and respect my young boss. He was a good guy but he had a weakness for skirt-chasing. Apparently (as in "allegedly"), he picked the wrong man's wife one night and was ambushed outside of a hotel following a fucking session. Contrary to Heidnik's delusions, I can assure you that detective Devlin was not involved in either the fucking or the shooting. There went my boss. I felt bad for him, but his demise stood in my mind as an ironic measure of how far I had come. He was acting like my old self. I had progressed to a point where I would never do anything that reckless and selfish. To my dismay, I had become a responsible adult.

And where did Gary M. Heidnik fit into my new life

and career? He didn't. The more I found my passion in my adolescent work, the less I wanted anything to do with Heidnik. Once upon a time, when I first started the Heidnik book, I was probably on the right track. It could have been a legitimate and admirable research project. It could have been my ticket to Redemption-ville. But the task of writing the definitive Heidnik forensic analysis was just too unstructured and required more self-discipline than I had at that time. I just couldn't get any words on paper. The combination of my writer's block and feeling dependent on Heidnik for his cooperation just added to my depression. When I finally dumped the project for the move to Illinois, I felt enormous relief. In hindsight, the difficulties of the Heidnik book fueled my worst fears of personal and professional failure. I also didn't like being a manipulator with Heidnik. I hated to pretend sympathy, interest, and friendship, and having to go along with his games just to keep him hooked. By the late fall of 1989, I was over Heidnik and the whole get-rich-quick book fantasy. I was invested in my career and finding my purpose.

But Heidnik was desperate to get me back and wouldn't quit. Letter #23 is his fourth attempt in six weeks. His tantrum in the previous letter had failed to elicit the desired response from me. He knows that he went overboard and is full of regret, not for insulting me, but for stupidly burning his own bridge. His purpose, as he says, remains precisely the same. He wants "equal treatment." In other words, he wants to restore his bond with me.

Nov 24, 1989

Dear Dr. Apsche,
 I think I know why we've been having a problem. It's a failure to communicate. Actually a matter of semantics.
 My fault though, not yours. I should have drawn on your superior education and asked you to explain something to me. I've

been using the words justice and fair play. they were the wrong words. I meant and should have used the word equal-treatment. That's the word I meant, not justice or fair play. There is a big difference. So I'm going to take advantage of your superior schooling. I'm asking you to explain to me the difference? Thank you.

Gary

    That's the whole letter. Short, muted, deferential. Very un-Heidnik. He gives the appearance of accepting the blame for our schism. "My fault though, not yours." But his supposed apology is not an apology at all. It is a prideful, face-saving ploy that minimizes his preceding rudeness as nothing more than "a matter of semantics." His message is carefully constructed to avoid any responsibility for his offensive conduct. He does not yield an inch from his original demand for "equal treatment." He simply reiterates his position. The only real difference between the previous letter and this one is that he is not screaming at me and respectfully requests my opinion on the matter.

    Of course, all this talk about "semantics" is just a charade. Heidnik is incredibly lonely and needy, and his true purpose is to restore the only intimate relationship available to him. As the letter concludes, however, Heidnik has no idea where he stands with me now. He does not even know what closing to use. Should I be formal? Should I make a joke like I usually do? Should I act as if nothing has changed? He avoids the decision entirely by leaving it blank. For the first time in his last thirteen letters, Heidnik does not conclude his letter with his usual bombast and attempt at humor.

LETTER #24
"The Quintessential Cruel Ghoul"

January 2, 1990

A few weeks later, in mid-December, I received a Christmas card from Heidnik. For whatever reason, I felt bad for the guy and caved. I sent him a letter acknowledging his card and wishing him well. I definitely did not want to restart our relationship so I was careful to keep it brief and as neutral as possible. Based on his response below, I must have also informed him that his imagined arch-enemy, Detective Devlin, had died from cancer. Given the foremost position of Devlin in Heidnik's paranoid delusions, one would expect a dramatic emotional reaction to this news. Instead, his initial response is calm, primitive denial. He doesn't believe me. He wants proof.

Otherwise, Heidnik is overjoyed to hear from me. His letter is ebullient and abounding with humor. He even drew a bottle of champagne and a noise-maker. It's a truly Happy New Year for Heidnik. His Jack is back. It is a time to celebrate.

Jan 2, 1990

Happy New Year!
Dear Dr. Apsche,
Thank you for your letter of Dec 28, 1989. I'm also glad to know you've gotten my letter and card. Thanks for acknowledging same.
We have a problem! I'm a schizophrenic-paranoid type. It's not for nothing I've acquired the moniker "paranoid." I've worked hard at it, and have "earned" it. ☺ That's where the problem rests now. You want me to "trust??" you, but you make promises and

don't keep them. You promised to <u>prove</u> to me that Detective Devlin has died. Do you remember that promise?? Well I'm still waiting!

I'm still convinced, (but only guessing) that he put pressure on you, and <u>forced</u> you to lie and <u>back off</u>. Now that you're living in close proximity* to Phila aren't* you worried about your personal safety, or however he convinced you to back off?? You were getting close to him, and he got scared*, desperate in fact, so he pressured you to "back off." He put pressure on my former attorney, Bulkin, to "back off." Remember?

He's dangerous, and nothing to fool with. He tried to kill me once (legally, of course). So I don't blame you for being in fear of your life and "backing" off.

This of course doesn't account for your "New interest" and display of courage, but it makes me curious and suspicious. So tell me. What gives??

There is a philosophy that no man is all bad. That there is some good in every man. Believe it or not, that also applies to "Marty" Graham. When I was in the "Bullpen" in Phila awaiting trial, we were locked up together, for a short while. About 5 inmates wanted to get "physical" with me. They were all black, of course. Marty came to my rescue and saved me from a beating. Even though it was 5 to 1, they didn't want to tangle with "Marty." He's not only big, but can be pretty mean, when he gets angry. He is a very imposing figure, when he decides to be, and apparently most convicts are basically* cowards. Since there was only 5 of them to 1, and they had no weapons and/or reinforcements, so they backed off. I've always been grateful to him for this, but have never thanked him. Although we are on the same block, I'm almost totally* isolated and only see him occasionally* for only a few seconds. You know "Hi," "Nice to see you," "Bye"! So when you see him or write him would you please mention this incident, my gratitude and tell him I said thanks. Also, feel free to mention this incident in your book. With all the negative publicity about Marty, he can use all the good "words" he can get ☺.

Also, if you want to have some fun, ask him about the "he-she" he was locked up with and the "blow job" he almost got. They were rushed for time, so he only got ½ a blow-job. I'll bet he cracks up laughing, when you mention this (that is when you stop laughing). ☺

By the way, guess what? I've finished my book (rough draft) and am now rewriting it and fine tuning it. It is over 500 pages and has 8 chapters. Chapter 8 is my tour-de-force. It switches from comedy to drama, and involves a shooting and a killing. ALL true of course. And believe it or not, I managed to give it a happy ending. The last two chapters are what gives my book real meaning, and turns it from a light-hearted comedy to something of substance, gut wrenching* substance!

Now to wrap up this letter, I'm enclosing a copy of a letter I wrote to a Dr. Kevorkian. Maybe you heard of him? He's the guy who was in the news recently for inventing a "suicide machine." When he heard I was dropping my appeal, and trying to be executed as quickly as possible, he wanted me to donate my body. He can't wait to get his scalpel* into me. He's the quintessential "cruel ghoul," and probably haunts graveyards.

Understand this letter is satire, pure satire and not to be taken seriously. The guy "pissed" me off, and I wanted to get back at him. After reading it, do you think I succeeded*?? Do you think he'll take my offer seriously?? Maybe take me up on it??

Also, after reading it you'll get an idea of the kind of "stuff" I can write and do write. I can hold a readers attention. No dried prunes, eh what??

      Still suspiciously yours
      Gary
Psst! Did you notice? B.S. Guess what these are??

This is a quirky and erratic letter, even for Heidnik. But he is clearly overjoyed to be reconnected to me once more. His mood is exuberant and he cracks jokes throughout. Even the upsetting news that Devlin has died will not ruin this glorious day of reconciliation – at least for now. His celebration is further heightened by the satisfaction of finally completing his

500 page "tour de force" novel, "40th Street Soaps."

It is surprising to hear Heidnik spontaneously recall the kindness of his fellow serial killer, Harrison "Marty" Graham. He has not mentioned Graham since Letter #3, but he remains genuinely touched by the fact that Graham protected him from a violent assault by five other African American inmates. Although three years have passed since the deed, Heidnik urges me to extend his gratitude. In a rare moment of authentic empathy and altruism, Heidnik wants me to "put a good word in" for Marty in my book. Psychologically, Heidnik's appreciation for the restoration of my therapeutic "protection" seems to have overflowed into appreciation for the physical protection he received from Graham.

Heidnik then changes the subject to his bizarre encounter with the famous, or infamous, "Dr. Death," Dr. Jack Kevorkian. Kevorkian had written to Heidnik on Death Row to ask him to donate his organs. This is an intriguing bit of history. At the time that Heidnik wrote this letter, Kevorkian was only beginning to attract media attention for his new "suicide machine." He had not yet used the device to assist the suicides of any of the 130 terminally ill patients that he would facilitate from 1990 through 1998. Physician-assisted suicide was the cause that made Kevorkian famous, but it was not his first "humanitarian" mission. In fact, his first cause was announced in 1987 when he published an article in the *Canadian Medical Association Journal* titled, "Capital Punishment and Organ Retrieval." In that article, he pronounced his belief that "if humans are to be executed, they should be permitted to partake of real retribution through [giving their] organs for transplantation." This is why Dr. Kevorkian wrote to Gary Heidnik in December 1989. Undoubtedly, Kevorkian hoped to gain national media attention for his organ retrieval cause by convincing the world's most notorious serial killer to donate his kidneys, lungs, liver, and heart to patients in need. Ironically, Heidnik considers Kevorkian to be a bigger nut than himself and mocks him as "the quintessential cruel ghoul."

Heidnik's response was to pull Kevorkian's chain with a prank letter, which he encloses for my comic approval. Like everything he writes, Heidnik is overly proud of his brilliant "satire." He then closes his three page letter with the boast that "I can hold a reader's attention. No dried prunes, eh what?" His closing remarks, signature, and postscript are particularly intriguing. It is an ambiguous mix of affection, humor, hostility, and suspicion. Six weeks before, he lambasted me as "Mr. Dried Prunes." Now he uses the same phrase as a term of endearment. This affectionate teasing is immediately followed by a cautious reminder that he is "still suspiciously yours, Gary." Clearly, Heidnik is deeply bothered by my message that Detective Devlin has died because it threatens to topple his entire castle of delusional beliefs.

Throughout his letter, Heidnik has been actively suppressing his negative emotions about Devlin's death in order to fully enjoy the moment of reconciliation. He will not allow his own paranoia to ruin his celebration. So he forces humor to push his suspicions from consciousness. As a postscript, Heidnik draws five turds and says, "Psst, did you notice? B.S. Guess what these are??" He is referring to the "B.S." in the prank letter that he just sent to Dr. Kevorkian. But even a junior Freudian would recognize this gesture as a primitive and infantile expression of Heidnik's suppressed anger. Like a little child, he is playing with his shit and wants to rub it in my face. Still hurting from my rejection of him one year ago, Heidnik literally wants to "mess" me up and make me suffer. It is my turn to wallow in stink and misery – like he has been feeling since the schism began.

LETTER #25
"My Last Letter to You"

January 1990

Heidnik's not quite "last" letter is undated, but it must have been written shortly after his letter of 1/2/90 in which he requested proof that Detective Devlin had died of cancer. Although he was momentarily ecstatic over his reconciliation with me, there was no way that Heidnik could continue to suppress his outrage over the Devlin news. As he says below, the imagined Devlin conspiracy "is an acid that turns my brain to mush." He has invested years of rumination to construct the impenetrable walls of his grand conspiracy theory. Devlin is the foundation stone of his entire paranoid delusional system. Devlin is the diabolical mastermind who had engineered his destruction. Devlin is the arch-villain who plotted and organized an army of conspirators to frame him, imprison him, and punish him – all for the purpose of stealing the fortune of his tax-evading church. Therefore the death of Devlin is absolutely incomprehensible for Heidnik.

He simply cannot allow the truth of this information, which he rejects as "<u>GARBAGE</u>. If Devlin is a fiction, then everything Heidnik believes is a fiction. If Devlin is nothing, then Heidnik's deepest convictions, and even his last purpose in life, are nothing. If Devlin disappears, Heidnik will vanish himself. If I sent a newspaper clipping of Devlin's obituary, Heidnik would dismiss the evidence as a forgery. There is only one way that Heidnik can maintain his cherished delusions. His trusted Dr. Apsche must have succumbed to the death threats or the financial seductions of the powerful Detective Devlin. I must have joined the Devlin conspiracy. I must be working for the enemy and telling this lie to fool Heidnik into dropping his guard over his precious treasure.

Heidnik begins his appeal (and attack) by addressing

me as the popular author Joe McGinniss, who had become an overnight success for his best-selling investigative book, *The Selling of the President*. By 1990, McGinness had completed two of his trilogy of true crime books, all of which were turned into successful TV mini-series. The first, *Fatal Vision*, in 1983, was another huge best seller. By comparing me to McGinness, Heidnik is both taunting and tempting me. On one hand, he compliments me as "a very capable, competent man, and your skills in investigating par excellence." He hopes to butter me up with visions of writing a best-selling investigative book, like Joe McGinness, and this will be just the beginning of lecture tours and more fame. "You need money," he says, "You like money!" All that I must do is reapply my investigatory talents to Heidnik's mission to prove the Devlin conspiracy.

Dear Apsche (alias Joe McGinniss)

This letter will prove beyond a shadow of a doubt how truly* naive* I am. It's analogous* to the older man who having been burned many times, and has no delusions about romantic love, but nevertheless seeks another liaison*, hoping against hope that this time things will be different, but inwardly knows he's wrong. After all there are some cases of love being true and certain.

Just by dubbing you with the nom de plume of Joe McGinniss, you know that I'm somewhat aware of the pitfalls and perils of the author-subject relation. The peripeteia* that all subjects undergo at the time of publication is nothing less than de Rigueur*, and thus when you delivered my peripeteia*, it was to be expected. So this is why am I writing* you now.*

This wrong that's been done to me hurts me so badly the pain is so insufferable I'm perhaps beyond help. This wrong is an acid that turns my brain to mush. There is here, something that goes way beyond the injustice Devlin and the others inflicted on me. They inflicted their injustices on all the rest of society. They not only *destroyed my life, but Anjeanette's, Maxine's, Alberta's and who knows how many other lives, and the reasons they did it were for racism, revenge, and most of all MONEY. Devlin is the most pernicious* of all. He steals under the panoply of his badge. He tried to do it to me and who knows how many others. You'd have to be very naive* indeed to think he's only stopped with me. He and the others are gnawing away at the very fabric of our society, pulling it and all of us down with them. So if you won't right this wrong for me, how about doing it for all those other victims, past and future.*

If you won't do it for altruistic reasons, then how about doing it for material reasons. You expose these malefactors and your* rewards of glory and specie will be truly* huge. You'd make a fortune on your book, lecture tours, etc. You need money! You like money! So here's an offer that's hard to deny. A chance to wax your own fortunes, as well as benefiting society. As the aphorism so succinctly* puts it: "A chance to do well while doing good."

You're a very capable, competent man, and your skills in investigating par excellence. Also, this is really a very difficult crime to solve, at least on the <u>surface</u>. Most of those involved are not professional* criminals* but amateurs. Also the fact that so many are involved makes it harder to keep a "dirty" secret. You've already done some of the ground work for my cries of "foul." I've given you a match, and you've already planted a few embers and they're beginning to feel the heat (I know). So all you have to do is fan the flames and burn these fallacious mansions down. Mansions built on lies, deceit, and most of all greed. It's all up to you now. I know they're feeling the pressure because of a few "feelers" I put out. Devlin is especially worried. But when you relate to me <u>GARBAGE</u> like Devlin has died of cancer, you completely* destroy your credibility and all the trust I've placed in you.

So this is going to be my last letter to you. I'll not rise to any more of your gambits*. I'm a fool, you know I'm a fool, and I know I'm a fool; BUT I'm not that BIG of a fool, and I don't intend to be hurt again.

However, I pray to God every night this injustice of Devlin's will be resolved in this world, NOT the next. If there's a chance it can be righted, you may be the one who can do it. I ask you,

importune you to do it, and pray to God that you will.
   Good luck and Good bye.
           Hopefully yours
           Gary

The news of Devlin's death has done nothing to weaken Heidnik's grand delusion of persecution. On the contrary, his delusion is stronger than ever and he raises it to the grandiose and absurd level of a threat to society itself. "Devlin and the others... are gnawing away at the very fabric of our society, pulling it and all of us down with them..."

He concludes his "last letter" to me with an impossible ultimatum. I must confess the lie that Devlin is still alive and rejoin Heidnik's mission to expose the forces of evil. But there is a problem. If I confess that I lied about Devlin's death, how can Heidnik ever trust me? Likewise, if I insist that the "lie" is truth, he also cannot trust me. He cannot win. Heidnik's grand persecutory delusion is the only "self" that he has left. If he gives up his delusion, he will cease to exist. Heidnik may be happy to have restored his relationship with me, but he cannot pay the price of his own psychological death. Fighting against his imagined arch-enemy is his only reason to live. Heidnik is as delusional as Don Quixote and Devlin is the windmill that fills his life with purpose.

Given his narcissistic personality, Heidnik must translate every external event into something important about himself, typically something that raises his own grandeur. So Heidnik tries to reverse his weakness into strength and regain control with an ultimatum: "This is going to be my last letter to you. I'll not rise to any more of your gambits. I'm a fool, you know I'm a fool, and I know I'm a fool; BUT I'm not that BIG of a fool, and I don't intend to be hurt again."

"Hurt" is the key word, the true driving emotion for Heidnik. For a moment, his ultimatum provides a surge of power and an illusory feeling of control. But then Heidnik weakens with the realization that his ultimatum is an all-or-nothing proposition. If it fails, he will lose me forever. So he softens his demand with a final prayer for reconciliation: "If there's a chance [our relationship] can be righted, you may be the one who can do it. I ask you, importune you to do it, and pray to GOD that you will... Hopefully yours, Gary."

No prayer was going to bring our relationship or Devlin back from the dead. I was content to accept his farewell. It had been 19 months since I first asked Gary to participate in a book about his case. At the outset of this project, I genuinely believed that I could discover the truth of why Heidnik did what he did. He never revealed it to me, or anyone, not even to himself. I had a strong hypothesis, but Heidnik deferred to his delusions. So I withdrew. I felt bad for him at times because he was profoundly alone. Despite my frequent irritation and disgust, I think I really understood and felt the human loneliness of Gary Heidnik.

I believe that ordinary people can sometimes do horrible things. No one is pure evil. That's a myth to sell on TV, but in reality we all have the capacity to do some horrible shit. Even the good guys in World War II, the Americans, fire-bombed Dresden, killing women, children, and every living thing. We destroyed hundreds of thousands of civilians at Hiroshima and Nagasaki. In Nazi Germany, the "normal lives" of the guards of the death camps have been well documented. They were ordinary men. They had mothers, fathers, wives, and children whom they loved, while they spent their days killing the mothers, fathers, wives, and children of innocent Jews. Are they simply evil or were they human beings with fears and flaws that allowed them to rationalize their atrocities? When we encounter people like Heidnik, we want a clear line that separates them from the rest of us. We want them to be purely evil monsters. It's not so simple. Those who abuse and destroy are the same as we are, but somehow able to commit horrible brutalities. Heidnik made sincere efforts to help people with intellectual disabilities. But he also kidnapped, raped, and tortured them. He was at least partly good for all his bad. Pure evil? Only from a moralistic point of view.

LETTER #26
"I've Got a Lot of Nerve, Don't I?"

January 18, 1992

Heidnik stayed true to his ultimatum. Two years passed and he never wrote another letter to me. It was I who broke the silence with a letter to him. By this time, I was finally writing my Heidnik book, *Probing the Mind of a Serial Killer*. For a variety of reasons, I felt compelled to send him a draft of part of the book. I suppose I was hoping that he would at least be able to confirm my hypothesis of how his sexual obsessions drove his sex crimes.

How was it possible for me to finally write the Heidnik book? What had changed? I suppose it was just time and self-confidence. After putting the book on the shelf for two years, I could return to the topic with a fresh perspective. The great success of my career with adolescents gave me the confidence and self-discipline to tackle the project again. It was still difficult. I forced myself to finish and I didn't care if it was half-assed in parts. The book was published in 1993. It barely made a splash. It wasn't even close to the best seller I had originally hoped for, but it was finished and I could move on.

Essentially, my theory was that Heidnik's masturbatory fantasies reached a satiation point where he felt compelled to fulfill his deviant sexual fantasies by acting them out in reality. The important point is that Heidnik's deviant process is grounded in the very same sexual process that operates for normal males. It is disquieting to think we're not so different from one of the world's worst sex criminals. The typical process for males begins when a sexual fantasy becomes reinforced through the pleasure of masturbation and orgasm. At some point, the repetition of that sexual fantasy reaches a saturation point, becomes boring, and loses its power to sexually arouse or to maintain arousal. The fantasy gets stale.

When this happens, the male feels compelled to either switch to a new fantasy, or elaborate on the current fantasy to spice it up, or possibly act it out in some fashion in real life.

Even a man who has one of the hottest movie stars in the planet can eventually get bored and start fantasizing about somebody else. Why else would Jesse James snub Sandra Bullock for a tattooed lady and string of bimbos? Why would Hugh Grant snub supermodel Elizabeth Hurley to have sex with a common LA street hooker? It is the same natural process of saturation where the sexual fantasy loses its appeal. The world is filled with the myriad ways that men seek sexual arousal and act out fantasies, all too often in deviant and damaging ways. It is well known that the #1 use of the internet is pornography – of every imaginable and unimaginable type. There are porn sites that cater to swingers, peeping toms, exhibitionists, S&M aficionados, people that dress as animals, you name it. The thing they share in common is the pursuit of arousal and the ecstasy of orgasm. But it starts with the individual's sexual fantasy.

The question is how and when does the natural pursuit of sexual pleasure cross over into unacceptable deviance and crimes that victimize other people. The key distinction between so-called normal and problematic behavior are (1) the content/severity of the sexual fantasy, and (2) the decision to act out that fantasy in a way that victimizes people. Thus a person can develop a serious problem if he becomes obsessive in masturbating to a particular harmful type of pornography or fantasy, such as child porn, rape, or bestiality. The process of repetitive masturbation to such deviant stimuli has the effect of strengthening and reinforcing the deviance. In Heidnik's case, he formed an exclusive attraction to African American women; he was turned on by bondage, group sex, and rape pornography; and he cultivated fantasies of sadistic dominance over women.

There is a very serious problem when a man's focus on the fetish or fantasy becomes so obsessive and excessive that it dominates his sexual <u>and</u> nonsexual life and becomes the only way that he can achieve arousal or orgasm. The more dangerous level is when that man becomes so obsessed with the specific sexual fantasy and porn type that he feels compelled to act it out in real life to achieve the desired arousal and orgasm. Typically, our moral values and learned respect for other people inhibits the acting out of sexual urges or fantasies in inappropriate ways. Heidnik lacked such normal self-control and inhibitions. Given his schizophrenic delusions, pathological personality problems, lack of experience with adults of normal intelligence, and his deviant sexual obsession with domination, Heidnik felt justified in kidnapping, raping, and torturing innocent women. As difficult as it may be for us to understand his obsessive mind, Heidnik did not regard his abuses as morally wrong – at least at the time that he committed them. That was our position at the trial when we failed to receive a verdict of "not guilty by reason of insanity."

At this point, you probably have formed your own opinion about Heidnik's level of sanity and culpability for his crimes. You've experienced Heidnik's inner thoughts and personality through these letters and have plenty of evidence to base your opinion on. You might agree or disagree with us. Either way, whether Heidnik knew exactly what he was doing or not, we cannot discount him as a pure evil monster. If we do, we fail to learn anything from this human tragedy. What if some wise and concerned adult had intervened when he saw little Gary being bullied at school? What if Gary had been protected from the cruel taunting? Maybe he would not have hidden himself in his room and immersed himself so deeply into his fantasies. And maybe, if he had had some help to make friends, his normal desires to be liked and feel competent would not have devolved into the pathological fantasies of power that eventually brought so much misery to the world.

My career with adolescents has taught me that

compassion and well-directed caring can save a troubled and anti-social kid before he devolves into a Heidnik. I was lucky to have a few special people who cared enough to save me from my own descent into self-destructive waste. It was my unique first-hand experience of the tragedy of Gary M. Heidnik, a troubled kid that no one cared to save, that helped direct me into the field of adolescent psychology and where I've been ever since.

Reading this final letter from Heidnik made me feel pity for a broken and sick human being. He is so diminished that he is nearly unrecognizable. Still hurting from my rejection of him nearly three years before, he keeps an emotional distance by being as formal as possible. Even addressing me as "Dr. Apsche" is not formal enough. For the first and only time in 26 letters, he writes out my title in full as "Doctor Apsche." Furthermore, to accentuate the need for formal distance, he writes his own name in full and even gives himself the title "Sr" for the first and only time: "Sr Gary M. Heidnik." In fact, he uses "Sr" twice, once in the header address and once in his final closing.

Sr Gary M. Heidnik
Jan 18, 1992

Dear Doctor Apsche,
I always thought it impossible but there is somebody with worse handwriting* than mine --- you. I can't even read your signature* and can only read ½ your letter. Would you mind trying again, but this time maybe typing or printing or something so I can read it.
ANON,
Sr Gary M. Heidnik

P. S. In that copy of Shakespeare you sent me, did you deliberately* rip out these pages in Anthony & Cleopatra and

OTHELLO and if so --- WHY??

P.S.S. I've got a lot of nerve don't I? --- that is to complain about somebody else's writing* ☺.

P.S.S.S. If you think my printing looks bad have look how level my handwriting is! ha ha, laugh hard, ha! [written in cursive]

Heidnik's final letter is barely a half-letter and it feels like he is only half-present. His handwriting is unstable, messy and sprawling. He seems too weak, cognitively and emotionally, to fully engage. He marshals one sentence to complain that my handwriting is illegible and a second sentence to politely request me to re-type my words. Then his letter is over. It is like he lacks the strength to even try to decipher my bad handwriting. Two sentences and he signs off.

But then he adds a postscript. It is a random paranoid question about the Shakespeare book that I gave him long ago. Then he thinks of a second postscript. It is a light joke about his own poor penmanship. Then he adds a third postscript. But he must already be exhausted by the exertion. For the first and only time in 26 letters, he writes his last words in cursive, the easiest way. It is like his brain is not working. He can only deliver short snippets of thought between lapses in concentration. I suspect that another long year in the isolation of death row has exacerbated his gross mental decline.

As a whole, Heidnik's final letter is frail and disjointed. Two sentences and three postscripts. There are hints of the former Gary Heidnik. Some paranoia. Some bombast. Some attempts at humor. There's even one instance of using a $25 word that he pulled from the dictionary – "ANON." He is faded in every faculty, truly half-present.

So why does Heidnik choose the capitalized word "ANON" for his final closing? Anon can mean "soon" or "shortly." Or it can mean "another time." Or it can be the abbreviation for "anonymous." Anonymous can be either someone who remains passively unknown or someone whose name has been actively withheld. All five meanings seem to fit. By asking me to rewrite my letter legibly, Heidnik may be hoping to speak to me again "soon or shortly." Or he is simply too weak and hopes that he may be able to engage me at "another time" when he has the necessary strength. Or he is literally "anonymous," a lost soul, a shadow of his former bold self. Or, finally, anon means that Heidnik actively "withholds" his name. In other words, he withholds his cooperation. It is a tiny, but decisive act of defiance. He cannot engage me. He will not engage me. That much he still controls – and for Gary M. Heidnik, control is, and always was, everything.

    Anon.

To Gary M. Heidnik
S1395
P.O. Box 33291
Pittsburgh, PA
Jan 15, 1992

Dear Doctor Apsche,

I always thought it impossible but there is somebody with worse handwriting than mine --- you. I can't even read your signature and can only read ½ your letter ~~~~~~~~

Trying again, but this time maybe typing or printing or something so I can read it.

ANON
So Gary M. Heidnik

P.S. In this copy of Shakespeare you sent me, did you deliberately rip out those pages in Anthony & Cleopatra and OTHELLO and if so --- WHY??

P.S.S. I've got a lot of nerve don't I? --- That is to complain about somebody else's writing ☺

P.S.S.S. If you like my pointy little ____ ___ ___ ___ ha ha, hy hey ha.

Copy of final hand-written letter from Gary Heidnik

Postscript

So my four year experience with Heidnik came in like a lion and went out like a lamb. My first Heidnik book was quietly published in 1993 and three years later, Heidnik was quietly executed by the Commonwealth of Pennsylvania. Ironically, in a case full of ironies, Gary escaped the electrocution that he so feared and was killed by lethal injection on July 6, 1999. By then my life had changed so much that I don't think I was even aware of his death. My marriage and stepfamily were healthy and strong. I was clean in body and spirit. I was confident and successful in my psychology career with youth.

Over twenty years later, my life has been blessed and wonderful. I'd like to think that, as Paul Simon sings, I'm "still crazy after all these years." I paint and write poetry and still love my collies and Bob Marley. Professionally I have accomplished about everything I could have hoped for. I've published many books and dozens of research articles. I've founded an international clinical journal and received various awards and acclaim. I'm also the Babe Ruth of Board Certifications because I'm pretty sure I have earned more than any psychologist on the planet. But, most of all, I am proud of my contributions to the field of adolescent mental health. I found a positive outlet for my bold and rebellious style by trying new treatment approaches. I pioneered the clinical application of mindfulness with adolescents and published *The Mindfulness Toolkit* for youth. I developed an innovative psychotherapeutic treatment called Mode Deactivation Therapy (MDT) that has proven to be extremely effective with adolescents with severe conduct and behavioral disorders, including aggression and sexual offenses. MDT is an evidence-based method that focuses on the interplay between trauma, personality factors, and belief systems in the development of behavior problems – the same processes that I learned from my analyses of Gary Heidnik.

Ironically, for better or worse, I might never have turned my life around if I had not gone through my crazy experience with Heidnik. And no, I'm sure as hell NOT going to dedicate this book in his memory! That honor belongs to my wife Joanne, my daughter Melissa and my stepchildren, Amy and Joe, all of whom I am immensely blessed by and proud of.

Jack A. Apsche

NOTE: JACK PASSED AWAY ON OCTOBER 12, 2014, SHORTLY AFTER THIS BOOK WAS TYPESET.

Summary Guide to Gary Heidnik's Letters

#	addressed to	Signed	Date	Pgs	Letter Title
1	-- none --	Respectfully, Gary M. Heidnik	8/12/88	1	I'm Not Available
2	Dr. Apsche	Gary M. Heidnik	10/14/88	1	Who's Exploiting Me?
3	Dr. Apsche	Gary	11/5/88	4	Special Olympics of Churches
4	Jack	-- none --	11/13/88	2	It Piques Me Extremely
5	-- none --	-- none --	11/19/88	11	The Vacuum of Belonging
6	Jack	Gary	11/24/88 likely	6	As Interesting as a Died Prune
7	Jack	Cogitatively yours, Gary	11/30/88	18	My Injustices of 78
8	Jack	Cogitatively yours, Gary	12/2/88	16	Is That Love or What?
9	Jack	Respectfully Gary M. Heidnik (author)	12/9/88	6	Now I'm Going to Play a Game on You
				1	40th Street Soaps (Prologue)
10	n/a	N/A	12/12/88	1	Here Lies Gary M. Heidnik
11	Jack	Your favorite lab specimen, Gary	12/16/88	6	A Distant Chord but No Music
12	Jack	Philologically yours, Gary	12/20/88 estimated	2	Prunes Could Turn Into Plums
13	Jack (Sherlock)	Egregiously Grieved, Gary M. Heidnik, etc.	12/23/88	28	Persecution is My Middle Name
14	Jack	Prolifically and relatively??? yours	12/24/88	14	I Promised You a Juicy Story
15	Jack	Electrically yours, Reddy Kilowatt	12/25/88	6	Put Yourself in a Criminal's Mind
16	page missing	Very truly yours, Gary	12/30/88 estimated	6	Let Her Know I Am Remorseful
17	Jack	Resurrectically yours, Lazarus Lazarus	2/4/89	4	Greetings from the Crypt
18	Jack	--page missing--	2/10/89	6+	Local Drug Lord
19	Jack	Missively yours, Lazarus	2/10/89	2	Don't Open That Can of Worms
20	Dr. Apsche	Veraciously Yours, Gary	10/17/89	1	Your Hostile Perspective

21	Dr. Apsche	Assiduously Yours, Gary	11/1/89	1	A Way to Expose Him from the Grave
22	Dr. Apsche (wise guy)	Pissed off, Gary	11/14/89	6	YOU That's Right YOU
23	Dr. Apsche	Gary	11/24/89	1	A Failure to Communicate
24	Dr. Apsche	Still suspiciously yours, Gary	1/2/90	3	The Quintessential Cruel Ghoul
25	Apsche (alias McGinnis)	Hopefully yours, Gary	Jan 1990	3	My Last Letter to Your
26	Doctor Apsche	ANON, Sr Gary M. Heidnik	1/18/92	1	I've Got a Lot of Nerve, Don't I?
26 Total Letters	Duration: 42 months – 8/12/88 thru 1/18/92				151+ Total pages

Other Books by the Authors

<u>Apsche and Jennings together</u>:

Apsche, J. and Jennings, J. (2013). *The Mindfulness Toolkit for Counselors, Teachers, Coaches and Clinicians of Youth*. Holyoke, MA: NEARI Press.

Jennings, J. and Apsche, J. (2013). *The Youth Companion to the Mindfulness Toolkit*. Holyoke, MA: NEARI Press.

Apsche, J. and Jennings, J. (2007). *Responsibility and Self-Management: A Client Workbook of Skills to Learn*. Holyoke, MA: NEARI Press.

Apsche, J. and Jennings, J. (2007). *Responsibility and Self-Management: A Clinician's Manual and Guide For Case Conceptualization*. Holyoke, MA: NEARI Press.

<u>Apsche</u>:

Apsche, J. (2014). *Tanning on Dangerous Beaches*. ePrintedBooks, Science Hill Ky.

Apsche, J. (2012). *Echo's from Vietnam and beyond*. ePrintedBooks, Science Hill Ky.

Apsche, J. (1993). *Probing the Mind of a Serial Killer*. Morrisville, PA: International Information Association, Inc.

Apsche, J. (2014). *Mode Deactivation Therapy: The Complete Guidebook for Clinicians*. Oakland, CA: New Harbinger.

Swart, J. and Apsche, J. (2014). *A Mindful Treatment for Families: Family Mode Deactivation Therapy*. New York: Springer Press.

Apsche, J. and DiMeo, L. (2012). *Mode Deactivation Therapy for Treating Aggression and Oppositional Behavior in Adolescents: An Integrative Methodology Using ACT, DBT, and CBT*. Oakland: New Harbinger Publications.

Jennings:

Jennings, J. (2005). *Stella's Secret: A True Story of Holocaust Survival.* Bloomington, IN: Xlibris.

Jennings, J. (2011). *Darkness Hides the Flowers: A True Story of Holocaust Survival.* Wayne, PA: Beach Lloyd Publishing.

Jennings, J. (2009). *I Choose Life: Two Linked Stories of Holocaust Survival and Rebirth.* Bloomington, IN: Xlibris.

Made in the USA
Monee, IL
23 January 2021